NUMERACY
FOR ALL
LEARNERS

The Mathematics Recovery book series

This book – *Numeracy for All Learners: Teaching Mathematics to Students with Special Needs* – is a significant and important addition to the current Mathematics Recovery series. The eight books in this series address the teaching of early number, whole-number arithmetic, and fractions in primary, elementary, and secondary education. These books provide practical help to enable schools and teachers to give equal status to numeracy intervention and classroom instruction. The authors are internationally recognized as leaders in this field and draw on considerable practical experience of delivering professional learning programs, training courses, and materials.

The books are:

Early Numeracy: Assessment for Teaching and Intervention, 2nd edition, Robert J. Wright, Jim Martland, and Ann K. Stafford, 2006.

Early Numeracy demonstrates how to assess students' mathematical knowledge, skills, and strategies in addition, subtraction, multiplication, and division.

Teaching Number: Advancing Children's Skill and Strategies, 2nd edition, Robert J. Wright, Jim Martland, Ann K. Stafford, and Garry Stanger, 2006.

Teaching Number sets out in detail nine principles which guide the teaching, together with 180 practical, exemplar teaching procedures to advance children to more sophisticated strategies for solving arithmetic problems.

Developing Number Knowledge: Assessment, Teaching and Intervention with 7–11 Year Olds, Robert J. Wright, David Ellemor-Collins, and Pamela D. Tabor, 2012.

Developing Number Knowledge provides more advanced knowledge and resources for teachers working with older children.

Teaching Number in the Classroom with 4–8 Year Olds, 2nd edition, Robert J. Wright, Garry Stanger, Ann K. Stafford, and Jim Martland, 2015.

Teaching Number in the Classroom shows how to extend the work of assessment and intervention with individual and small groups to working with the whole class.

Developing Fractions Knowledge, Amy J. Hackenberg, Anderson Norton, and Robert J. Wright, 2016.

Developing Fractions Knowledge provides a detailed progressive approach to assessment and instruction related to students' learning of fractions.

The Learning Framework in Number: Pedagogical Tools for Assessment and Instruction, Robert J. Wright and David Ellemor-Collins, 2018.

The Learning Framework in Number presents a learning framework across the whole K-to-5 range and provides three sets of pedagogical tools for the framework – assessment schedules, models of learning progressions, and teaching charts. These tools enable detailed assessment and profiling of children's whole-number arithmetic knowledge and the development of specific instructional programs.

Teaching Early Numeracy to Children with Developmental Disabilities, Corinna F. Grindle, Richard P. Hastings, and Robert J. Wright, 2021.

This practical guide for teaching numeracy is based on core concepts from *Teaching Number* (aka 'the green book') that have been adapted for children with developmental disabilities.

Numeracy for All Learners: Teaching Mathematics to Students with Special Needs, Pamela D. Tabor, Dawn Dibley, Amy J. Hackenberg, and Anderson Norton, 2021.

Numeracy for All Learners builds on the first six books in the series and presents the knowledge, resources, and examples for teachers working with students with special needs form Pre-K through secondary school.

NUMERACY FOR ALL LEARNERS

TEACHING MATHEMATICS TO STUDENTS WITH SPECIAL NEEDS

PAMELA D. TABOR

DAWN DIBLEY

AMY J. HACKENBERG

ANDERSON NORTON

SAGE Publications Ltd
1 Oliver's Yard
55 City Road
London EC1Y 1SP

CORWIN
A SAGE company
2455 Teller Road
Thousand Oaks, California 91320
(0800)233-9936
www.corwin.com

SAGE Publications India Pvt Ltd
B 1/I 1 Mohan Cooperative Industrial Area
Mathura Road
New Delhi 110 044

SAGE Publications Asia-Pacific Pte Ltd
3 Church Street
#10-04 Samsung Hub
Singapore 049483

Editor: James Clark
Senior assistant editor: Diana Alves
Production editor: Katherine Haw
Copyeditor: Neville Hankins
Proofreader: Bryan Campbell
Indexer: Martin Hargreaves
Marketing manager: Dilhara Attygalle
Cover design: Wendy Scott
Typeset by: C&M Digitals (P) Ltd, Chennai, India
Printed in the USA

Library of Congress Control Number: 2020938401

British Library Cataloguing in Publication data

A catalogue record for this book is available from the British Library

ISBN 978-1-5264-9196-1
ISBN 978-1-5264-9195-4 (pbk)

At SAGE we take sustainability seriously. Most of our products are printed in the UK using responsibly sourced papers and boards. When we print overseas we ensure sustainable papers are used as measured by the PREPS grading system. We undertake an annual audit to monitor our sustainability.

To Bob

To Ron, Jeremy, and Zack

To Jim, Josh, and Anna

To Erik, Nikolas, and Amaya

To Caroline and Eleanor

Contents

About the Authors

Dr. Pamela D. Tabor holds a Bachelor of Science degree in elementary education and Bible from Kentucky Christian University, a Master of Arts degree in elementary education from East Tennessee State University, and a Doctor of Philosophy in mathematics education from Southern Cross University, Lismore, NSW, Australia. Her supervisor was Robert J. Wright, the developer of Mathematics Recovery. Her current position is that of Research and Evaluation Specialist for the US Math Recovery Council (USMRC) in which she has the pleasure of working with instructional leaders from districts around the United States and internationally to think deeply about the impact of Math Recovery in their school contexts. Previously, she spent nearly two decades as a school-based math specialist, interventionist, and instructional coach. In that capacity she worked with administrators, teachers of mathematics, teachers of special education, students, and parents to improve the quality of mathematics instruction in a public elementary school in Maryland. She is also a co-author of the Math Recovery series book *Developing Number Knowledge*, a contributor of *Teaching Number in the Classroom with 4–8 Year Olds*, one of the original developers of USMRC's Add+VantageMR Professional Development Courses, and one of the developers of USMRC's Student Numeracy Assessment Progressions (SNAP).

Dawn Dibley, a special educator with 30 years of experience as a music therapist, classroom teacher, and mathematics coach is currently an instructional coach for the US Math Recovery Council. From the time of her initial training as a Math Recovery Intervention Specialist in 2007, she began exploring the use of the Learning Framework in Number (LFIN) in teaching numeracy to students with disabilities. She spent several years facilitating the USMRC's Add+VantageMR Professional Development Courses to specifically address the concerns of teachers of students with special needs. She holds a Bachelor's degree in *Music Therapy* and Master's degrees in music therapy and developmental cognitive disabilities from the University of Minnesota.

Dr. Amy J. Hackenberg taught mathematics to middle and high school students for nine years in Los Angeles and Chicago, prior to earning a PhD in mathematics education from the University of Georgia. She is currently an associate professor of mathematics education at Indiana University Bloomington. She conducts research on how middle school students construct fractions knowledge and algebraic reasoning and on how teachers can learn to develop productive student–teacher relationships. In her current project she is investigating how to differentiate instruction for diverse middle school students (see https://idream.sitehost.iu.edu/), studying her own teaching as well as working with practicing teachers. She is the proud co-author of the Math Recovery series book, *Developing Fractions Knowledge*.

Dr. Anderson Norton is a professor in the Department of Mathematics at Virginia Tech. His research focuses on building models of students' mathematical development. This work has generated inter-disciplinary collaborations with psychologists and neuroscientists. Prior to this volume, he served as chair of the steering committee for the North American Chapter of the International Group for the Psychology of Mathematics Education, and is co-editor on a pair of publications bridging psy-chology and mathematics education, and co-author of the Math Recovery series book, *Developing Fractions Knowledge.*

Acknowledgements

The authors wish to acknowledge the members of the Math Recovery community who have contributed to the critical conversations necessary to produce this book. The authors specifically wish to thank the US Math Recovery Council, Kurt Kinsey, Lucinda "Petey" MacCarty, and Jennifer Scholla for their thoughtful feedback to this work and for granting permission to include the new Learning Framework in Number for the Classroom. The feedback provided on earlier versions of Chapter 12 by Jaclyn Vallier, Mikel Vallier, Joan Cable, Margie Broman, Ron Tabor, Sara George, Zack Tabor, Noelle Tabor, Jackie Amato, Marria Carrington, and Dara Glazer was particularly helpful. Dawn wishes to acknowledge the support of the students and staff of Independent School District 196, Rosemount–Apple Valley–Eagan, Minnesota as well as the helpful feedback given by members of the Math Recovery community who attended conference sessions where ideas presented in this text were originally shared. A special thank you to Cindy Johnson who loaned us a camera to photograph students and instructional settings and to Kate Anderson who stepped up to take photos when COVID-19 interfered. We also wish to thank the parents and students who graciously allowed us to include their photographs in this book including Frank Cacich and Eleanor Allen. Many of the instructional settings discussed in this book are available from the US Math Recovery Council store (https://www.mathrecovery.org/store). We appreciate US Math Recovery Council graciously allowing us to use images of their products.

Foreword

Robert J. Wright

I can think of no one more suited to the task of lead writer for a book focusing on numeracy for all learners than Dr Pamela Tabor. For a good number of years Pam Tabor has been a leading light in the development of Mathematics Recovery (MR) professional development programs and implementations of those programs in the United States and beyond. In particular, she has brought an elaborated research perspective to the MR programs. Several writers have highlighted the need for a book that fairly and squarely addresses the important task of building a rapprochement between the fields of mathematics education and special education. Pam Tabor and co-authors Dawn Dibley, Amy Hackenberg, and Anderson Norton have produced such a book. They begin with a description of the Learning Framework in Number (LFIN) which has been used extensively as an organizer of the field of teaching number ranging from earliest counting to arithmetic and beyond, that is, the whole number and arithmetic typically taught in the first four or five years of school. Several chapters in the book draw significantly on the LFIN and MR, ensuring that, at the very least, the book can enable application to a broad range of needs in special education, of current material and approaches to teaching number that are prominent in mathematics education.

The LFIN occurs in two forms – one for application to intensive instruction for intervention and the other for application in the classroom. Common to these two forms are three important kinds of pedagogical tools – assessment schedules, tables of learning progressions, and teaching charts. The authors also overview professional practices and principles that are used widely in MR, a program focusing on intensive and extensive professional learning which provides an appropriate setting for several chapters in this book.

The book includes an illuminating chapter on the implications of brain research for teaching and learning mathematics, highlighting the potential of this research for generating important insights applicable to a diverse range of mathematics learners. The chapter on functional mathematics, also known as life skills mathematics, provides a detailed overview of an extensive body of research on 'the mathematics used by people without disabilities in day-to-day life.'

An important theme of the book is its focus on constructivism – not as a theory of teaching but rather as a theory of how humans come to know. Application of the theory of constructivism to teaching involves the notion that students build new knowledge when they reorganize their thinking through solving novel problems. In this approach the teacher's role is to create situations at the cutting edge of students' current levels of knowledge that are likely to elicit mathematical reasoning.

The book includes a focus on assessing and teaching students with disabilities. Processes of assessment can involve making adjustments to the tasks presented to students that take account of particular disabilities. In the case of teaching, activities are provided that enable the building of conceptual understanding for all students. This typically involves making accommodations and modifications to instructional tasks according to students' particular constructions and teaching students with different learning needs in a common instructional activity. Also included is an informative discussion of dyscalculia, a topic which has received much focus in recent years. According to research findings, around 5% of students who would otherwise be expected to succeed in mathematics encounter extreme difficulties in progressing their mathematical knowledge in parallel with that of their peers.

An overview of current research and practice associated with differentiating instruction is provided and five supportive teaching practices are described: using research-based knowledge of students' mathematical thinking; providing purposeful choices and different pathways; inquiring responsively during group work; attending to small-group functioning; and conducting whole-class discussions across different thinkers. The book provides an exposition on students with other special needs. These include students who are part of a traditionally marginalized or underserved population, students living in poverty, English learners (ELs), students who suffer from math anxiety, and students with exceptional abilities and talents in mathematics. The book describes strategies and perspectives teachers might use to better meet the needs of these students, as well as their reflections on these issues. This has the purpose of raising awareness, promoting discussion and pointing the reader to additional resources.

Pam Tabor, Dawn Dibley, Amy Hackenberg, and Anderson Norton have written a book that is noteworthy for the inclusion of, on the one hand, very practical material that is immediately applicable and, on the other hand, elaborated technical material which requires serious study. Given the depth and scope of this book I have no doubt that the book will appeal to a wide range of readers and it would make an ideal text for courses at both undergraduate and graduate levels. Finally, the book is an excellent addition to the MR series.

Bob Wright EdD
Developer,
Mathematics Recovery®

Introduction

This book has been several years in the making. Dawn Dibley has pioneered the work of modifying the Math Recovery professional development Add+VantageMR® for special educators in her school district. An out-growth of that work was the development of several different conference presentations over the years at the US Math Recovery Council National Conferences covering different aspects of using Math Recovery theory, pedagogy, and tools within the realm of special education. Pam Tabor had the pleasure of attending a number of these sessions. After attending one of Dawn's sessions, Pam suggested Dawn should write a book. The timing wasn't quite right, and Dawn politely, but firmly, declined. A year later, after another standing-room-only session, Pam again suggested Dawn should write a book and this time offered to help. That same year Amy Hackenberg and Anderson Norton also presented their current work at the conference. All of these sessions presented different components of a cohesive work that was simply demanding to be written. During his keynote address at the 2019 US Math Recovery Council Conference in Providence, Rhode Island, Andy ended his address with a slide unveiling the cover of the new work still in the writing phase. The need for the book was confirmed as conference participants began asking the publisher how they could order the book.

The goal of this book is to present a radically different way to approach special education from the perspective of **constructivism**. The work is based on the premise that all students deserve the right to construct meaning of **numeracy** and must be afforded the appropriate educational opportunities in which this is most likely to happen. The authors of this work see Math Recovery as a vehicle of improved **equity** of access to quality mathematics instruction and learning. Students with disabilities and other special needs have historically underperformed on nearly every measure of success (see, for example, Mader & Butrymowicz, 2020; Nation's Report Card, 2007; National Center for Learning Disabilities, 2020). While Math Recovery theory, pedagogy, and tools do not constitute a magic wand, we do believe they have a profound impact on student learning when used by skillful teachers with a passion for helping their students learn and grow.

This book builds on a rich legacy of the other books in the Math Recovery series. The purpose here is not to supplant the content of the previous books in the series. Rather, we aim to view the content of the other books through a particular lens. We will use excerpts from the previous books to illustrate how modifications and accommodations might be employed to improve access for all students. We have employed a color-coding system to draw the readers' attention to the original source book. It is our intention that this book be used in tandem with the other books in the series. We hope this book will spark honest conversation and critical dialogue that will lead to a revolutionary shift in the way students with special needs are typically taught mathematics. We invite you to join us on this journey of change and growth for the good of all students.

Intended Audience

It is our hope this book will be useful to a wide array of educators and administrators. Three groups, in particular, are likely to use this book. The first group includes members of the Math Recovery community who seek to understand how Math Recovery pedagogy and practice might be used when working with students with special needs. The second group comprises special educators and administrators who have no previous experience with Math Recovery but who wish to better meet the needs of their students in mathematics. These teachers and administrators are encouraged to learn more about the US Math Recovery Council at www.mathrecovery.org. Academics, undergraduate, and graduate education students made up the final group. This book will work well as a textbook in both undergraduate- and graduate-level courses.

A Personal Note from Dawn

In the summer of 2007 I embarked on a professional development journey that challenged my understanding of mathematics and how it should be taught. I had spent the previous two years as the teacher of a small class of students with autism and cognitive disabilities. Prior to that, I had been a music therapist, before earning my teaching license in developmental/cognitive disabilities. The students in my class all had academic goals in the area of mathematics ranging from naming shapes and reading **numerals** to two-digit addition/subtraction (with and without regrouping) and learning their multiplication facts. I did the best I could. I consulted my state academic standards, I consulted my colleagues, and wished there was a program that would tell me what to do next. I consulted my students' **Individualized Education Programs (IEPs)** and tried to figure out how to work on their current goals/objectives and what I should do if they did or didn't achieve their goal by the next scheduled IEP meeting. That all changed in the summer of 2007 when I started professional development to become a Math Recovery Intervention Specialist. The training was a requirement of my new position as a math coach for elementary special education teachers in my district. At the end of the first day of training, I had several thoughts: I needed to go back to my students because I was starting to understand what experiences I should have been providing for them, I needed to learn more, and I needed to share what I was learning with other special education teachers. While I wasn't able to return to my classroom, I have been able to continue learning about how students develop their understanding of mathematics, I have been able to share what I've learned with my special education colleagues, and I have been able to work with students across my district who have a variety of abilities and disabilities. As with many aspects of education, I've discovered what works with one student, or even most students, doesn't work with every student. I've become increasingly curious, and my colleagues know I enjoy hearing about their challenging students. Every student gives us an opportunity to learn something new. I'm moving forward with the beliefs that all students can learn, and all students give us something to build on; our job is to find what it is.

Color Coding Used in the Book

Throughout the book, sections have been quoted and referenced from the other books in the Math Recovery Series. Color coding has been used to help the reader more easily locate the related discussion in the previous books:

Blue = *Early Numeracy: Assessment for Teaching and Intervention* (hereafter *EN*) (Wright, Martland, & Stafford, 2006a)

Green = *Teaching Number: Advancing Children's Skills and Strategies* (hereafter *TN*) (Wright, Martland, Stafford, & Stanger, 2006b)

Purple = *Teaching Number in the Classroom with 4–8 Year Olds* (hereafter *TNC*) (Wright, Stanger, Stafford, & Martland, 2015)

Red = *Developing Number Knowledge: Assessment, Teaching and Intervention with 7–11 Year Olds* (hereafter *DNK*) (Wright, Ellemor-Collins, & Tabor, 2012)

Orange = *Developing Fractions Knowledge* (hereafter *DFK*) (Hackenberg, Norton, & Wright, 2016)

Gray = *The Learning Framework in Number* (hereafter *LFIN*) (Wright & Ellemor-Collins, 2018)

The Learning Framework in Number for the Classroom

This chapter introduces the **Learning Framework in Number for the Classroom** and discusses how the framework provides direction for the teaching and learning of numeracy.

Wright et al. have previously written about the three grand organizers for arithmetic and rational number instruction: the Guiding Principles for Instruction, the Domains of Arithmetic and Fractions, and the **Dimensions of Progressive Mathematization** (see Hackenberg et al., 2016; Wright et al., 2006a; Wright et al., 2006b; Wright et al., 2012; Wright et al., 2015). The Guiding Principles and the Dimensions of Progressive Mathematization will be covered in Chapter 3. The Domains of Arithmetic and Fractions are the critical topics of learning and instruction that are encompassed in the Learning Framework in Number.

Wright, Martland, and Stafford first broadly published the initial Learning Framework in Number in 2000 as adapted from the 1996 Count Me In Too Project in New South Wales, Australia (NSW Department of Education and Training, 1996). This framework grew out of a rich tradition of constructivist research in early number conducted by Steffe and his colleagues (see, for example, Steffe, Cobb, & von Glasersfeld, 1988) at the University of Georgia and the research Wright (1989) conducted in New South Wales, Australia. The original Learning Framework in Number articulated the progressions of student development over four domains of early number: Stages of Early Arithmetical Learning (SEAL), Number Word Sequences and Numeral Identification, Other

Aspects of Early Numeracy (the predecessor of structuring number), and Early Multiplication and Division. Since the publication of that initial Learning Framework in Number in the first book in the Math Recovery series, additional research has led to several updates and elaborations of the initial framework to include domains relevant to older students and classroom settings. Wright and Ellemor-Collins (2018) codify this Learning Framework in Number for an intervention teaching setting. Ellemor-Collins, Kinsey, MacCarty, and Wright (forthcoming) will articulate on the most recent iteration of the Learning Framework in Number for the Classroom. Figure 1.1 presents the summary schemata for the new Learning Framework in Number for the Classroom.

The Learning Framework in Number for the Classroom covers four major areas of whole number instruction: Number Words and Numerals, Addition and Subtraction to 20, Addition and Subtraction to 100, and Multiplication and Division and one for Fractions. Within each area, the Learning Framework in Number for the Classroom presents two domain progressions that articulate the direction or trajectory (Simon, 1995) of learning and teaching across zones of numeracy development in each domain. Each zone is characterized by different types of thinking and behaviors. By carefully assessing students, teachers can develop a profile of the students' current numeracy development and identify the next appropriate instructional goals. For example, if the student can successfully produce the forward number word sequence from 1 to 7, that student would be in the beginning of Zone A for the forward number word sequence. An appropriate educational goal for the student would be to develop facility with the number word sequences in the range of 1 to 10 which would progress the student to Zone B. Chapter 6 will cover using the Learning Framework in Number to write Individualized Education Program (IEP) goals. For a detailed discussion of the Learning Framework in Number for the Classroom including an elaboration of each whole-number domain, see Ellemor-Collins et al. (forthcoming).

The Learning Framework in Number was first expanded into the domain of fractions by Hackenberg, Norton, and Wright. The authors present the research undergirding this portion of the Learning Framework in Number for the Classroom in their book, *Developing Fractions Knowledge* (2016). The book delves into the development of **fragmenting**, part–whole reasoning, fractions as measurement, reversible reasoning, fractions as numbers, and operations with fractions bridging into algebraic thinking. This research then forms the foundation of the *Add+VantageMR Fractions Course* by the US Math Recovery Council which contains the fraction domain of the Learning Framework in Number (US Math Recovery Council, 2016). For more information on this course, see https://www.mathrecovery.org/professional-development/addvangtage-mr-fractions.

Conceptual Understandings and Conventions of Mathematics

There are two types of mathematical knowledge included in the Learning Framework in Number for the Classroom. One type is the socially constructed **conventions of mathematics** and can only be known if one is informed of the convention. These are because someone decided they would be so. One example of a convention is the names that we call numerals. 'Five' must be learned as the name for the symbol 5 or the quantity ⁙ in English-speaking cultures. No student can construct this name without being informed of the information. Other examples of socially constructed conventions are the forward and backward sequences of numbers and the meaning of mathematical symbols. The second type of mathematical knowledge is the **conceptual understanding** that must be

THE LEARNING FRAMEWORK IN NUMBER
for the classroom

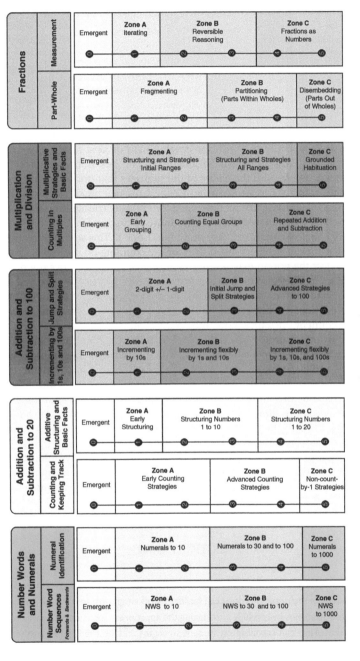

Figure 1.1 Learning Framework in Number for the Classroom schemata

Source: Ellemor-Collins et al. (forthcoming)

constructed by each student, such as strategies for adding and subtracting. While some domains of the Learning Framework in Number for the Classroom deal more with conventions of mathematics than others, one cannot say that any one domain is solely dependent on conventional or conceptual knowledge. These types of knowledge are highly dependent on each other. For example, while there is a socially constructed convention of mathematics surrounding the order of the forward number word sequence and the names of those numbers, students can also develop conceptual understanding about the patterns of those numbers and how the numerals are related to each other. Similarly, while developing additive strategies is dependent on the construction of conceptual knowledge, it is also dependent on those socially constructed conventions that give definition to the names of the numbers involved in the additive tasks and the numerals and symbols used to record their thinking.

With this caveat in mind, we can characterize certain portions of the Learning Framework in Number for the Classroom as more concerned with the development of new, more sophisticated conceptual understanding than others. For example, what distinguished one zone from another on the left-hand side of Addition and Subtraction to 20 is the nature of the strategies that students use to solve additive and subtractive tasks in the range of 1 to 20. Students in Zone A use perceptual and figural strategies to solve additive tasks. These students have not yet developed a composite concept of number. They are said to be pre-numerical in their thinking (see Chapter 9 for more discussion of this topic). As students develop an initial concept of composite numbers, they move into Zone B. This sort of thinking is evidenced by the emergence, without explicit, direct instruction, of the counting-on strategy for addition. Students construct for themselves the notion that 'seven' will always be seven and does not need to be counted each time to create seven. They also understand that seven contains within it six, and within six is five, and so on. They begin to see they can simply name the next number word (count-on) to determine the **sum** of 'one more' situations. Finally, as students begin using **units** greater than one to solve additive tasks without needing to count by ones, they move into Zone C. Solution strategies in Zone C would include a range of non-count-by-one strategies such as the use of doubles, near doubles, making 10, compensation, and the like, all of which involve mentally operating with different units or composite groups.

While students employ conventional knowledge in each zone in the domain, the characteristic that distinguishes between the strategies indicative of each zone is the nature of their conceptual knowledge as indicated by the additive strategies they employ. At any given moment, students may be at different zones in various domains across the Learning Framework in Number for the Classroom. For example, a student might be in Zone C on the Number Word Sequences, Zone B in Number Identification, and Zone A on Addition and Subtraction to 20 Counting and Keeping Track. Conversely, another student might be developing non-count-by-one strategies to solve addition and subtraction tasks (Zone C), but the student's lack of mastery in distinguishing between the numerals in the range to 20 (Zone A) might severely hamper the student's success with problems in a written context.

Conclusion

If teachers have knowledge of the Learning Framework in Number for the Classroom and use the zones to plan for the needs of their students, they can facilitate student growth toward the emergence of ever-more sophisticated strategies by carefully introducing the appropriate instructional activities for that child at just the right time. They can capitalize on student strengths and intervene to strengthen areas lagging behind. Chapter 9 will discuss several manageable strategies which teachers may employ to make sure students within a heterogeneously grouped classroom are presented with the appropriate instructional experiences given their zone in the domains of the Learning Framework in Number for the Classroom.

2

Professional Principles and Practices

Today's teachers benefit from a variety of research, resources, and practices to guide our instruction. At times the plethora of new ideas can seem overwhelming, and it can be difficult to determine how best to meet the needs of our students. This chapter will examine professional principles and practices from the disciplines of mathematics education and special education, to see how they align with the Learning Framework in Number, presented in Chapter 1. It will also address the assessment and instructional practices introduced in the other books in the Math Recovery series.

The Council for Exceptional Children and the National Council of Teachers of Mathematics are professional organizations supporting special education teachers and teachers of mathematics. Both organizations have outlined standards and practices for their members. The National Academies of Sciences, in its publication *Adding it Up: Helping Children Learn Mathematics* (Kilpatrick, Swafford, & Findell, 2001) and the National Governors Association, in their **Common Core State Standards for Mathematics** (*CCSSM*, 2010b), offer additional guidance on instructional practices for teachers of mathematics. This chapter will connect our assessment and teaching practices to the suggested practices of these organizations and publications.

Additional information on assessment practices can be found in Chapter 5, and information on instructional practices can be found in Chapters 3 and 10 of this book. We hope that the examples laid out in this chapter will give guidance for teachers as they evaluate the instructional resources and methods available and work to align their instruction with recommended practices.

CEC Code of Ethics (CEC, 2015)

The Council for Exceptional Children (CEC) is a professional organization for special education teachers in the United States. The organization provides guidance and support for teachers as they meet the diverse needs of students with disabilities. Will teachers who use the assessment and instructional practices promoted in this book be upholding the code of ethics promoted by the CEC? We contend that our practices align with and support these specific ethical principles.

1.   **Maintaining challenging expectations for individuals with exceptionalities to develop the highest possible learning outcomes and quality of life potential in ways that respect their dignity, culture, language, and background. (CEC, 2015, p. 1)**

Students will develop the highest possible learning outcomes when instruction is based on their current skills and conceptual understanding and these Guiding Principles of Instruction as presented in *LFIN*:

- Guiding Principle 1: Initial and ongoing assessment…
- Guiding Principle 3: Teaching just beyond the cutting edge…
- Guiding Principle 5: Engendering more sophisticated strategies
- Guiding Principle 6: Observing the child and fine-tuning teaching. (LFIN, p. 92)

(See Chapter 3 for more information on the Guiding Principles of Instruction.)

2.   **Maintaining a high level of professional competence and integrity and exercising professional judgment to benefit individuals with exceptionalities and their families. (CEC, 2015, p. 1)**

We do not promote a cookie cutter approach to instruction, in which teachers follow a specific program or script when providing instruction. Instruction for all students must be geared toward students' specific needs as determined by one-to-one assessments designed to help teachers determine students' current abilities. Then, implementing 'Guiding Principle 4: Selecting from a bank of teaching procedures' (*LFIN*, p. 92), teachers use their professional judgment to design a program of instruction that will meet the needs of each student.

3.   **Promoting meaningful and inclusive participation of individuals with exceptionalities in their schools and communities. (CEC, 2015, p. 1)**

The previous books in the Math Recovery series were written to provide meaningful mathematics instruction to all students. The Learning Framework in Number allows us to look at the abilities of all students and plan appropriate instruction. In the classroom, this means all students assessed to be working in a particular zone of the Learning Framework in Number, regardless of their perceived abilities or disabilities, will benefit from instruction designed to engender their movement to the next zone. It also means that teachers will have the knowledge and ability to modify classroom activities to meet the needs of all students in the classroom. Additionally, students benefit from participating in learning activities with students who may be at a zone above or below them. The opportunities to learn from other students is a benefit to all.

4. **Using evidence, instructional data, research, and professional knowledge to inform practice. (CEC, 2015, p. 1)**

By using the Learning Framework in Number (Chapter 1), assessment, (Chapter 5), and instructional practices (Chapters 3 and 10) presented in this book, teachers are able to determine their students' current conceptual understanding and provide appropriate learning opportunities. The Learning Framework in Number also provides a way to monitor the growth of students, providing important data for future instructional decisions.

CEC Standards for Professional Practice (CEC, 2015)

The CEC Standards for Professional Practice are organized into various categories. The standards for teaching and assessment are most relevant to this discussion.

"**1.1 Systematically individualize instructional variables to maximize the learning outcomes of individuals with exceptionalities (CEC, 2015, p. 1).**"

As mentioned above, the Learning Framework in Number, assessment techniques, and instructional strategies in this series enable teachers to meet the learning needs of all students. In this book we provide additional guidance in making adaptations to meet the needs of students with exceptionalities.

"**1.3 Use periodic assessments to accurately measure the learning progress of individuals with exceptionalities, and individualize instruction variables in response to assessment results (CEC, 2015, p. 1).**"

The **Teaching and Learning Cycle** (see Figure 2.1), as presented in Wright et al. (2006b, pp. 52–56) and Wright et al. (2015, pp. 12–13), emphasizes the need for initial and ongoing assessment. All instruction should begin with, and build on, the student's current understanding. Teachers then use their knowledge of the Learning Framework in Number (see Chapter 1) to determine the next steps in developing conceptual understanding. In addition to the Learning Framework in Number, the Dimensions of Mathematization, discussed in *DNK*, *DFK*, *LFIN*, and Chapter 3 of this book provide guidance on how to build on a student's current conceptual understanding. Using tasks such as those presented in *TN*, *TNC*, *DNK*, *DFK*, *LFIN*, and Chapter 10 of this book, teachers design instructional settings, activities, tasks, and games to engender new conceptual understanding. During instruction, teachers are constantly monitoring the conceptual understanding of their students and using the Learning Framework in Number to determine if instruction needs to be adjusted.

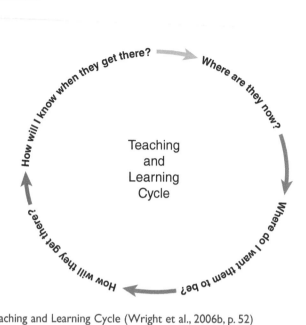

Figure 2.1   The Teaching and Learning Cycle (Wright et al., 2006b, p. 52)

"1.4 Create safe, effective, and culturally responsive learning environments which contribute to fulfill-ment of needs, stimulation of learning, and realization of positive self-concepts (CEC, 2015, p. 1)."

Readers are referred to Chapter 12 of this book for a discussion of how the techniques discussed in this series create culturally responsive learning environments.

"1.5 Participate in the selection and use of effective and culturally responsive instructional materials, equipment, supplies, and other resources appropriate to their professional roles (CEC, 2015, p. 1)."

Guiding Principle 4: Selecting from a bank of teaching procedures (*LFIN*, p. 92), encourages teachers to use their professional judgment in selecting the tools and activities that will be most appropriate for their students. *TN*, *TNC*, *DNK*, and *DFK*, as well as Chapter 10 of this book, provide suggestions for materials and activities. These suggestions are illustrations of the types of activities teachers have found successful when working with students. As stated in Guiding Principle 6: Observing the child and fine-tuning teaching (*LFIN*, p. 92), teachers need to continually monitor the student's response to instruction and adjust instruction to meet the student's needs.

"1.6 Use culturally and linguistically appropriate assessment procedures that accurately measure what is intended to be measured, and do not discriminate against individuals with excep-tional or culturally diverse learning needs (CEC, 2015, p. 1)."

Readers are referred to Chapter 12 of this book for a discussion of how the techniques discussed in this series meet the cultural and linguistic needs of students.

Adding It Up: Helping Children Learn Mathematics (Kilpatrick et al., 2001)

This publication, by the National Research Council, focuses on numeracy instruction for K–8 students and their teachers. It highlights five intertwined components of mathematical proficiency and how students and teachers can develop these proficiencies. We find that these five proficiencies align with the instructional practice promoted by the books in the Math Recovery series.

The five strands of mathematical proficiency presented in *Adding It Up* are:

- Conceptual Understanding
- Procedural Fluency
- Strategic Competence
- Adaptive Reasoning
- Productive Disposition.

Adding It Up indicates that these strands are interconnected, they support each other, and as teachers we must ensure that students have opportunities to engage with all of the strands. We will look at each strand and illustrate how the assessment and instructional practices promoted in this series support each strand.

Conceptual understanding

"Conceptual understanding refers to an integrated and functional grasp of mathematical ideas" (Kilpatrick et al., 2001, p. 118). In order to build conceptual understanding, students must have the opportunity to connect new ideas to what they already know. The Teaching and Learning Cycle referenced above under CEC Standard for Professional Practice 1.3 outlines a process for teachers to assess and monitor the conceptual understanding of students as they plan instruction to engender the growth of conceptual understanding.

The Guiding Principles, presented in the books in this series and outlined in Chapter 3 of this book, also support teaching for conceptual understanding. The Guiding Principles that specifically address teaching for conceptual understanding are elaborated in:

- Guiding Principle 2: Initial and ongoing assessment
- Guiding Principle 3: Teaching just beyond the cutting edge…
- Guiding Principle 5: Engendering more sophisticated strategies
- Guiding Principle 6: Observing the child and fine-tuning teaching…
- Guiding Principle 8: Encouraging sustained thinking and reflection. (LFIN, p. 92)

Teachers can observe whether students are using and developing their conceptual understanding by looking for the Characteristics of Children's Problem Solving, presented in *TN*, *LFIN*, and Chapter 3 of this book. Characteristics that may indicate conceptual understanding are:

- Cognitive reorganization
- Anticipation

- Curtailment
- Re-presentation
- Spontaneity, robustness, and certitude
- Asserting autonomy
- Child reflection. (*LFIN*)

Procedural fluency

"Procedural fluency refers to knowledge of procedures, knowledge of when and how to use them appropriately, and skill in performing them flexibly, accurately, and efficiently" (Kilpatrick et al., 2001, p. 121). While all strands of mathematical proficiency are intertwined, there is a very strong connection between conceptual understanding and procedural fluency. Conceptual understanding should precede the habituation of basic facts and the learning of procedures. As stated in *Adding it Up*, "once students have learned procedures without understanding, it can be difficult to get them to engage in activities to help them understand the reasons underlying the procedure" (Kilpatrick et al., 2001, p. 122).

The Learning Framework in Number illustrates how students build on their conceptual understanding to develop procedural fluency. For example, students who begin learning about addition by counting visible objects will progress through the stages to using known facts to help them solve unknown problems.

In *DNK*, readers are introduced to "phases of instruction" for Place Value (pp. 110–120) and Multiplication (pp. 149–155). Teachers who use these phases in planning instruction will provide students with opportunities to develop procedural fluency based on their conceptual understanding and then use that procedural fluency to develop new understanding. For example, after students "have developed flexible mental strategies for multiplying two 1-digit factors we advocate a systematic approach to developing automatized knowledge of basic facts" (*DNK*, p. 153). Students can then build on this habituation of basic facts to develop strategies for multiplication and division of multi-digit factors.

The Dimensions of Mathematization, mentioned briefly under Conceptual Understanding, outline ways that teachers can modify tasks to increase or decrease the sophistication of mathematical thinking required. The following dimensions from *DNK* and *LFIN* are important for moving from conceptual understanding to procedural fluency:

- Increasing the complexity
- Distancing the setting
- Notating and formalizing
- Refining strategies
- Structuring numbers. (*LFIN*, p. 18)

Moving through these dimensions allows students to use their conceptual understanding and procedural fluency to solve new problems or represent their thinking in more formal ways. For example, when teachers increase complexity, they use a skill that students have developed, such as adding to the next **decuple** (46 + 4), and increase the complexity by adding across the decuple (46 + 5). This gives students the opportunity to use what they know in solving a new type of problem.

The Guiding Principles related to procedural fluency are:

- Principle 5: Engendering more sophisticated strategies...
- Principle 7: Incorporating symbolizing and notating. (LFIN, p. 92)

Principle 7: Incorporating symbolizing and notating, is related to the **notating** and **formalizing** Dimension of Mathematization. Students may begin by using drawings and jottings to represent their thinking when solving problems. Over time, as their understanding develops, students can be introduced to more formal **algorithms**.

Students who have developed procedural fluency will exhibit the following Characteristics of Children's Problem Solving from *TN* and *LFIN*.

- Anticipation – knowing that their strategy will produce a correct answer.
- Curtailment – no longer needing previously used strategies.
- Spontaneity, robustness, and certitude – using a strategy independently, across a range of problems, and with confidence.

Strategic competence

'Strategic competence refers to the ability to formulate mathematical problems, represent them, and solve them' (Kilpatrick et al., 2001, p. 124). 'For day-to-day instruction, we advocate an approach based on inquiry, that is, on posing and solving problems' (*DNK*, p. 19). Fostering students' abilities to solve problems is at the heart of Guiding Principle 1: 'Children routinely are engaged in thinking hard to solve numerical problems which for them are quite challenging' (*TNC*, p. 6). This principle promotes teaching that involves giving students problems 'for which the children do not have a ready-made solution' (*TNC*, p. 6). Guiding Principle 8: Encouraging sustained thinking and reflection (*LFIN*, p. 92), emphasizes the need for **wait-time** after a problem is presented and after students have given a response. Giving wait-time for students to solve problems sends the message that real problems require sustained thinking. Providing wait-time after a solution has been presented sends the message that the student, not the teacher, can take responsibility for determining if the solution is correct. Post-posing wait-time and post-responding wait-time are two of the Key Elements of One-to-One Instruction presented in *LFIN*. Initially, students may feel frustration when teachers do not step in to help with difficult problems or do not immediately acknowledge their responses; however, child engagement and child reflection are two Characteristics of Children's Problem Solving that indicate their developing strategic competence.

Adaptive reasoning

'Adaptive reasoning refers to the capacity to think logically about the relationships among concepts and situations' (Kilpatrick et al., 2001, p. 129). There are two Dimensions of Mathematization (*DNK*, pp. 14–19) that address this mathematical proficiency:

- Structuring Numbers promotes the development of an expanding web of relationships between numbers and concepts.

- Generalizing describes the process in which students see patterns and make conjectures based on their observations. 'When students develop number concepts, number relationships, and computation strategies, they are typically generalizing from a few cases to many cases' (DNK, p. 19).

Adaptive reasoning can be developed through explaining and justifying answers. Asking students to explain their thinking and justify their answers is an important aspect of the initial and ongoing assessment process used to determine students' conceptual understanding.

Productive disposition

'Productive disposition refers to the tendency to see sense in mathematics, to perceive it as both useful and worthwhile, to believe that steady effort in learning mathematics pays off, and to see oneself as an effective learner and doer of mathematics' (Kilpatrick et al., 2001, p. 131). This mathematical proficiency aligns with Guiding Principle 9: Aiming for children's intrinsic satisfaction (LFIN, p. 92), and can be observed when students are exhibiting the Characteristic of Children's problem solving, enjoying the challenge. When teachers are aware of the conceptual understanding of their students and use the Learning Framework in Number to implement Guiding Principle 3: Teaching just beyond the cutting edge (LFIN, p. 92), students will have the opportunity to solve meaningful problems that will advance their competence and enjoyment of mathematics. 'Developing a productive disposition requires frequent opportunities to make sense of mathematics, to recognize the benefits of perseverance, and to experience the rewards of sense making in mathematics' (Kilpatrick et al., 2001, p. 131). The assessment and instructional techniques presented in the Math Recovery series of books provide these opportunities to all students.

Standards for Mathematical Practice (National Governors Association Center, CCSSM, 2010b)

The Standards for Mathematical Practice are a component of the **Common Core State Standards** which have been adopted by many states and territories in the United States. While not all states have adopted these standards, most states have adopted standards that are closely aligned. These Standards for Mathematical Practice are based on the Process Standards, developed by the National Council of Teachers of Mathematics and The Strands of Mathematical Proficiency outlined in *Adding It Up*.

1.   **Make sense of problems and persevere in solving them.**

"Mathematically proficient students start by explaining to themselves the meaning of a problem and looking for entry points to its solution" (CCSSM, p. 6). Solving problems is an important aspect of assessment and instruction. Assessment tasks are designed to elicit students' most sophisticated strategies for solving problems. Teachers use information from assessments to determine students' current level of understanding and design instruction that will engender their movement to the next level. Based on Guiding Principle 1: Enquiry-based/problem-based teaching (LFIN, p. 92), this instruction will be based on tasks and problems for which students do not immediately know the answer.

When students struggle with a problem, teachers may use one or more of the Key Elements of One-to-One Instruction, from *LFIN*, to guide students through an impasse:

- 9. Reformulating a task
- 10. Scaffolding during a task
- 11. Introducing an additional setting during solving
- 12. Post-posing wait-time
- 13. Post-responding wait-time
- 14. Re-posing the task
- 15. Rephrasing the task
- 16. Focused prompting
- 17. Giving encouragement to a partly correct response. (LFIN, p. 98)

(See Chapter 3 for information on the Key Elements of One-to-One Instruction.)

2.   Reason abstractly and quantitatively.

"Mathematically proficient students make sense of quantities and their relationships in problem situations" (CCSSM, p. 6). Our approach to instruction moves from working with perceived items to bare numbers. One example of this is our approach to addition and subtraction to 100, outlined in *DNK*. Teachers first ensure that students have the foundational knowledge of **structuring numbers** to 20, which is learned through the use of visual models such as five-, ten-, and twenty-frames, and math racks. Students are also given time to develop conceptual place value, which is the ability to use mental strategies for adding and subtracting tens and ones. These mental strategies are first developed in the context of materials so that students are able to see and reason about the quantities being added and subtracted. Students then use their knowledge of structuring and conceptual place value to add and subtract one-digit numbers to and from two-digit numbers. Again, these early lessons involve the use of materials, giving students the opportunity to develop a mental image, which can be used when solving problems with bare numbers. As students develop mental strategies to solve bare number problems, their thinking may be represented by notations, such as the **empty number line** for **jump strategies** or drop-down notation for **split strategies**. Further discussion of notating strategies can be found in *DNK*.

3.   Construct viable arguments and critique the reasoning of others.

"Mathematically proficient students understand and use stated assumptions, definitions, and previously established results in constructing arguments" (CCSSM, p. 6). Common questions asked during assessment are: "How do you know?" "If you didn't know the answer, how could you figure it out?" and "Do you have another way to figure it out?" Students are given experience from their first opportunities solving problems to construct viable arguments. Through activities and games students listen to and critique the reasoning of other students as they refine their ability to construct their own arguments.

4.   Model with mathematics.

"Mathematically proficient students can apply the mathematics they know to solve problems arising in everyday life, society, and the workplace" (CCSSM, p. 7). Readers are directed to Chapter 4 of this book for a discussion of numeracy and functional mathematics. Students are better equipped to use mathematics in everyday life when they have constructed conceptual understanding of mathematics.

5.   Use appropriate tools strategically.

"Mathematically proficient students consider the available tools when solving a mathematical problem" (CCSSM, p. 7). Students are exposed to a variety of settings during the course of instruction, and they are encouraged to see and use the similarities between settings. For example, a teacher may flash a ten-frame to a group of students. Some of the students will be asked to show the quantity on their fingers. Other students will represent the quantity on a math rack. A third group will write or select the number that represents the quantity they see. Because students are exposed to a variety of tools, they are able to select the tools that will be most beneficial to them in solving problems. In addition to physical tools, students are constantly building a repertoire of mental strategies and ways to notate their thinking. They can determine if a problem such as 200 – 98 is most efficiently solved by using the standard algorithm with pencil and paper, or if a mental strategy will be more efficient.

6.   Attend to precision.

"Mathematically proficient students try to communicate precisely to others" (CCSSM, p. 7). As mentioned in Practice 3, students are often given opportunities to explain their thinking and listen to the thinking of others. Teachers use the Key Elements of One-to-One Instruction, presented in Practice 1 above, to encourage students in refining their explanations.

7.   Look for and make use of structure.

"Mathematically proficient students look closely to discern a pattern or structure" (CCSSM, p. 8). As students' understanding of computational strategies increase, they make use of their understanding to solve problems more easily. For example, students who are just beginning to understand the process for solving subtraction problems may need to count backward to solve the problem 10 – 2. However, more advanced students can use their knowledge of composing and decomposing numbers to ten and their knowledge of inverse operations in using 8 + 2 to solve 10 – 2.

8.   Look for and express regularity in repeated reasoning.

"Mathematically proficient students notice if calculations are repeated, and look both for general methods and for shortcuts" (CCSSM, p. 8). This mathematical practice is related to the Structuring Numbers and Generalizing Themes of Progressive Mathematization. Using the theme of Structuring Numbers, students notice and use relationships between numbers to build a web of relationships between numbers. Using the theme of Generalizing, students notice and use patterns when solving problems. For example, students use the answer to 6 + 4 to solve the problems 16 + 4, 26 + 4, etc. In this example, students are using their knowledge of combinations to ten, to solve higher decade addition.

Principles to Actions: Ensuring Mathematical Success for All (National Council of Teachers of Mathematics, 2014a)

The primary message of this publication is "effective teaching is the nonnegotiable core that ensures that all students learn mathematics at high levels and that such teaching requires a range of actions at the state or provincial, district, school, and classroom levels" (National Council of Teachers of Mathematics, 2014a, p. 4). The authors have identified eight Mathematics Teaching Practices which they believe represent "a core set of high-leverage practices and essential teaching skills necessary to promote deep learning of mathematics" (National Council of Teachers of Mathematics, 2014a, p. 9). Since many of these teaching practices are related to the Mathematical Proficiencies from *Adding It Up* and the Standards for Mathematical Practice from the Common Core State Standards for Mathematics, we only cover unique connections here and refer the reader to previous sections of this chapter for connections that have already been discussed.

Establish mathematics goals to focus learning

> Effective teaching of mathematics establishes clear goals for the mathematics that students are learning, situates goals within learning progressions, and uses the goals to guide instructional decisions (National Council of Teachers of Mathematics, 2014a, p. 12)

Our focus is on numeracy instruction which provides a strong and necessary foundation for the other strands of mathematics. The Learning Framework in Number (see Chapter 1) illustrates the various domains of number learning and the developmental progress students make as they increase their skills and understanding. This framework and our understanding of students' current attainment guide us as we establish mathematics goals to focus learning.

Implement tasks that promote reasoning and problem solving

> Effective teaching of mathematics engages students in solving and discussing tasks that promote mathematical reasoning and problem solving and allow multiple entry points and varied solution strategies. (National Council of Teachers of Mathematics, 2014a, p. 17)

Refer above to:

- Conceptual Understanding from *Adding it Up: Helping Children Learn Mathematics*
- Standards for Mathematical Practice 1. Make sense of problems and persevere in solving them, from *Common Core State Standards for Mathematics*.

Use and connect mathematical representations

> Effective teaching of mathematics engages students in making connections among mathematical representations to deepen understanding of mathematical concepts and procedures as tools for problem solving. (National Council of Teachers of Mathematics, 2014a, p. 24)

The Learning Framework in Number outlines the progressions of student development across various domains of mathematics. During assessment and instruction, we monitor the progress of students through these various domains. These domains represent symbolic, verbal, and quantitative representations of number. It is our goal that students connect these representations: that is, understanding that the symbol '5' can represent five objects, and those objects can be counted by using the verbal sequence 'one, two, three, four, five.' These connections continue as students connect 3 × 5 with the verbal expression 'three times five' and the quantity represented by three groups with five objects in each group. Students also connect their verbal strategies for adding or subtracting bundles of ten and single sticks with a visual representation such as an empty number line. Students are encouraged to make connections between different visual representations of quantity. (See Standards for Mathematical Practice 5: Use appropriate tools strategically.)

Facilitate meaningful mathematical discourse

Effective teaching of mathematics facilitates discourse among students to build shared understanding of mathematical ideas by analyzing and comparing student approaches and arguments. (National Council of Teachers of Mathematics, 2014a, p. 29)

Refer above to:

- Standards for Mathematical Practice 3: Construct viable arguments and critique the reasoning of others.
- Standards for Mathematical Practice 6: Attend to precision, from Common Core State Standards for Mathematics.

Pose purposeful questions

Effective teaching of mathematics uses purposeful questions to assess and advance students' reasoning and sense making about important mathematical ideas and relationships. (National Council of Teachers of Mathematics, 2014a, p. 35)

Two of the Key Elements of One-to-One Instruction address the importance of posing purposeful questions. These are querying both incorrect and correct responses (LFIN).

Students should not assume that their response is incorrect just because their teacher questions their response. Teachers should not assume that students have conceptual understanding just because they give a correct response. Posing purposeful questions allows us to understand the strategies students are using to solve problems. The questions we pose can also engender the development of more sophisticated strategies.

For additional information on posing purposeful questions, refer above to:

- Standards for Mathematical Practice 3: Construct viable arguments and critique the reasoning of others.

Build procedural fluency from conceptual understanding

Effective teaching of mathematics builds fluency with procedures on a foundation of conceptual understanding so that students, over time, become skillful in using procedures flexibly as they solve contextual and mathematical problems. (National Council of Teachers of Mathematics, 2014a, p. 42)

Refer above to:

- Conceptual Understanding from *Adding It Up*.
- Procedural Fluency from *Adding It Up*.

Support productive struggle in learning mathematics

Effective teaching of mathematics consistently provides students, individually and collectively, with opportunities and supports to engage in **productive struggle** as they grapple with mathematical ideas and relationships. (National Council of Teachers of Mathematics, 2014a, p. 48)

The following Guiding Principles from *LFIN* support productive struggle:

- Guiding Principle 3: Teaching just beyond the cutting edge (LFIN, p. 92).
  This principle encourages teachers to focus instruction just beyond students' current knowledge. Problems are presented that build on and extend students' strategies.
- Guiding Principle 6: Observing the child and fine tuning (LFIN, p. 92).
  Considering the results of initial and ongoing assessment, teachers design instructional tasks based on their hypothesis of students' current understanding. As students begin working, teachers observe students for signs that the task is too easy or too difficult. If the task appears to be too easy or difficult, teachers may use the Dimensions of Progressive Mathematization (see Chapter 3 for more information.) to increase or decrease the rigor of the task. If the task appears to be too difficult for students (students are struggling but it is not productive), teachers may implement one or more of the Key Elements of One-to-One instruction:
  - 11. Introducing an additional setting during solving
  - 12. Post-posing wait-time
  - 13. Post-responding wait-time
  - 14. Re-posing the task
  - 15. Re-phrasing the task
  - 16. Focused prompting
  - 17. Giving encouragement to a partly correct response
  - 18. Directing to check
  - 19. Querying an incorrect response. (*LFIN*, p. 98)

Teachers also need to consider that the task presented was not within students' capacities to solve the problem at this time. In other words, the teacher's hypothesis about students' current understanding was incorrect. In that case, teachers may decide to release students from the task and move on to a new task or activity.

Elicit and use evidence of student thinking

Effective teaching of mathematics uses evidence of student thinking to assess progress toward mathematical understanding and to adjust instruction continually in ways that support and extend learning. (National Council of Teachers of Mathematics, 2014a, p. 53)

The Learning Framework in Number outlines a developmental sequence for the acquisition of numeracy knowledge. Teachers listen and watch for evidence of students' current development and, using the Learning Framework in Number, they anticipate what knowledge is on the horizon for each student. Students are encouraged to explain or show their strategies for solving problems, proving evidence of their current understanding.

For additional information on this mathematics teaching practice, refer above to:

- Standards for Mathematical Practice 3: Construct viable arguments and critique the reasoning of others.
- CEC Code of Ethics Principle 6: Using evidence, instructional data, research, and professional knowledge to inform practice.
- CEC Standards for Professional Practice 1.3: Use periodic assessments to accurately measure the learning progress of individuals with exceptionalities and individualize instruction variables in response to assessment results.

Conclusion

This chapter has examined the professional standards and practices of two groups of educators we believe will interact with the content of this book. We have attempted to illustrate how the assessment and teaching practices outlined in this book and in other books in the Math Recovery series align with these practices. Readers are encouraged to consider these principles and practices as they evaluate resources for instruction.

3

Good Instruction for All Students

In this chapter we will explore instructional practices introduced in the existing books in the Math Recovery series and advocate for their use in teaching students with disabilities.

In searching the research literature, method books, and websites, teachers will find a variety of strategies for teaching mathematics. Some methods are recommended specifically for students with disabilities and others are recommended for the general student population. When teachers explore new and effective ways to help students construct an understanding of mathematics, they will also encounter methods designed to guide students through mathematical procedures. These procedural methods may help students get answers, but they often rob students of the opportunity to solve problems. The existing books in the Math Recovery series provide a collection of instructional practices that can be implemented by all teachers to support students in constructing their understanding of mathematics.

Guiding Principles for Classroom Teaching

The Guiding Principles for Classroom Teaching were first introduced in *TN*, pp. 25–31, and referred to as The Guiding Principles of MR Teaching. With the publication of *TNC*, pp. 5–8, the same set of principles became Guiding Principles for Classroom Teaching. This is an indication of the appropriateness of these principles for any type of instructional setting. Summaries of these guiding principles are included in *DNK*, pp. 19–20, and *LFIN*, pp. 92–93. *DFK*, pp. 5–8, includes a discussion of Guiding Principles for Instruction, which illustrates the appropriateness of these principles across domains of numeracy instruction. The Guiding Principles for Classroom Teaching, as presented in *TNC*, pp. 5–8, are:

1. The teaching approach is inquiry based, that is problem based. Children routinely are engaged in thinking hard to solve numerical problems which for them are quite challenging.
2. Teaching is informed by an initial, comprehensive assessment and ongoing assessment through teaching. The latter refers to the teacher's informed understanding of children's current knowledge and problem-solving strategies and continual revision of this understanding.
3. Teaching is focused just beyond the 'cutting-edge' [sic] of the child's current knowledge.
4. Teachers exercise their professional judgement in selecting from a bank of teaching procedures each of which involves particular instructional settings and tasks, and varying this selection on the basis of ongoing observations.
5. The teacher understands children's numerical strategies and deliberately engenders the development of more sophisticated strategies.
6. Teaching involves intensive, ongoing observation by the teacher and continual **micro-adjusting** or fine-tuning of teaching on the basis of her or his observation.
7. Teaching supports and builds on children's intuitive, verbally based strategies and these are used as a basis for the development of written forms of arithmetic which accord with the child's verbally based strategies.
8. The teacher provides the child with sufficient time to solve a given problem. Consequently, the child is frequently engaged in episodes which involve sustained thinking, reflection on her or his thinking and reflecting on the results of her or his thinking.
9. Children gain intrinsic satisfaction from their problem solving, their realization that they are making progress and from the verification methods they develop. (*TNC*, p. 6)

These Guiding Principles will be discussed in more detail, including how they might contrast with some existing practices in teaching students with disabilities.

Guiding Principle 1

The teaching approach is inquiry based, that is problem based. Children routinely are engaged in thinking hard to solve numerical problems which for them are quite challenging. (*TNC*, p. 6)

This principle is in contrast to Gradual Release of Responsibility, also known as 'I do, We do, You do,' in which teachers model a skill, then guide students through the skill, and finally release the students to perform the skill independently (Fischer and Fray, 2014). There are some situations in which this instructional technique may be appropriate such as learning the names of numerals or the forward and backward sequence of numbers. However, when students are solving problems that are challenging for them and build on their previous knowledge, we advocate for beginning with 'You do.' Students should be given sufficient wait-time (Guiding Principle 8) to build on their current knowledge (Guiding Principle 2) to solve problems. The success of this Guiding Principle is dependent on teachers utilizing Guiding Principle 5 and posing problems that will 'engender the development of more sophisticated strategies.' The following characteristics of problem-centered lessons are presented in *TNC*:

- Activities should require children to use strategic thinking rather than automatic or procedural responses. There are times when you might design activities to enhance factual knowledge but activities should largely involve problematic rather than routine tasks.

- Activities should allow children to use their current number knowledge. If the activities are too advanced, there is a risk that children will become frustrated in attempting to undertake the activities.
- Children should acquire some mathematical knowledge from engaging in an activity. If the tasks are too simple, children will not have an opportunity to advance their number knowledge. (*TNC*, pp. 12–13)

Guiding Principle 2

Teaching is informed by an initial, comprehensive assessment and ongoing assessment through teaching. The latter refers to the teacher's informed understanding of children's current knowledge and problem-solving strategies and continual revision of this understanding. (*TNC*, p. 6)

In order to build on what students know, we need to determine their current knowledge, skills, and understanding. Initial and ongoing assessment are key. We do not wait until the next formal assessment to change our instructional goals; rather the instructional goals change as students acquire new understanding and exhibit this understanding through problem solving. Through their interactions with students, teachers are able to constantly assess formatively as they are teaching. Using their knowledge of the Learning Framework in Number, teachers can set realistic goals and systems for collecting data on student progress needed for writing Individualized Education Programs (IEPs), parent conferences, and progress reports. (See Chapter 5.)

Guiding Principle 3

Teaching is focused just beyond the 'cutting-edge' [*sic*] of the child's current knowledge. (*TNC*, p. 7)

Steffe (1991) refers to this **cutting edge** as the zone of potential construction. Implementing this principle successfully requires Guiding Principle 2, initial and ongoing assessment, and Guiding Principles 5 and 6, the ability to make adjustments in teaching to engender more sophisticated strategies. The mathematics with which students engage should make sense to them. When students are confused about how to solve the problems presented to them, teachers need to return to what makes sense for the student and progress from there. For some students, the zone of potential construction can seem very thin; it is our job as teachers to tinker with instructional activities to meet the needs of each student.

Guiding Principle 4

Teachers exercise their professional judgement in selecting from a bank of teaching procedures each of which involves particular instructional settings and tasks, and varying this selection on the basis of ongoing observations. (*TNC*, p. 7)

This Guiding Principle is in contrast to scripted lessons or any resource in which teachers are expected to turn the page and teach the next lesson. The Guiding Principle recognizes the professionalism of teachers and their ability to design and adapt lessons based on the needs of students.

Guiding Principle 5

The teacher understands children's numerical strategies and deliberately engenders the development of more sophisticated strategies. (*TNC*, p. 7)

Building on the strategies currently used by students, teachers present problems that will promote the use of a more advanced strategy. For example, if a student is currently counting from one to determine the quantity of counters under two screens, the teacher might make the first quantity large enough that the student is dissuaded from counting the collection from one. If the second quantity is just one or two, the student may find it easier to just say the first quantity and count on one or two more. This is in contrast to telling students, 'Put the big number in your head and count on.' This guiding principle acknowledges that all students are capable of learning and improving their understanding of mathematics.

Guiding Principle 6

Teaching involves intensive, ongoing observation by the teacher and continual micro-adjusting or fine-tuning of teaching on the basis of her or his observation. (*TNC*, p. 8)

Guiding Principle 6 begins with teacher observations as students are solving problems. The information needed by teachers will not be apparent from watching students complete worksheets or listening to them reciting known facts. Teachers need to watch as students solve genuine problems and ask questions to determine the students' strategies. Based on their observations, teachers can make small adjustments to the task or ask questions to promote the development of a more advanced strategy. The ability to micro-adjust is also important for teachers to meet the needs of a class in which students are using a range of strategies. Through micro-adjusting, teachers can adapt the same activity to meet the needs of students with a variety of abilities.

Guiding Principle 7

Teaching supports and builds on students' intuitive strategies and these are used as a basis for the development of written forms of arithmetic which align with the students' intuitive strategies.

This principle has been modified from the principle as introduced in the existing books to honor the fact that not all students are verbal. Neurotypical students may utter counting sequences as they solve problems or may be able to explain their strategies. Non-verbal students may express their strategies in a variety of means such as sign language, **Augmentative and Alternative Communication** (AAC) system for communication, drawing pictures, or demonstrating with **manipulatives**, depending on their particular disability. Students who are non-verbal, while they do not utter sequences and cannot verbally explain the thinking associated with their strategy, do possess intuitive, informal strategies that should form the basis of any emerging written forms of arithmetic.

Guiding Principle 8

The teacher provides the child with sufficient time to solve a given problem. Consequently, the child is frequently engaged in episodes which involve sustained thinking, reflection on her or his thinking and reflecting on the results of her or his thinking. (*TNC*, p. 8)

Students need time to solve problems and the opportunity to think about how they were successful or unsuccessful in solving problems. This principle is connected to Principles 3 and 5 in that students must be given problems that build on their current understanding, and are accessible, so that solving the problem is challenging yet possible. Students come to realize that the answers to problems are not just something they know or do not know, rather the solution is something they can figure out. Students who have been unsuccessful solving problems in the past, because the problems were not appropriate for their current understanding, will need to build stamina for solving problems. The intrinsic satisfaction gained from solving problems, Guiding Principle 9, will encourage students to persevere in solving problems.

Guiding Principle 9

Children gain intrinsic satisfaction from their problem solving, their realization that they are making progress, and from the verification methods they develop. (*TNC*, p. 8)

Rather than receiving rewards from the teacher, such as food or stickers, students are rewarded by the awareness that they are making progress in their ability to solve new and challenging problems.

Key Elements of Intensive One-to-One Instruction

Twelve Key Elements of Intensive One-to-One Instruction were introduced in *TN*, pp. 31–37, and referred to as Key Elements of Individualized Teaching. Based on the research of Tran (2016) the Key Elements of Intensive One-to-One Instruction were expanded in *LFIN*, pp. 96–100, to include 26 key elements which are organized by the stages of teachers and students working through a task: (1) before posing a task, (2) posing a task, (3) during solving a task, and (4) after solving a task. Tran (2016) defines a key element of instruction as 'a micro-instructional strategy used by a teacher when interacting with a student in solving an arithmetical task' (p. 25). Tran identifies four functions of the key elements of instruction (see p. 26). The first is organizing on-task activity which involves selecting materials and activities that will engage the students in learning mathematics. The second function is responding to students' thinking or answering by providing support or asking questions to promote further discussion. The third function is to adjust the challenge of a task. This adjustment might result in making the task more accessible or more challenging, depending on the needs of the students. The final function is providing opportunities for students to gain intrinsic satisfaction from solving tasks. Students gain intrinsic satisfaction by successfully solving tasks that are challenging to them, having the opportunity to check that their solutions are correct (as opposed to relying on confirmation from the teacher), and being aware of the progress they are making.

Tran (2016) also identified 'problematic teacher behaviors' which are presented in *LFIN*, pp. 100–101). Although these key elements and problematic teacher behaviors have been derived from observations of one-to-one instruction, they offer guidance for all teacher–student interactions, especially instruction focused on intervention. The 26 key elements, as presented in *LFIN*, are as follows.

Before posing a task:

1.   Stating a goal

Teachers generally have short-term and long-range goals for their students. Stating a goal is the process of sharing a goal with students. The goal should be a short-term goal that seems achievable to the teacher and the students. Examples include, 'Let's work to identify all the teen numbers,' or 'I think you can learn all the combinations that make ten.' Stating an achievable goal helps focus students' attention and helps them experience a sense of accomplishment when the goal is achieved.

2. Pre-formulating a task

When teachers pre-formulate a task, they are preparing the student for the task or tasks that follow. Pre-formulating helps students focus on important aspects of the task. One way that teachers might pre-formulate a task is by referring to work that students have done previously and how it connects to the current task. Teachers might also pre-formulate a task by explaining how they will be using materials and setting up the activity.

3. Introducing a setting

Tran (2016) identifies four categories of settings: materials such as counters, arithmetic racks, or numeral rolls; informal writing such as an empty number line or arrow notation; formal writing such as addition or subtraction expressions presented horizontally or vertically; and verbal tasks. Introducing a setting to students serves two purposes: students learn about the setting, and teachers learn what students know or do not know about the setting. It is important to realize that students and teachers might not understand a setting in the same way. When presenting a setting, teachers can ask questions to determine what students already know and how they may have interacted with the setting in the past. Possible questions include:

a. Have you seen this before?
b. Does this remind you of anything you have seen before?
c. Do you know what it's called? (This can be followed by telling students the name of the setting, if necessary.)
d. What do you notice about this?
e. How do you think this might help us when we are solving problems?

If students are non-verbal or have complex communication needs, teachers can spend time watching how the student interacts with the new setting.

4. Referring to an unseen setting

Referring to an unseen setting is an important element when students are moving from the use of materials to more abstract problems such as bare number problems. By reminding students of materials they have used to solve similar problems, teachers can help students visualize the materials and use that visualization to assist in solving the current problem. For example, when presenting students with a problem like $56 + 13$, a teacher might remind them of the work they have done adding bundles and sticks or beads on the 100-bead string.

5. Linking settings

When teachers introduce a new setting, it can be helpful to link the new setting to a setting the students have encountered previously. Teachers should not assume that students will make the same connections between settings that teachers are making. Examples of settings that might be linked are: a **numeral roll** and a 100-chart, 20-frames and an arithmetic rack, bundles and sticks and a 100-bead string.

6. Directly demonstrating

Since we want students to be problem solvers, we do not recommend directly demonstrating strategies for solving problems. However, teachers may need to demonstrate the use of various settings, such as an arithmetic rack or how to play a game, such as dominos.

7. Scaffolding before

'Scaffolding refers to statements or actions on the part of the teacher to provide support for a student in an interactive teaching session' (Wood et al., 1976, as cited in Tran, 2016, p. 94). When teachers scaffold before presenting a task, they include scaffolds they anticipate students will need as they present the task. Providing scaffolds can be especially helpful for students who have not previously experienced success with problem solving. Scaffolds can be strategically removed as students demonstrate they are capable of solving more complex problems.

Posing a task:

8. Color coding, **screening,** and **flashing**

These three instructional techniques are important aspects of Math Recovery teaching. Many teachers are familiar with the concrete–representational–abstract sequence for teaching numeracy concepts. The strategy of screening answers the question, 'How do we move students from concrete–representational to abstract?' Screening involves presenting concrete materials and then covering them (screening) with a piece of cloth or cardboard so that items are no longer visible. Screening prevents students from using the materials to solve the problem. One or both screens can be removed, if needed, to support students in solving the problem. Screening also allows students to check their answers by lifting the screen(s) to verify their answers. Flashing is related to screening in that students are able to see an image briefly before it is hidden from view.

Many readers will be familiar with **subitizing**, the ability to determine a quantity without counting. Flashing a collection of dots dissuades students from counting dots individually and encourages them to see and use groups of dots in determining the total. **Color coding** can be used in conjunction with screening and flashing. When presenting screened tasks, teachers can use different colors to represent the **addends**. Color can be used when flashing dot images to highlight groups of dots.

9. Reformulating a task

Reformulating a task involves restating or adding additional information before students have solved a problem. Teachers might emphasize important information or remind teachers of similar problems that have been solved in the past. This is in contrast to re-posing or scaffolding which occurs after students have not been successful in solving a problem. Teachers need to exercise caution in reformulating tasks so as not to interrupt students' thinking as they attempt to solve problems.

During work on a task:

Responding to a partly correct response, an incorrect response, or an impasse.

10. Scaffolding during

Scaffolding during a task is necessary when students are not successful solving a task. Scaffolding can include providing students with additional information, access to tools, or making previously screened items visible.

11. Introducing an additional setting during solving

Settings are the materials and situations used in presenting and solving tasks. Introducing an additional setting is also referred to as within-task setting change. This element is usually employed when students need additional help in solving a task. Teachers choose the tool or visual model that will provide the student with the support needed to successfully complete the task. When changing settings or introducing a new setting, teachers need to consider the new setting from the students' perspective and avoid making assumptions that students will perceive the new setting the same way teachers do. Introducing an additional setting can also be used to help students see the connection between different settings. For example, if students have been solving two-digit addition and subtraction problems using bundles and sticks, a teacher might introduce a 100-bead string, to show students how the two tools are related. Similarly, students who are solving addition and subtraction tasks with screened objects will need to see how this setting relates to written or verbal addition and subtraction problems. Teachers should not assume that students will see the similarities between settings. For some students, these connections may need to be made explicitly.

12. Post-posing wait-time

Post-posing wait-time and post-responding wait-time are both part of post-task wait-time originally presented in *TN*. Post-posing wait-time involves giving students time to think about the problems presented. This element assumes that teachers are utilizing Guiding Principle 1, that students are routinely solving problems for which they do not immediately know the answer. Students who are not accustomed to solving problems may need to build their stamina for solving problems. Teachers will need to observe students and select tasks and settings that are appropriate for them (Guiding Principles 4 and 6). Teachers also need to observe students' behaviors closely to determine if students are working on the task presented or if they have given up. Determining the appropriate amount of post-posing wait-time for specific students can be tricky and may require some trial and error. Waiting too long may result in students giving up and wasting instructional time, but not giving enough post-posing wait-time might result in the interruption of student thinking.

13. Post-responding wait-time

Teachers should also implement the element of post-responding wait-time. This gives students time to reflect on their strategies and answers, whether they are correct or incorrect. Post-responding wait-time also helps students realize that they do not need to depend on teachers to tell them if they are correct or incorrect. Many students have become accustomed to teachers giving immediate responses to their answers, relieving students of the responsibility of verifying their answers. In a whole-class or small-group setting, it is critical that the teacher develops this norm to allow processing time. Placing a finger to the lips can become a cue to students to maintain a moment of reflective silence.

14. Re-posing the task

    When teachers repose a task, they do not provide additional information, they are simply repeating information that students request or highlighting information that will be helpful for students as they work on the task. It may be helpful for some students to have important information written down for them so they can refer to it as they are working on the task.

15. Rephrasing the task

    Teachers may find it necessary to rephrase a task if students seem confused by the initial presentation. Teachers rephrasing a task do not provide additional information or change the setting, they are simply using different words to make the task clearer to students. This may be particularly important for **English learners** (ELs). See Chapter 12 for more on ELs.

16. Focused prompting

    Focused prompting involves asking open-ended questions about specific aspects of a task to see what students notice. An important aspect of focused prompting is that teachers ask students what they notice rather than telling students what to notice.

17. Giving encouragement to a partly correct response

    Teachers should give encouragement to students as they are solving problems and highlight the portions of the task that are being solved correctly. For example, if a student uses a counting-on strategy to solve an addition problem, but skips some numbers in the sequence, the teacher might respond, 'Counting on the next numbers sounds like a good idea; let's check the numeral roll to make sure you're saying all the numbers in the correct order.'

18. Directing to check

    Students can be directed to check their answers, whether they are correct or incorrect. This element is also referred to as child checking. The process of checking might involve using a tool such as a numeral roll or removing a screen so that objects become visible and can be counted. The process of checking helps students realize that answers to problems can be verified and that they do not need to rely on others to determine if answers are correct or incorrect.

19. Querying an incorrect response

    Teachers might question an incorrect response for two reasons. First, they might question the response to promote reflection so that students realize their mistakes. Another reason for questioning an incorrect response is to gain information on the strategies used and to discover why the error was made. This information will help the teacher scaffold the task or make micro-adjustments to the task.

20. Correcting a response

    Correcting a response is another key element that should not be overused. It might be used when quickly giving students the correct answer to a question will help students move on to other elements of the task.

Responding to a correct response

21. Querying a correct response

After students give a correct response, teachers may want to question the strategy used to solve the problem. This gives teachers insight into the sophistication of the strategies used by students. Teachers may also want to know if students have additional strategies for solving a problem. Being questioned about correct answers may be a new experience for students, and they may assume that if teachers are questioning their answer, it must be wrong. Querying a correct response gives students experience explaining their thinking and helps them develop certitude in their responses. Students who do not have experience explaining their thinking will benefit from listening to classmates explain their thinking. Additionally, teachers can model the language students might use by verbalizing what they observed students doing as they solved the problem. Students who are non-verbal can be asked to show how they determined an answer or draw a picture of their solution.

22. Affirming

Teachers can affirm correct answers or effort exhibited by students in working toward an answer. Verbal and non-verbal affirmations might be given at the completion of a task or as students are working. The affirmations can take the form of specific feedback and help provide language that students can use in solving future problems. For example, the first time a student counts back to solve a subtraction problem, the teacher might respond, 'I heard you use backward counting to solve that problem; that was a great idea!' This affirmation can be followed by a direction for the child to verify that the answer was correct.

23. Confirming, highlighting, and privileging a correct response.

Teachers can confirm, highlight, and privilege a correct response when students seem uncertain of their answer. Letting students know they are correct can get them beyond the concern of getting the correct answer and move on to focusing on the strategy used.

After a task:

24. Recapitulating

Recapitulating refers to the activity of teachers summarizing or highlighting strategies used by students. Recapitulating is helpful when students who do not have experience explaining their strategies can hear teachers explain strategies that were observed. Teachers can also use recapitulating as an opportunity to introduce more precise mathematical vocabulary to describe students' strategies.

25. Explaining

After students have completed a task, teachers can engage them in conversation about the strategies used. Teachers can extend the students' thinking and highlight new or significant strategies used by students. Teachers need to be aware of students' current understanding, so their explanations align with students' current strategies.

26. Giving a meta-explanation

A meta-explanation does not necessarily refer to a specific task but might relate a series of tasks to mathematics in general. For example, after working on a series of combinations to ten, a teacher might remark that knowing the combinations to ten will be helpful in solving many kinds of problems.

A key element that is included in *TN*, but is not included in Tran's expanded list, is teacher reflection (Wright et al., 2006b, p. 35). Although teachers should have a plan for each lesson, teacher observations and reflections may result in changing the problems posed or the scaffolds provided to students. Teacher reflection may not be an observable action, but the observable teacher actions that occur during work on a task and after a task will not be possible if teachers are not closely observing and questioning students to determine their current understanding and strategies. At the conclusion of a lesson, teacher reflection will influence the goals and tasks posed at the beginning of the next lesson.

In her observations of intensive one-to-one interventions, Tran (2016) also identified problematic teacher behaviors.

Problematic teacher behaviors **when presenting a task.**

- Flagging a task as being difficult or easy:

Tasks presented as being either difficult or easy can cause students to become anxious. If a task is presented as being easy, students may become concerned that they will not be able to solve an easy task and might experience added stress if they are not able to successfully complete the task. If a task is presented as being difficult, this can also raise anxiety if students are concerned about their ability to solve the task.

- Simultaneously making more than one request.

Teachers need to pose problems clearly so that students know what the teacher is asking. Asking students to respond to more than one question can be confusing to students.

Problematic teacher behaviors when providing support.

- Interrupting the student

This behavior is related to the key element of post-posing wait-time. Teachers need to make sure that students have time to think and take care not to interrupt student thinking by re-posing, re-phrasing, re-formulating, or scaffolding before it is necessary.

- Rushing or indecent haste:

This problematic behavior is related to the previous behavior of interrupting and is contrary to the key element of post-posing and post-responding wait-time.

- Miscuing or districting the student:

This problematic teacher behavior occurs when a teacher attempts to scaffold a task but provides information that is misleading to students or distracts them from a strategy they are attempting.

Giving a 'back-handed' compliment:

The key element of affirming can become problematic when a teacher expresses surprise when students have successfully solved a problem. 'I didn't think you would be able to do that' can send the message that the teacher did not have confidence in the student's problem-solving abilities.

Adding the key elements and eliminating the problematic teacher behaviors will enhance instruction for students with disabilities.

Dimensions of Mathematization

The Dimensions of Progressive Mathematization are discussed in *DNK*, pp. 15–19, *DFK*, pp. 11–14, and *LFIN*, pp. 16–20 and 94–96. 'Progressive mathematization means the development of mathematical sophistication over time.' (*DNK*, 2012, p. 15)

The discussions of progressive mathematization in the prior books in the series give teachers a roadmap for increasing or decreasing the rigor of problems presented to students by following the various dimensions. As teachers observe the strategies used successfully by students, they can adjust subsequent tasks along one or more dimensions to advance the types of problems students are able to solve. 'Mathematical knowledge is developed by progressively formalizing informal but meaningful strategies.' (Gravemeijer, 1994, as cited in Drijvers, 2003, p. 52)

In the same manner, teachers can adapt problems and scaffolds, based on the Dimensions of Mathematization, to make problems more accessible to students. 'Typical of progressive mathematization is that students in every phase can refer to the concrete level of the previous step in the mathematization process and infer meaning from that' (Drijvers, 2003, p. 52). This may be the key in utilizing the Dimensions of Progressive Mathematization for teachers of students with disabilities. Do the problems presented to students make sense to them? If not, how can the dimensions provide guidance in making adjustments to tasks so that students can connect to previous tasks and strategies that make sense to them? Rather than progressive mathematization, teachers of students with disabilities may need to consider **folding back** by returning to a previously developed state and building from there (Martin et al., 2005; Pirie, 1989). Teachers and students may fold back to a previously developed state when students encounter a problem that is not accessible with their current understanding. Folding back allows students to build on and extend their current understanding.

Table 3.1 outlines the Dimensions of Mathematization, as presented in *LFIN*, and provides examples of progressive mathematization and folding back. It is our intention that teachers should recognize ways they can make tasks more accessible to students who are struggling.

Table 3.1 Dimensions of Mathematization: progressive and folding back

Dimension of Mathematization	Progressive mathematization	Folding back
Extending the range	Working with larger numbers	Attempting the task with smaller numbers. The numbers chosen can be determined by the forward and backward number word sequences known by students, the numerals students can read, and/or the combinations and partitions known by students

Dimension of Mathematization	Progressive mathematization	Folding back
Varying the orientation	Solving a variety of problems, using the same numbers, presented in a variety of orientations. For example: $4 + 2 = ?$ $4 + ? = 6$ $6 - 2 = ?$ $6 - ? = 4$	Beginning with formats understood by students and relating new orientations to orientations that were previously understood by students
Increasing the complexity	Presenting problems that require more steps to complete, for example, moving from addition and subtraction tasks that do not require regrouping to tasks that require regrouping	Making problems less complex. For example, adding a single-digit number to a two-digit number instead of adding two, two-digit numbers
Distancing the setting	Moving from a visible setting to a screened setting and then bare numbers	Working from a bare number task, asking students to visualize a previously used setting and, if necessary, making the setting available to students
Notating and formalizing	Using more formal notation, such as a standard algorithm This can also include moving from teachers recording students' thinking to students recording their own thinking	Allowing students to use notation that makes sense to them such as drawing pictures, an empty number line, or arrow notation
Refining strategies	Using more efficient strategies	Allowing students to use strategies that make sense to them, even if they do not seem efficient to teachers or other students
Structuring numbers	Developing an organized network of number relationships	Recognizing the relationships that students are able to use and selecting problems that utilize those relationships
Unitizing	Organizing individual items into more complex and abstract units	Recognizing that some students need to count individual units to make sense of problems
Decimalizing	Recognizing that 10, 100, 1,000, etc., are special units to be constructed and used in solving problems	Recognizing that some students may not have constructed a unit of 10. Students may not realize that one ten and ten ones represent the same quantity
Organizing and generalizing	Noticing and using patterns when solving problems. Students are able to make generalizations such as adding an even number and an odd number will produce a sum that is an odd number	Recognizing that some students may not make the same observations as their peers. Patterns and generalizations that seem obvious to adults may not be obvious to all students. Teachers may need to prompt students to attend to relationships that their peers notice without prompting

Characteristics of Children's Problem Solving

Characteristics of children's problem solving will be evident when teachers are utilizing the Guiding Principles, key elements of instruction, and the domains of progressive mathematization to plan instruction. The characteristics of children's problem solving identified in *TN, p. 26*, are as follows.

Cognitive reorganization

Students are able to employ new strategies and solve problems that were previously inaccessible to them. These new strategies are available to students because they have developed this new understanding, not because they are mimicking a procedure. This is not to say that they cannot learn from witnessing strategies modeled by teachers and fellow students, rather students should take on new strategies because they make sense and are usable for the student in solving problems. Using the Guiding Principles of problem-based teaching, teaching just beyond the cutting edge, and encouraging sustained thinking and reflection will give students the opportunity to build on previously acquired strategies.

Anticipation

Students anticipate the strategy they will use to solve a problem, and they anticipate that the strategy will be successful. In the case of cognitive reorganization, students may be trying a strategy for the first time and, as a result of their new understanding, they anticipate that the strategy will work. Students might also anticipate that a strategy they have used in the past will help them to solve a new kind of problem. Teachers who use the Key Elements of referring to an unseen setting and scaffolding before presenting a task will engender the anticipation that a strategy will help students solve a task successfully.

Curtailment

This characteristic involves the realization, on the part of students, that previously used strategies are no longer needed to solve a problem. Perhaps the easiest example to observe is students who no longer need to count from one to solve an addition problem. Students realize that they can count on from the first addend rather than count the first addend from one. The Guiding Principle of engendering more sophisticated strategies and the Key Element of focused prompting can guide students toward the curtailment of strategies that are no longer needed by students.

Re-presentation

Re-presentation (von Glasersfeld, 1984) signifies a specific cognitive reorganization that occurs when students can replay a previous experience to solve problems (Wright et al., 2006a, p. 191). Instead of needing to see, and perhaps touch, physical items to determine a quantity, students can mentally replay previous experiences and reflect on that activity. The Key Element of color coding, screening, and flashing when presenting problems will develop the cognitive shift of re-presentation.

Spontaneity, robustness, and certitude

Spontaneity refers to students' ability to implement a problem-solving strategy without the need of scaffolding or focused prompting from the teacher. We anticipate that just as students decrease their reliance on perceptual materials to solve problems, they will also decrease their reliance on teacher assistance. See the following characteristic, asserting autonomy for more information on spontaneity. When students are able to use a strategy to solve a wide range of problems or are able to use a variety of settings to solve similar problems, they have demonstrated robustness in the use of that strategy. Teachers can promote robustness by utilizing the Dimensions of Progressive Mathematization, varying the orientation, and distancing the setting. Students are demonstrating certitude when they solve a problem with confidence, knowing that their answer is correct. Are students giving the answer with a questioning tone? Are they looking at the teacher's face for affirmation? If the teacher does not respond immediately, do students change their answer? These are signs that a student lacks certitude. Using the Key Elements of post-responding wait-time and directing to check will give students the message that they are responsible for determining the correctness of their answers.

Asserting autonomy

One way that students demonstrate spontaneity is by asserting autonomy. Statements such as 'Don't tell me,' or 'Don't show me,' indicate that students are ready to solve problems on their own. These statements can also indicate curtailment as students are preventing teachers from reminding them of strategies or tools they do not need to use. Students might also assert autonomy when teachers use the Key Element of directing to check by asserting that they do not need to check, they are sure of their answer.

Child engagement

An important characteristic of children's problem solving is that students are actively engaged in solving problems. They are not watching demonstrations of problem solving or completing pages of problems using the same strategies. Teachers who use Guiding Principle 3, teaching that is focused just beyond the cutting edge, will promote child engagement by presenting problems that are challenging, yet accessible. For many students who are developing their understanding of mathematics, child engagement must involve the use of physical settings that will help students make sense of the problems presented.

Child reflection

This characteristic is connected to Guiding Principle 8, providing the child with sufficient time to solve a given problem, and will occur when teachers utilize the Key Elements of post-posing and post-responding wait-time. Teachers can encourage reflection by using the Key Elements of querying a response, whether the response is correct or incorrect, and engaging in the Key Elements of recapitulating, explaining, and giving a meta-explanation after a task. It can be difficult for students and teachers to take the time needed to think about a problem. Many students have been given the message that they either know the answer or do not. They have not built the stamina necessary to figure out the answer to a problem to which they do not immediately know the answer. Teachers feel pressure to cover a lot of content, especially with students who have demonstrated significant holes in their learning. They feel a sense of urgency to move on to the next problem or topic, demonstrating the problematic teacher behavior of rushing or indecent haste.

Enjoying the challenge of problem solving

Students who are actively engaged in solving problems that are challenging, yet accessible, will enjoy the challenge. Just as people playing a video game enjoy the challenge of beating a level only to be rewarded with a slightly more difficult level, students can enjoy solving a series of progressively more challenging tasks. As stated in Guiding Principle 9, 'Children gain intrinsic satisfaction from their problem solving, their realization that they are making progress and from the verification of the methods they develop' (*TNC*, p. 8). Teachers and students may find it helpful to keep a record of the types of problems solved and the strategies used by students. This can be done by keeping a video record of students solving increasingly difficult tasks, or keeping a notebook where students record or dictate their strategies to be recorded by an adult. Both methods are a way to keep a record of student progress for teachers, students, and parents.

Conclusion

Teachers who utilize the Guiding Principles and Key Elements as they deliver instruction and plan lessons utilizing the Learning Framework in Number and the Dimensions of Mathematization will provide students with opportunities to engage in meaningful problem solving to advance their skills and strategies.

4

Numeracy and Functional Mathematics

In this chapter we will examine the meanings of functional mathematics and how they might be the same or different as academic skills. We will consider specific skills that have been identified as functional and illustrate how aspects of the Learning Framework in Number support the acquisition of functional skills.

What Is Functional Mathematics?

Functional mathematics, also known as life skills mathematics, is 'the mathematics related to living, working, participating, and accessing services in everyday life' (Bouck, Park, & Nickell, 2016a, p. 25). Functional mathematics skills can be divided into four domains: community, recreation, domestic, and vocational (Brown et al., 1979). In the simplest terms, functional mathematics can be thought of as the mathematics used by people without disabilities in day-to-day life (Dymond & Orelove, 2001). The ultimate goal of functional skills instruction for students with disabilities is to enable them to participate in the four domains of community, recreation, domestic, and vocational with as few restrictions as possible.

In Australia, functional mathematics is referred to as numeracy: 'To be numerate is to use mathematics effectively to meet the general demands of life at home, in paid work, and for participation in community and civic life' (Department of Employment, Education, Training and Youth Affairs, 1997, p. 15). Numeracy involves using mathematics to 'achieve some purpose' such as 'successfully altering a recipe for a different number of people, checking change in a transaction and planning the funding and timing aspects of a group social outing' (1997, p. 14). The preparation for the numeracy (functional mathematics) needs of adults begins with teaching mathematics concepts and skills (Faragher & Brown, 2005). Numeracy is not just a concern for students with disabilities but for all students who are transitioning into adulthood.

Similarly, the UK views functional skills as a set of skills that are necessary for all students:

> The introduction to *Functional skills standards: mathematics* states that: 'The term *functional* should be considered in the broad sense of providing learners with the skills and abilities they need to take an active and responsible role in their communities, in their everyday life, workplace and in educational settings. Functional mathematics requires learners to be able to use mathematics in ways that make them effective and involved as citizens, able to operate confidently in life and to work in a wide range of contexts. (QCA, 2007, p. 19)

Numeracy is also used in the UK to describe the types of skills needed to use mathematics in everyday life:

> Numeracy involves skills that aren't always taught in the classroom – the ability to use numbers and solve problems in real life. It means having the confidence and skill to use numbers and mathematical approaches in all aspects of life. Numeracy is as important as literacy. In fact, it's sometimes called 'mathematical literacy'. (National Numeracy, n.d.)

Academic Standards and Functional Goals

When the Education for All Handicapped Children Act of 1975 was initially implemented in the United States, instruction for students with disabilities was generally based on the developmental age and skills of the student. A 12-year-old student with a developmental age of 5 years would be taught a curriculum typically taught to a 5-year-old student. This practice changed in the 1980s when a greater emphasis was placed on preparing students with disabilities to function as independently as possible, in the least restrictive environment, when they became adults. The focus of instruction changed again in 1997 with the adoption of the Individuals with Disabilities Education Act (IDEA). IDEA 1997 and the most recent update in 2004 stipulate that all students will have access to the general curriculum, preferably in inclusive settings, and be assessed on academic standards (Alwell & Cobb, 2009; Dymond & Orelove, 2001; Moljord, 2018).

Given the new requirements to address academic standards, teachers need to balance the inclination to prepare students with disabilities for transition to adulthood with the expectation that students will have access to the general curriculum. Considering the need to address both of these requirements, teachers may attempt to embed functional skills into academic content or embed academic content into functional skills (Collins et al, 2010; Dymond & Orelove, 2001). As we will illustrate in this chapter, the skills needed to function independently are complex and require knowledge that is included in the Learning Framework in Number.

Our position is that academic goals related to the development of early numeracy are functional goals, since an understanding of number and operations is necessary to maximize independence. All parents want their children to become independent and have options for careers and living situations. For parents of students with disabilities, the level of independence students attain will have a significant impact on the housing and vocational opportunities available to them in the future.

How do we decide if an academic skill will lead to necessary functional skills? 'Accuracy in counting, recognising numerals, telling time, and understanding quantity are important if individuals with mental retardation are to achieve employment, independent living, competence in basic skills, and successful integration into school and community settings' (Butler, Miller, Lee, & Pierce, 2001, p. 21). The preparation for the numeracy (functional mathematics) needs of adults begins with developing an understanding of numbers and operations. Academic skills based on the Learning Framework in Number are functional and will prepare students to understand and use mathematics as adults.

Next, we will look at some specific areas that teachers and researchers have identified as being important for students as they prepare for adulthood.

Money

The ability to make purchases is necessary for independent living. A meta-analysis of purchasing skill instruction concluded that 'the demands of basic math skills (e.g., counting, adding) often limits the ability of students with disabilities to master purchasing skills' (Xin, Grasso, Dipipi-Hoy, & Jitendra, 2005). The authors noted that students needed the prerequisite skills of counting and adding to benefit from purchasing instruction. Beyond making purchases, independent living requires the ability to save money and make a budget. These more advanced money skills require the knowledge of all four basic operations (Kirk, Gallagher, & Coleman, 2015). According to the Money Advice Service, 2% of the population in the UK has a learning disability; 40% of the population with a learning disability are unsure of coins, notes, and their value; 86% are confused about their income, benefits, and expenses; and 74% rely on others to control their finances.

Here is a list of the money ideas and skills typically required in the primary grades:

- Recognizing coins.
- Identifying and using the values of coins.
- Counting and comparing sets of coins.
- Creating equivalent coin collections (same amounts, different coins).
- Selecting coins for a given amount.
- Making change.
- Solving word problems involving money. (Van de Walle, Karp, & Bay-Williams, 2013, p. 399)

The names and values of coins are social conventions that students need to learn, just as they learn the names of numerals, letters, and objects in their environment. For many students with disabilities, learning to label coins with names and values will require repeated exposure and practice. Whenever possible, students should have the opportunity to use real coins and bills. Some 'school money' is a particularly poor representation of real coins and bills. School money does not accurately give students additional clues such as weight and texture that adults routinely use in identifying coins. Using the school money simply adds additional, unnecessary barriers to an already challenging topic. While students may learn the verbal or symbolic label for the value of a coin, for example, 'five cents,' 5¢, or $.05 for a nickel in the United States, that does not guarantee that they understand that one nickel represents a quantity of five, without having five objects to count. This understanding requires that students are able to understand a quantity without needing to see individual objects. In the case of coins that have a value of more than one, the coin is essentially acting as a screen, preventing students from seeing the individual objects that represent the quantity.

With respect to the Learning Framework in Number (see Chapter 1), students should demonstrate that they are transitioning from Zone A to Zone B and are able to solve addition tasks with screened objects in order to be successful counting coins. If counting coins is introduced prematurely (that is, prior to the student being able to solve screened tasks), the instruction is likely to be very procedural in nature and highly frustrating for the student. Delaying the introduction of coins until after the student is successful with screened tasks will allow the student to be more likely to experience initial success and will ultimately take less instructional time to master.

Students will be able to count coins more easily if they are familiar with the number word sequences needed for counting coins. Initially students will need to know the sequences for counting collections of like coins; counting by ones for pennies, fives for nickels, tens for dimes, and twenty-fives for quarters. This skill can be practiced using the following activities from *TNC*.

ACTIVITY IA3.1: Count Around

Intended learning: To extend knowledge of forward number word sequences.

Materials: None

Description: Children stand in a circle and count around, each child saying the next number in the sequence. Start the count at one. The child who says the number 12 sits down. The next child begins the sequence again at one. The activity continues until only one child is left standing.

- Extend to crossing decuples.
- Use shorter or longer sequences.
- Vary the range of numbers (for example, start at 45 and sit down on 53).
- Extend to backward number word sequences.

Notes

- Children might omit numbers, say them in the incorrect order or not be able to give the next number, particularly when crossing a decuple.
- Ask questions such as: Who will sit down next? Who will say 5? Who will be left standing?
- Suitable for whole class or groups. (*TNC*, p. 42)

Suggestions for making connections to counting money:

- When counting by one, replace saying *five* (ten or twenty-five) with saying *nickel* (dime or quarter). The person who says the name of the coin sits down.
- When counting by five, ten, or twenty-five, replace saying one *hundred* with saying *one-dollar*. The person who says *one-dollar* sits down.
- For an added challenge, students can change the sequence they are saying based on the coin the teacher displays.

ACTIVITY IA3.3: Counting Choir

Intended learning: To count in ones, tens and hundreds.

Materials: Baton, a set of cards (labeled *ONES, TENS, HUNDREDS*).

Description: Divide the class into three groups. The teacher takes the role of the conductor holding a baton (pointer). The teacher begins the count, for example 21, 22, 23, 24, and then points the baton at one of the groups who continue the count in unison, for example 25, 26, 27… until the teacher points the baton at another group. This group in turn continues the count. The teacher moves the baton from group to group pseudorandomly bringing in sections of the choir. Similarly with other starting numbers. Give one group a card labeled *ONES*, the second group a card labeled *TENS*, and the third a card labeled *HUNDREDS*. The teacher begins the count again, for example, 7, 8, 9, and then points to the *ONES* group. The *ONES* group continues the count in ones, for example, 10, 11, 12, 13. The teacher moves the baton to the *TENS* group. The *TENS* group continues the count in tens, for example, 23, 33, 43, 53. The teacher then moves the baton to the *HUNDREDS* group. The *HUNDREDS* group continues the count in hundreds, for example, 153, 253, 353, 453. Similarly with other start numbers. Vary the activity by counting on ones only, in ones and tens, extending to counting in thousands, or counting backwards by ones, tens, or hundreds.

Notes

- Suitable for whole class or large group.
- Children can be grouped according to their facility in counting by ones, tens and hundreds.
- Children might experience difficulties when crossing decuples or going beyond 999. (*TNC*, p. 43)

Suggestions for making connections to counting money:

- Instead of labeling groups *ONES, TENS*, and *HUNDREDS*, use the labels *PENNIES, NICKELS, DIMES, QUARTERS*, and *DOLLARS* (substitute the appropriate currency).
- Pictures of coins can be used instead of words to label the groups.
- Include the use of *dollars* and *cents* when saying the sequence. Using the example above, the *PENNIES* group will say ten cents, *11 cents, 12 cents, 13 cents*; the *DIMES* group will continue *23 cents, 33 cents, 43 cents, 53 cents*. Next the *DOLLARS* group will say *1 dollar, fifty-three cents; 2 dollars, fifty-three cents; 3 dollars, fifty-three cents; 4 dollars, fifty-three cents.*
- Students can hold the coin or bill that represents the counting sequence for their group and hold it up in the air when their group is counting.

Making purchases is the most commonly researched functional skill (Weng & Bouck, 2014), and this task generally requires that students produce the amount of money needed to make a purchase. When students are counting money, they are mentally adding the value of each coin or bill without being able to see individual objects. To count a collection of dimes and pennies, students will need to be in Zone B, of Incrementing by 1s, 10s, and 100s on the Learning Framework in Number. To count collections of dollar bills, dimes and pennies, students will need to be in Zone C. To successfully count a collection that includes a variety of coins, students will need to be moving from Zone B to Zone C in Jump and Split Strategies. When students are learning to count mixed collections of coins, teachers should connect the coins, initially dimes and pennies, to other base-ten materials.

The following activities, from previous books in this series, provide examples of combining functional skill of counting money and academic content of addition and subtraction.

Activity IA5.1: Incrementing and Decrementing by Tens with Screened Bundling Sticks

Intended learning: To flexibly increment and decrement by tens in a quantitative context.

Instructional mode: Longer, inquiry mode for individuals or groups.

Materials: Bundling stick – many bundles and loose sticks, screen (cloth or sheet of foam).

Description: Establish that each bundle contains ten sticks. Briefly display and then screen three bundles of sticks (see Figure 4.1). *How many bundles of sticks? How many sticks are there altogether?* Add another bundle under the screen. *How many sticks now?* Allow the child to check as needed. Continue to add bundles until there are 130 sticks. *How many sticks now? How many bundles now?* Remove a bundle. *How many sticks now?* Continue removing a bundle and asking for the total number of sticks and bundles until there are zero sticks under the screen.

Briefly display and then screen two bundles and four extra sticks. *How many sticks are there altogether?* Add another bundle under the screen. *How many sticks now?* Continue to add bundles until there are 124 sticks. *How many sticks now?* Continue removing a bundle and asking for the total number of sticks and bundles until there are four sticks under the screen.

Responses, variations and extensions:

- This task is designed to enable students to connect to a quantitative context, forward number word sequences (incrementing), and backward number word sequences (decrementing).
- Tracking the progressions on a 200 chart or ENL enables students to describe patterns and link quantities and numerals.
- When incrementing off the decuple, students often have difficulty with the 'teen' numbers. Beginning in the twenties will facilitate children recognizing the oral pattern of the numbers in the sequence (e.g. twenty-four, thirty-four, forty-four…).
- Bridging the century and century plus ten frequently poses a difficulty. For example, students may increment '87, 97, 107, 207'. The bundling of ten tens into a bundle of one hundred (mega bundle) will facilitate child checking. Remove the last ten added in the sequence and ask, *How many was that?* When the child responds 107, ask, *Where is the one hundred?* When the student indicates the ten tens, add a big rubber band to form the mega bundle. Place the mega bundle back beside the seven extra. *How many was that altogether?* Add another then. *Now how many?* If the student persists in stating 207, unscreen the collection to compare the relative size of the mega bundle (hundred) to the ten bundle. *So do we have two mega bundles?* Remove the mega bundle and ask *How many now?* [17] Replace the mega bundle. *Now how many?*
- If necessary, the rubber bands may be removed from the bundles in order for the student to verify the number of sticks. The use of groupable base-ten materials is critically important until

the student develops a mental construct of composite units and can regard tens and hundreds as units that are easily mentally composed and decomposed.

- Repeat the process with other collections (e.g. starting with five sticks) and track the increments and decrements on a 200 chart or empty number line (ENL). *What do you notice about all these numbers? How are the numbers the same? How are they different?*
- Modify the procedure by adding two bundles of ten at a time. Extend this by adding three or four bundles at a time. Record on the ENL or 200 chart.
- Once students can simultaneously conceive base-ten materials as both one ten and ten ones, use pre-grouped base-ten materials such as dot strips or base-ten blocks.
- Repeat the process by incrementing and decrementing by hundreds
- Repeat the process by incrementing and decrementing by mixed tens and hundreds. (*DNK*, pp. 89–90)

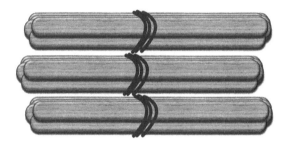

Figure 4.1 Bundles of ten sticks

Transitioning to money

- Initially, teachers may want to pair dimes and pennies with the bundles of ten and single sticks, or other base-ten materials, to make the relationship explicit for students.
- When students are able to complete the activity with pre-grouped materials, use coins in place of the base-ten materials.
- Dollars can be substituted for the mega bundle.

Activity IA9.5: Playing with Money

Intended learning: To use the setting of money to support learning of 2-digit addition and subtraction.

Materials: One dollar notes (or coins) and ten dollar notes (or play money).

Description: Children play in pairs or individuals with a set of $1 notes (or coins) and $10 notes.

- Make these amounts: $24, $56, $99, and so on.
- Make $48. How many dollars to make $50? Make $34. 'How much will I take away to make $30? And so on.

- Make $43. Make $30 and $13. *How much is this?* Have children make $50 and $14. *How much is this?* Give similar tasks ($60 and $12, $20 and $16, etc.). Follow up with some mental tasks of this type (without using money).
- Demonstrate an addition task using money without bridging the decuple (e.g. $34 and $23). Give some of these tasks and follow up with similar mental tasks.
- Demonstrate an addition that bridges the decuple (e.g. $37 and $25). Have children make these amounts. *How much altogether?* See if some children have $50 + $12. Do others have $62? Discuss these results.
- Give other 2-digit additions. After each task, give the children a mental task to see if they can solve the addition without using the money.
- Advertisements can be cut out of newspapers. Have children cut out or bring in items, or create pictures with the cost next to them. The children select two items to buy and take the numbers of tens and ones indicated in the cost. They then count the total number of tens and the total numbers of ones to find the total cost of the two items.

Notes

- Ten cent and one cent coins can be used if available in the currency.
- This activity is suitable for whole class, small group, or one-to-one.
- Children can add 3-digit numbers by using $100 bills (£100 notes).
- Children can also select more than two items to buy.
- Using $5 bills (£5 notes) as well would encourage adding using five as a reference point.
- Teachers may prefer to introduce this activity via newspaper advertisements and setting up a shop. (*TNC*, p. 172)

Adaptations

- Students can show the amount of money needed to purchase one item.
- Students can work together, one student assembling the coins and another student assembling the bills.
- Some students can use other base-ten materials, such as bundles and sticks, to represent the amount. The group can then compare the base-ten pieces to the money.

Activity IA5.7: Withdrawing Money from the Automated Teller Machine

Intended learning: To subtract decuples from a given number.

Instructional mode: Shorter, inquiry mode for whole class or small group.

Materials: ATM graphic, chart paper and pen or chalkboard and chalk, base-ten materials as needed.

Description: Introduce the context of using an ATM machine to withdraw cash from a bank account. *Who can tell me what an Automated Teller Machine or ATM is? Yes, it is a machine that allows you to deposit* *or withdraw cash from your bank account. I went to an ATM last night to withdraw some cash. Do you know it would only allow me to withdraw increments of £20, £50, or £100. Why do you think that was? Yes, they only stock £20, £50, and £100 bills in the machine. I thought about that. If my balance was £457 and I withdrew £20, what would my balance be? How could I figure that out? If students lack a strategy, prompt with If I were going to make 20 using these base-ten materials, how would I do that as quickly as possible? How can we use that idea to help us with this problem? Solve other problems of increasing complexity.*

Responses, variations, and extensions

- This task is best introduced when students are facile at adding or subtracting ten from any number.
- For less facile students, the machine could have £10 bills and the initial balance could be less than £100.
- Some students may need base-ten materials to support their reasoning about the quantities.
- The ENL is an excellent tool for notating student thinking during whole group discussions.
- School money or base-ten materials can be used to support students' reasoning. (*DNK*, pp. 96–98)

The Empty number line can be used to model students' thinking, if they are using a jump strategy, when counting collections of coins. (The reader is referred to *TNC* and *DNK* for further discussion of two-digit addition and subtraction strategies.) The use of the ENL allows students in the classroom to see and compare the ways their classmates count coins. As seen in Figure 4.2, coins can be added to the ENL to help other students in the class understand their classmate's thinking. It is important to note that the ENL should be used to notate the mental strategies used by students and should not be taught procedurally to solve the task (Wright et al., 2015).

Begin with collections of two kinds of coins and add additional kinds of coins as students become proficient.

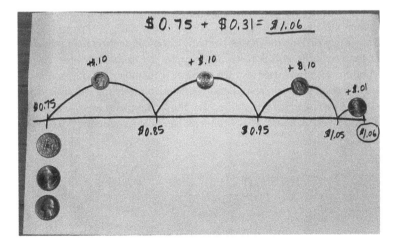

Figure 4.2 Teacher notation of student strategy for solving addition of money on ENL

One technique that eliminates the need for students to count coins when making purchases is known by the names 'one-more-than,' 'dollar more,' or 'next dollar' strategy (Denny & Test, 1995; Test, Howell, Burkhart, & Beroth, 1993). The basic premise of this strategy is that students count out the number of dollars needed and then add one more dollar to cover the cents. The technique was initially designed for students to make purchases using only one dollar bills. Using this strategy, students need to be able to read prices (numeral identification), understand the price in verbal form, and count with **one-to-one correspondence** to produce the correct number of bills. Students also need to know the **Number Word After** the number of dollars indicated by the price to add one more dollar. Some students have difficulty adding the additional dollar so an adaptation is to put aside one dollar for the cents pile and then count the number of dollars indicated by the price (Test et al., 1993). Shopping with a large number of one dollar bills is not practical so the technique has been adapted, for students who are able, to include five, ten, and twenty dollar bills (Denny & Test, 1995). To use larger bills, students need the ability to count on from five, ten, or twenty dollars. This requires knowledge of the forward number word sequence, the number words after five, ten, and twenty, and the conceptual understanding required for counting on. Based on the Learning Framework in Number, students using this strategy will need to be in Zones A or B in Number Word Sequences and Numeral Identification, depending on the cost of the items they want to purchase. Students will also need to be in Zone B of Counting and Keeping Track. Students utilizing this technique to make purchases will need to depend on the honesty of store employees to deliver the correct change, since determining the amount of change the purchaser receives is not part of the strategy.

To determine how much change should be received when making a purchase, the customer needs to determine the **difference** between the amount owed and the amount paid. The standard way to count back change is to count up from the amount owed to the amount paid. To understand this strategy, students need to understand that addition (adding up from the amount owed to the amount paid) and subtraction (subtracting the amount owed from the amount paid) are inverse operations. The Learning Framework in Number indicates that this understanding happens when students are in Zone C of Counting and Keeping Track. Additionally, these students will need to be in at least Zone B and preferably Zone C of Additive Structuring and Basic Facts. The ENL (see Figure 4.2) can also be used to model the thinking of students as they determine the amount of change they should receive when making a purchase.

In addition to simply making purchases, students can increase their independence and maintain a budget when they have the ability to compare prices for items they want to purchase (Bouck et al., 2016b). A number line was used to teach students with autism to compare prices when making purchases. Using the number line in conjunction with video modeling was successful for all but one student in the study. The researchers concluded that the student who was not able to use the strategy lacked number sense (Weng & Bouck, 2014). Students can practice ordering prices using the following activity from *TNC*.

ACTIVITY IA3.2: Numbers on the Line

Intending learning: To sequence numerals.

Materials: A length of rope or string, pegs, numeral cards.

Description: Place a set of numeral cards from 16–25 face down on the floor, in a pile in pseudo random order. Ask a child to take a card and peg it on the line. Ask a second child to take the next card from the pile and place it appropriately on the line. Continue until all the numbers have been pegged on the line in the correct sequence. Ask children to read the numbers aloud to check. If any numbers are in the wrong place, discuss and ask a child to re-position.

- Use shorter or longer sequences.
- Vary the range of numbers, for example 126 to 135.
- Read the sequences backwards as well as forwards.
- Extend to non-consecutive numbers, for example 46, 48, 51, 54, 60.

Notes

- When children are about to place their card, ask questions such as: Is it more or less than…? Will you place it to the left or right of…? Which two numbers should it go between?
- Vocabulary includes: more, less, higher, lower, before, after.
- Suitable for whole class or groups. (*TNC*, pp. 42–43)

Suggestions for making connections to money

- Write dollar amounts on the cards, $1.00, $2.00, $3.00, etc.
- Write cents on the cards, beginning with sequences familiar to the students and transitioning to amounts that do not fit into a sequence familiar to students. For example, begin with 5¢, 10¢, 15¢, 20¢… and other familiar sequences such as counting by tens or twenty-fives. Transition to non-consecutive values such as $.05, $.12, $.21, $.30, etc.
- Write cents both ways, for example, 5¢ and $.05.
- Write cards with dollars and cents, for example, $4.38.
- Have students read the cards as they clip them on the line.

Telling Time

Telling time on an analog and digital clock is another functional math skill for all students.
   Much of the knowledge needed to tell time on an analog clock can be connected to the Learning Framework in Number:

- Identification of the numerals 1 to 12 – Zone A in Numeral Identification.
- Number word sequences to sixty, by fives and ones – Zone B in Number Word Sequences.
- The understanding that each numeral on the clock has two meanings, the hour and a multiple of five for the minutes – Zone B in Counting in Multiples.
- Telling time on a digital clock requires **numeral identification** to 59 – Zone B in Numeral Identification.

Additional knowledge required for telling time on an analog clock includes:

- Which direction the hands go.
- The hands move at different speeds.
- The short hand indicates the hour and the long hand indicates the minutes.

Two activities presented in the previous section on money can be adapted to help students who are learning to tell time. During Count Around (*TNC*, p. 42) students can each hold a train of five connecting cubes as they count by fives. 'One hour' can be substituted for 'sixty' and that student will sit down. Sixty of the cubes, twelve groups of five, can be placed in a circle to form a giant clock where each cube represents one minute (McMillen & Hernandez, 2008).

When students are learning to tell time to the minute, for example, the time 5:18, they might either count the minutes by ones or count by fives and switch to counting by ones to count the last three minutes. The activity Counting Choir (*TNC*, p. 43) can be used to give students the opportunity to practice switching from counting by fives to counting by ones. Students counting by fives can be given trains of five connecting cubes to hold and students counting by ones can hold single cubes.

Determining elapsed time is another opportunity to incorporate the ENL to model student thinking (see Figure 4.3). With the emphasis usually placed on one hundred, students may have difficulty remembering the importance of the number sixty, as in sixty minutes to make one hour, when working with time. Students should determine the jumps that make the most sense for them as they are determining elapsed time. *TNC* points out that students should be 'facile with addition and subtraction in the range of 1-20,' to become proficient with using jump strategies (Wright et al., 2015, p. 136). The ability to compose and decompose numbers will allow students to count coins and solve elapsed time problems more efficiently than if they need to complete these tasks counting by ones.

Teachers should vary the orientation (Wright & Ellemor-Collins, 2018, p. 19) of elapsed time problems, for example:

- Cassie walked from 1:10 until 1:25. How many minutes did she walk?
- The movie starts at 2:10 and it will take Cassie 20 minutes to walk to the movie theater. What time should Cassie leave her house?
- Cassie left her house at 9:25 for a fifteen-minute walk to the store. What time did she get to the store?

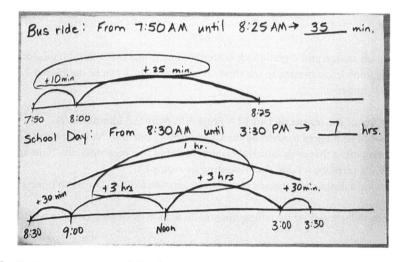

Figure 4.3 Teacher notation using ENL of student thinking to solve elapsed time problems

Domestic Skills

Students with disabilities may experience various difficulties using recipes, including reading instructions, following direction, and using various utensils (Brunosson, Brante, Sepp, & Sydner, 2014). The authors also found that lack of numeracy skills can interfere with the ability to follow a recipe and that typically developing students can have difficulty dealing with fractions in recipes. Even cooking with recipes adapted for students with disabilities requires students to read numerals and count (see Figure 4.4).

Figure 4.4   Picture communication symbols by Tobii Dynavox

Source: Available from: https://goboardmaker.com/ (accessed April 1, 2020)

Beyond following a basic recipe, increasing or decreasing the number of servings needed will require adjusting the measurement of all ingredients by the same proportion. The following activity adapted from *DFK* illustrates the understanding required to successfully make these adjustments. The original activity called 'Making $\frac{1}{4}$ of a Recipe' can be found on pages 138–139 of *DFK* and is intended for students who are developing an understanding of multiplying fractions which is Zone C in the Fractions-Measurement domain. This adaptation of the activity, based on 'Finding an Equal Share', *DFK*, p. 65, will be accessible to students who are working in Zone B of the Fractions: Part-Whole domain.

Intended learning: Students will learn to take a unit fraction of a whole.

Instructional mode: Students working individually or in pairs with instruction from the teacher.

Materials: A cardboard rectangle that represents a whole cup of honey and a variety of shares made from this cup of honey that are $\frac{1}{2}$ of the cup, $\frac{1}{3}$ of the cup, $\frac{1}{4}$ of the cup, $\frac{1}{8}$ of the cup, etc. It can be helpful to have very thin lines or arrows running parallel to the longer edges of the rectangles so that students know which way to orient the parts. (See Figure 4.5.)

Description: Pose the 'Muffin Problem' to all students. Tell them: A honey wheat muffin recipe requires one cup of honey. However, Nikolas wants to make $\frac{1}{2}$ of the recipe. How much flour does he need? Tell the students that the rectangle is one cup of honey. Which part shows the size of $\frac{1}{2}$ cup of honey?

Notes

- Various tasks in *DFK* can be adapted to a recipe context to give students opportunities to increase and apply their knowledge of fractions in relation to this functional skill.
- Tasks can also be adapted to provide students with experiences in doubling or tripling recipes.

Figure 4.5   Materials for 'Finding the Equal Share Problem'

Source: Hackenberg (2013)

Recreation

Recreation, or leisure, is one of the four domains of basic skills (Dymond & Orelove, 2001). Students should have opportunities to explore recreational activities that are interesting to them and be exposed to new opportunities. As with typically developing students, the ways a person can spend their leisure time are endless. In an effort to increase socialization, teachers and caregivers may promote activities that provide opportunities for interactions with family and community members. This section will focus on some activities that will be supported and enhanced by students' progress on the Learning Framework in Number, as well as activities that can promote an understanding of number and operations.

The leisure domain can be broken down into the following categories:

- Exercise
- Games, Crafts, and Hobbies
- Events
- Media
- Other. (Wilcox & Bellamy, 1987)

We will focus on the first two categories to illustrate how skills from the Learning Framework in Number are used in recreation or leisure activities. As teachers, it is our responsibility to provide learning opportunities so that students will have the skills needed to participate in activities that interest them.

Exercise can involve individual or team sports and activities. Many forms of exercise such as walking, running, or cycling can be enjoyed without incorporating mathematics, although participants may enjoy comparing how long or how fast they completed the activity. A timer or stopwatch can be used to integrate reading numerals, comparing times, and perhaps working on elapsed time problems. A fitness tracker can be used to measure the distance traveled and provide another opportunity to read and compare numbers. Even a simple pedometer can provide students with a way to measure and track progress on walking or running. Competitive endeavors require keeping score, and enjoyment of the activity can be enhanced when everyone understands and can participate in the process of keeping score. Ten-pin bowling is an example of a sport with various levels of participation and opportunities to incorporate mathematics. Keeping track of the score in bowling can be complex when bonuses for strikes or spares are earned and need to be added to the score. Participants may enjoy keeping track of how many pins they knock down and how many more pins they need to knock down in each frame. Since there are ten bowling pins, this activity can help students who are working on Structuring Numbers 1 to 10, which is Zone B of the Additive Structuring and Basic Facts domain on the Learning Framework in Number.

Games, crafts, and hobbies can also be enjoyed individually or with a group. Many learning activities in the previous books in this series involve playing games with a partner or small group. Participation in these activities not only develops math skills, but also provides opportunities for students to interact with others and develop social skills. A walk down the game aisle in a department store or a web search for games can give ideas for the types of games available and the math skills outlined in the Learning Framework in Number needed for participation. Bingo is a game that can be played by school children and is also enjoyed by adults. In its simplest form, participants need to have the ability to identify numerals.

Bingo in the United States typically uses the numerals 1–75, which will require a participant to be in Zone B of the Numeral Identification domain. In an instructional setting, teachers can create boards to match the numeral identification ranges available to the student. Dominos is a game with many variations. To play a basic version of the game, students need the ability to match the various dot patterns used on the domino tiles. The difficulty of a game can be adjusted by using tiles with smaller or larger collections of dots. The ability to subitize regular dot patterns is included in Zone A of the Additive Structuring and Basic Facts domain. The game can also be used as an instructional activity by having students say the quantity of dots as a tile is played or playing tiles so that the connecting tiles equal a target number. To play board games such as Chutes and Ladders (Snakes and

Ladders outside the US), Sorry, or Trouble, players need to be able to read numerals on a die, spinner or card (Zone A of the Numeral Identification domain) and count, with one-to-one correspondence, to move their tokens along the gameboard (Zone A of the Counting and Keeping Track domain). There is an endless variety of games, traditional and electronic, and new games are continuously being developed. The use of games as an instructional technique gives students the opportunity to develop academic skills and learn a leisure skill that can be continued into adulthood.

Conclusion

This chapter has focused on functional mathematics skills that students will need as they transition to adulthood. These skills will increase students' independence and allow them to become active members of their communities. Mathematics should also be incorporated into the school lives of students. There are many opportunities to incorporate mathematics throughout the day. Many class-rooms incorporate a calendar time into the school day. During this time students can practice count-ing forward and backward, discuss the date for yesterday and tomorrow (**Number Word Before** and **Number Word After**), collect a stick each day, and make bundles of ten to keep track of the number of days in school.

Students who need to work on one-to-one correspondence can be asked to pass out materials to classmates. Students can practice reading room numbers and bus numbers. A student might be asked to deliver a message to the teacher in room 205. Students can be given the responsibility for taking attendance or completing the lunch count. Mathematics can easily be incorporated into snack or lunch time. *How many grapes did you get? How many grapes will you have after you eat one?* Incorpo-rating mathematics throughout the school day increases the amount of time spent on mathematics instruction and shows the students that mathematics is important in their daily life. As stated earlier in this chapter, teachers may attempt to embed functional skills into academic content or embed academic content into functional skills. Both options will increase the opportunities to see mathematics as an important part of their lives and build skills for independence.

5

Assessing Students with Disabilities

This chapter discusses considerations for modifications and accommodations in assessment tasks presented in the other books in the Math Recovery series.

All students can build on their current mathematical understanding to construct a deeper understanding of mathematics. The challenge for educators is determining: (1) a student's current understanding and (2) how we might engender the next concept. If we are going to provide appropriate opportunities for a student to construct new knowledge, we need to find a foundation on which to build. Too often when working with students, especially students with disabilities, we determine what a student cannot do. Knowing what a student cannot do gives us a goal to work toward, but it does not give us a place to start.

Based on the two types of mathematical knowledge discussed in Chapter 1, we have two types of goals for students: (1) teaching important skills and knowledge of the conventions of mathematics and (2) building on the student's current conceptual understanding to engender the construction of new, more sophisticated conceptual understanding. Both types of goals require knowledge of what the student is currently able to do and what the next logical step is for that student. Determining appropriate goals for a student requires that we assess a student's understanding of socially constructed conventions and conceptual understanding.

Universal Screening

In addition to using assessments to identify the learning needs of students with disabilities, some assessment tasks may be useful as a **universal screener** in identifying students who need further assessment or intervention. Wilkins, Woodward, and Norton (2020), in a large-scale, longitudinal study, demonstrate the strong predictive nature of the Stages of Early Arithmetical Learning to forecast success in later grades in numeracy and mathematics in general. Those students in Zone B of Counting and Keeping Track (see Chapter 1) by the end of second grade were much more likely to develop multiplicative reasoning and a measurement scheme of fractions in fourth and fifth grade than those who were in Zone A or Emergent. Those in Zone C were even more likely than those in Zone B. Furthermore, the more advanced the zone at the end of second grade, the more likely the student would meet or exceed grade-level expectations on the state mathematics achievement test in fourth and fifth grade. It is, therefore, reasonable that a few items carefully designed to identify a student's Stage of Early Arithmetical Learning could function very well as an early universal screener to identify students likely in need of diagnostic assessment and intervention.

Administering Assessments

Administering assessment tasks to some students may present challenges because of the students' disabilities. In this chapter we will explore assessment tasks from other books in the Math Recovery series to illustrate the types of modifications and accommodations that may be necessary when assessing students with disabilities. We will not present every assessment task, nor will we be able to predict every accommodation or modification that may be required. Instead, we offer some general guidelines followed by examples.

Considerations for assessment accommodations and modifications

When accommodations or modifications are needed, teachers should ask:

- What is the essential element of the task that must be preserved?
- What aspect of the task might make it inaccessible to the student?
- What presentation accommodations or modifications can I make to lend accessibility and yet preserve the intent of the task?
    - Does the student need the task to be more perceptual?
    - How can I use different materials to help the student be more successful?
    - Does the student have the prerequisite vocabulary to complete the task?
    - Will the student be successful with smaller/simpler quantities?
- What supports are needed to enable students to demonstrate their content mastery?
    - What response options will be helpful for the student?
        - Verbal?
        - Written?
        - Demonstrating with manipulatives?
- Is the student able to generate a response independently or will it be helpful to provide choices?
- How will we use information gained from these modified tasks to provoke the student to build new and more sophisticated knowledge and understanding?

Some students will need accommodations to access the assessment tasks. When tasks are accommodated for students, the student expectations remain the same, but the presentation might be altered, or the student might be given alternate response options. Although the following list is not meant to be exhaustive, some accommodations of the tasks from the previous books in the series might include:

- Sign language or cued speech for students who are deaf.
- Sitting directly across from a student who is deaf/hard of hearing, as opposed to sitting side by side.
- Printed instructions for students who are deaf/hard of hearing.
- Printed instructions may also be helpful for students with auditory processing difficulties.
- Braille for students who are blind.
- Adding a tactile component to visual models for students who are visually impaired (VI) (see Figure 5.1).

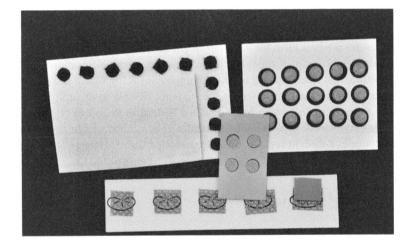

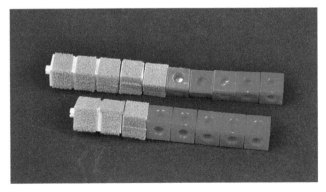

Figure 5.1 Tactile components can be added to visual models for students with visual impairments: (a) VI multiplication; (b) VI structuring

- Giving more time for students to see 'flashed' images may be helpful for students with visual processing disorders.
- Larger manipulatives can be used for students with fine motor difficulties.
- Breaking the assessment into smaller chunks might be helpful for students with attention difficulties.
- Scribing for students as they explain their answer might help students who have short-term memory difficulties.

After an initial assessment using assessment tasks from the other books in the Math Recovery series, it may seem that a student cannot accomplish any of the tasks suggested. On such occasions, teachers need to dig deeper to determine what a student can do and how students might demonstrate their knowledge and understanding. Finding out what a student can do might require modification of the original task. When a student is not able to complete a task, the question must become, 'What can the student do?' Uncovering what a student can do will require teachers to be observant, pose different questions, and offer different types of support.

The tasks presented in this chapter are followed by suggestions of what teachers should look for beyond correct and incorrect answers. Also presented are modified or alternative tasks to help determine the student's current level of performance. The list of ideas for modification is not exhaustive but is intended to give teachers ideas for how they might modify tasks. The ultimate goal will be for the student to successfully complete the original task. The suggested modifications can help teachers plan a path for instruction. Determining what students can do is important not only for designing instructional activities, but also for knowing what students are able to do, and what accommodations they need, to guide us in writing Individualized Education Programs (IEPs); see Chapter 6. Using the Learning Framework in Number (see Chapter 1) as a guide, we can determine the sophistication of the strategies a student is currently using and what the next step in learning might be for that student.

Number Words and Numerals

We begin by determining what knowledge the student has of number words and numerals. For a discussion of the various skills included in this topic, refer to:

- *EN*, pp. 22–24
- *TNC*, pp. 33–36
- *DNK*, pp. 25–34
- *LFIN*, pp. 51–52.

Task Group A3.1: Forward Number Word Sequences

Materials: None.

What to do and say: Start counting from one. I will tell you when to stop. Stop the child at 32. Start counting from forty-seven. Stop the child at 55. And so on. (*TNC*, p. 37)

Similarly, for Backward Number Word Sequences, starting at various numbers and counting backward.

Some students will have a very limited range of numbers they can say in the sequence, and even learning the sequence forward to or backward from ten will seem like a big undertaking. What should we notice, and what questions should we ask when students are attempting to say the sequence of numbers to ten?

- Does the student say only numbers when saying the sequence? Does the student know that the counting sequence does not include letters or other words?
- Is the student able to say any string of numbers in the correct sequence?
- Is the student able to say the sequence as the teacher touches each numeral?
- When starting from numbers other than one, does the student count in the correct direction to produce the backward or forward sequence?
- Does the student recognize if the teacher is saying a forward or backward number word sequence?
- Is the student able to repeat sequences said by the teacher? What is the length of the sequences the student can repeat?
- Some students may not understand the instructions, or they may not understand the need to 'count' when there is nothing to count. Although we are interested in the number word sequence, and not the ability to count objects, some students will do better saying the number word sequence when they have objects to count.
- When saying forward and backward sequences, some students may be able to say short sequences, but not long extended sequences. What is the length of the sequence the student is able to say?
- If the student is non-verbal:
  - Is the student able to arrange printed numerals in the correct sequence? This requires that students are able to recognize the numerals and sequence them in counting order. In this case, the printed numeral becomes both the symbolic and the verbal aspect of the number.
  - Is the student able to use an alternative form of communication to express the number word sequence?
  - Is the student able to recognize whether someone (a teacher or another student) says the sequence of numbers correctly or incorrectly?
  - Can the student demonstrate they are using the correct number sequence by correctly determining the quantity of a collection?
  - Is the student able to point to or touch numerals, as the teacher says the sequence?

Vignette

When asked to start counting, Maria responded, '1, 2, 3, 6, 8, 10!' Although Maria did not successfully count to ten, her response shows us what she knows about saying the forward sequence of numbers:

(Continued)

- The first three numbers were in sequence.
- As she continued saying numbers, the numbers were in the correct order, even though she omitted some numbers in the sequence.
- She only said numbers. She did not say letters. She knows that numbers are used for counting.
- Her excitement in saying '10!' indicates that she knows ten is an important number.

Early strategies for addition and subtraction, counting on and counting back, require that students are able to say the number after or before a given number. This may be difficult if students consider the sequences of numbers merely a sequence of sounds without meaning assigned to the individual number words.

Task Group A3.2: Number Word After

Materials: None.

What to do and say: I am going to say a number and I would like you to say the number that comes right after that number I say: What comes after six? After eleven? And so on. (*TNC*, p. 37)

Similarly, for Number Word Before, asking students to say the Number Word Before a given number. Similar tasks can be found in:

- *EN*, pp. 36 and 41
- *LFIN*, pp. 40–41.

If a student is not able to say the number word after or before a given number, a teacher might wonder:

- Can the student produce the next number after the teacher says a short series of numbers?
- Can the student write the next number after a series of written numbers?
- Given a sequence of numeral cards, can the student say which number comes next?
- Given a sequence of numeral cards, can the student select the card with the next number, from a field of three cards? (See Figure 5.2.)
- Given a numeral card, is the student able to point to where the number before or after that number should be placed?

Task Group A3.5: Numeral Identification

Materials: Sets of numeral cards from 1 to 10, not in numerical order. Similarly, a set of numeral cards from 11–20, and a set of cards for selected numerals in the range of 21 to 100 (about 12–15 of these).

What to do and say: Display the cards in turn. *Tell me the number on the card.* (*TNC*, p. 39)

Figure 5.2 'What is the number after 14?'

Source: The 0–100 Card Deck & Trio Card are products available from US Math Recovery Council

Some students may not be able to identify numerals, that is, produce the name of a numeral as it is shown to them in isolation. However, they will be able to recognize numerals, that is, select the correct numeral when given a collection of numerals arranged in a non-sequential order and asked to find a specific numeral. Some students may only be able to identify or recognize a limited number of numerals. When assessing for this knowledge, teachers will want to keep track of which numerals the student can identify or recognize. The numerals known by a student might not be in any sequence and seem a random collection to the assessor. Are there any similarities between the numerals a student can identify or recognize?

If students have difficulty identifying or recognizing numerals, a teacher might wonder:

- Can the student match duplicate copies of the same numerals?
- Can the student sort numerals? For example, give several cards with the numerals 1, 2, and 3, can the student put the 1s, 2s, and 3s in separate piles?
- Can the student sort numerals from other symbols such as letters, @ symbols, and the like?
- Can the student distinguish between commonly confused symbols such as Ps and 9s?

The behaviors described above will indicate the extent to which the student can discriminate between different numerals.

Identifying or recognizing numerals is an important skill for non-verbal students who use an AAC system for communication. Teachers may question whether students who use AAC are really identifying numerals because their verbal expression involves selecting a numeral on their communication device. When shown a numeral and asked, 'What number is this?', the student responds by touching the numeral on the communication device. Has the student identified the numeral or merely matched the symbol that was shown? If the verbal prompt, 'Show me the number five', is given, the student will touch the numeral 5 on the communication device. This is considered numeral recognition, a less advanced skill than numeral identification. Students using assistive technology should be given opportunities to respond in both ways. Students will be able to further demonstrate their knowledge of numerals when they communicate about quantity.

Counting, Addition, and Subtraction Strategies

When students know a portion of the forward number word sequence from one to ten, they have the potential to use that sequence to determine the quantity of a collection. For a discussion of this topic, refer to:

- *EN*, pp. 52, 53–54, 56–57
- *TNC*, pp. 53–57 and 92–96.

Task Group A4.3: Establishing the Numerosity of a Collection

Materials: About 30 counters all of one color.

What to do and say: Place out a collection of 12 counters. *How many counters are there?* Similarly, 15, 18, or 8 counters. (*TNC*, p. 58)

If the student is successful counting a collection of one color, a similar task can be tried with a collection of two colors.
  Similar tasks can be found in:

- *EN*, pp. 47–48
- *LFIN*, p. 46.

Students who are not able to establish the numerosity of a collection (count perceived items) may not know the sequence of number words used in counting (see Task Group A3.1, above), they may not have one-to-one correspondence between the counting words and the objects being counted, and/or they may not know that the last number in the counting sequence signifies the quantity of the collection.
  In our experience, teachers may not realize that a student does not have the **Cardinality Principle** because, after observing the student's counting behavior, the teacher does not follow up with the important question, 'How many are there?' In fact, teachers may promote the idea that we are looking for counting behavior rather than determining a quantity by telling the student, 'Count these,' rather than asking, 'How many are there?' Teachers may be so interested in the student's counting behavior that they promote the use of counting when it is not necessary. For example, in the case of small quantities of objects arranged in a familiar pattern, the student might know the quantity without counting or the quantity may be so small that the student does not need to count it. When

students are counting, the teacher will want to determine whether there is a maximum quantity the student is able to count before one-to-one correspondence or the sequence of numbers breaks down.

Vignette

A teacher presented Zachary with a collection of seven counters and asked, 'How many are there?' Zachary proceeds to laboriously count the items, exhibiting one-to-one correspondence and a strategy of keeping track of which items had been counted. As he uttered the word 'Seven,' he glanced up at his teacher. The teacher responded with 'So, how many are there?' Upon hearing the question, Zachary proceeded to count the items a second time, again stopping on the seven and glancing at his teacher. A third time the teacher asked, 'So, how many are there?' A third time Zachary commenced to count.

One could argue a lack of certitude in his response caused Zachary to recount to verify his answer. From subsequent interactions, it became apparent that Zachary thought the question 'How many are there?' was a prompt for him to complete some counting activity, not to identify a quantity.

If a student is not able to determine the quantity of a collection, a teacher might wonder:

- Does the student know the sequence of counting words needed to count this collection?
- Does the student have one-to-one correspondence between the counting words and the objects being counted?
- Is the student able to answer the question 'How many are there?'
- If the objects are rearranged, does the student know that the quantity remains the same and the objects do not need to be recounted?
- Does the student have a way to keep track of which objects were counted?
    - Does the student miss some objects when counting?
    - Does the student count some objects more than once?
- Does the student have the fine motor coordination necessary to manipulate the objects being counted?
- Is the student able to say the counting words as the teacher touches each object?
- Is the student able to touch each object as the teacher says the counting words?

Vignette

Nathan is a non-verbal student with autism who uses an Augmentative and Alternative Communication (AAC) system to communicate. He is able to make meaningful requests using his AAC

(Continued)

device and will also select random symbols impulsively. His teacher was writing an evaluation report and wanted to determine goals for his next IEP. The assessment was given with the assessor and Nathan both sitting on the floor. Nathan had a basket of picture cards that he enjoyed looking at during the assessment. These cards were incorporated into the assessment when he was asked to indicate how many objects were on a card. Nathan was first asked to locate numerals on his communication device. Although this is technically **numeral recognition** as opposed to numeral identification, this is an important skill for students using AAC.

Nathan was able to locate numerals up to 30. When asked for a numeral greater than 30, the numeral selected represented the last part of the numeral that was said. For example, when asked to find the numeral 34, Nathan selected the numeral 4. Nathan will be able to demonstrate more complete understanding of the numerals when he is able to use them to communicate the quantity of a collection. He did not use his communication device to say the Forward Number Word Sequence, and he was not able to say the number after a number given by the assessor. He was able to use his device to complete a forward sequence of numbers said by the assessor. Nathan was not able to demonstrate an understanding of the Backward Number Word Sequence.

When shown a collection of objects (pictures of objects on a card) and asked, 'How many?', Nathan tapped some of the objects on the card and then selected a number on his communication device. He did not tap all the objects and did not select the correct numeral to represent the quantity. His behavior indicates that he understands the expected response to the question 'How many?' Nathan was able to put his hand on the assessor's hand as she touched each object on the card and said a numeral for each object. He was then able to select the correct numeral on his communication device. As a result of this assessment, Nathan's teacher decided that his next IEP would include goals to recognize two-digit numerals greater than 30, say the number after a given number in the range of 1–10, and that he would demonstrate the ability to determine the quantity of a collection of up to five objects.

The following task will assess whether students need perceptual objects to count or whether they have constructed figurative images that will allow them to solve tasks in which materials are hidden from view by an opaque cover. We begin by showing and then covering two collections of objects and asking the student to determine the total of the two collections.

For further discussion of this topic refer to:

- *EN*, pp. 60–73
- *TNC*, pp. 55 and 92–94.

Task Group A6.1: Additive Tasks Involving Two Screened Collections

Materials: A collection of counters of one color (red) and a collection of another counter (blue); two [opaque] screens of cardboard or cloth.

What to do and say: Briefly display and then screen eight red counters. *Here are eight red counters.* Briefly display and then screen five blue counters. *Here are five blue counters. How many counters altogether?* Similarly, with collections such as 9 red and 3 blue, 15 red and 2 blue, 11 red and 4 blue, and so on. (*TNC*, p. 97)

Missing addend, subtraction, and missing **subtrahend** tasks can be presented as above, using counters and opaque screens. These tasks are presented so the student can see the objects momentarily before they are then placed under an opaque screen, such as a piece of cardboard or fabric, so the student is not able to count the objects to determine the new quantity. The tasks are generally presented with small flat counters, which may be tempting for some students to play with or scatter around and push off the table. To simplify the assessment process, the teacher may choose to use larger objects such as connecting cubes and hide them under plastic bins. Another option is to have cards with the appropriate numbers of dots or coding stickers, which will be easier for the teacher to manipulate than individual counters.

If students are not able to determine the correct quantity, their answer can still give information about their understanding of addition and subtraction.

If a student is not able to determine the correct quantity when the items are fully screened, a teacher might wonder:

- Can the student determine the total quantity when a smaller quantity of items is placed under each screen?
- Is the student able to use counters to show the quantity of items hidden under each screen?
- Is the student able to determine the total quantity if the counters are placed in a domino pattern? (Placing counters in a domino pattern is generally not recommended during assessment, as it provides extra support for the student.)
- Can the student determine the quantity when one of the screens is removed?
- Can the student hold a small quantity of objects in each hand and determine the total number of objects held?

Structuring: Non-count-by-one Strategies

While counting forward and backward is an important strategy for addition and subtraction, we do not want students to be stuck counting by ones to solve problems. The tasks in this section assess the student's ability to see and use groups in solving addition and subtraction problems.

Many students use their fingers as tools for solving math problems. Fingers may be used to represent quantities that the student cannot see. For example, when presented with the expression 4 + 2, a student might put up four fingers on one hand, two fingers on the other hand, and count all the fingers to determine a total of six. Another student might use fingers differently to solve the same problem, using two fingers to keep track of two counts while counting up from four to six. Fingers can also be a path toward unitizing, thinking about the individual fingers on one hand as a group of five fingers.

For further discussion of this topic, refer to:

- *TNC*, pp. 73–74
- *EN*, pp. 26–27 and 106–107.

Task Group A5.2: Making Finder Patterns 6 to 10

Materials: None.

What to do and say: *Can you show me six fingers?* Similarly, 9, 7, 10, 8. (*TNC*, p. 76)

Students may have difficulty making **finger patterns** because of their lack of experience using fingers, because they do not understand that fingers can be used to represent a quantity, and/or because of diminished fine motor control. Some students may not have 10 fingers. If students are not able to make the requested finger patterns we will want to determine the following:

- Can they manipulate the fingers of paper hands or gloves to show finger patterns?
- Can they say the quantity of fingers when shown a finger pattern? Did they count the fingers or recognize the finger pattern without needing to count?
- Can they say the quantity of fingers when a finger pattern is flashed (shown quickly)?
- Can they point to a picture of a finger pattern when a quantity is specified?
- Can they imitate finger patterns shown to them?
- Can they match pictures showing the same finger patterns?
- Can they match pictures showing finger patterns to numerals?

Students who use sign language for communication use their fingers to express number words. In this task, we are asking students to use their fingers to express quantity. Students and sign language interpreters will need to be aware of how students are being asked to use their fingers. Are students being asked to express a number or a quantity?

Task Group 4: Five Frame Patterns

The five frame is simply that: a horizontal or vertical frame of five squares upon which a number of spots has been placed. The card is flashed for half a second. ...The objective of the task is to assess the child's facility with partitions of five. For example, do they know the patterns on the five frame? Related to this is whether they can say the number of spots seen and the number of empty squares without counting them? [*sic*] The first question is open ended to allow the child the opportunity to tell you as much as possible. The assessor could probe to see if they have more to tell. If not, then the second question can be posed.

Flash the five frame.

a. What did you see?
b. How many spots did you see? (*EN*, p. 109)

Similar tasks can be done with five-wise and pair-wise ten-frames and ten-wise and pair-wise twenty-frames.
   Similar tasks can be found in:

- *EN*, pp. 109–113

- *TNC*, pp. 77–80
- *DNK*, pp. 62–63.

If a student is unable to quantify the various spatial patterns, a teacher might wonder:

- Can the student determine a quantity when the cards are not flashed?
  - o Does the student need to count the dots?
  - o Does the student know the quantity without counting?
- When quickly shown a spatial pattern, can the student point to a matching spatial pattern card, from a field of three or more cards?
- When quickly shown a spatial pattern, can the student make the pattern with chips or draw it on paper?
- Can the student sort a set of dot pattern cards; in other words, does the student discriminate between the different patterns?
- Is the student able to match a dot pattern card to a numeral card?
- Can the student match a dot card to a card with the same quantity but a different configuration? Does the student appear to be counting each card or can the student determine the quantity without counting each object?

After establishing that students can name the number of dots and empty spaces on the presented five-frame and ten-frame cards, without counting, teachers will want to determine whether students are able to use that knowledge to determine the combinations and partitions of numbers to five, ten, and twenty, without counting. Tasks will be presented as verbal problems and written addition and subtraction expressions.

For further discussion of this topic, refer to:

- *TNC*, pp. 74–75
- *DNK*, pp. 50–53.

Task Group A5.6: Partitions of 5 and 10

Materials: None.

What to do and say: I will say a number and you say the number that goes with it to make five: 3, 4, 2, 1. I will say a number and you say the number that goes with it to make ten: 9, 5, 8, 3, and so on. (*TNC*, p. 79)

Similar tasks can be found in:

- *EN*, pp. 112–113
- *LFIN*, pp. 43–44 and 53–56
- *DNK*, pp. 63–67.

Verbal tasks can be challenging for students with verbal comprehension difficulties. The student may know the combinations but not understand the prompt given by the teacher.

If a student is not able to respond to the verbal prompt, a teacher might wonder:

- Does the student respond correctly, but use a counting strategy to determine the answer? In this case, the student understands the verbal prompt but does not yet know the partitions to five and ten.
- Can the student respond to the verbal prompt, without counting, when given a five- or ten-frame as a visual cue?
- Can the student respond to written problems, using partitions of five and ten, without counting? (See Figure 5.3.)
- Given a collection of addition expression cards, can the student select the expressions that equal a requested quantity? For example, 'Which of these expressions equal 5?'

$$7 + \_\_\_ = 10$$

$$9 + \_\_\_ = 10$$

$$5 + \_\_\_ = 10$$

$$8 + \_\_\_ = 10$$

$$3 + \_\_\_ = 10$$

Figure 5.3   Written equations for combinations to ten

Conceptual place value, addition, and subtraction to 100

Students who have demonstrated the ability to conceptually count on and count back to solve addition and subtraction problems are cognitively ready to extend their learning into conceptual place value and multiplicative thinking. Students should also be learning to use doubles and combinations to 5, 10, and 20 to solve addition and subtraction problems without counting by ones. These initial experiences in unitizing – thinking in groups rather than individual items – will pave the way toward conceptual place value, multiplication, and division.

Task Group A5.2: Incrementing and Decrementing by Tens on the Decuple

Materials: A screen of card or cloth, and bundling sticks, including 12 bundles.

What to do and say: Increment as follows. Show one bundle then place it under the screen. *How many sticks are under there?* Show a second bundle then place it under the screen. *Now how many sticks are there (altogether)?* Continue, adding one or two bundles at a time under the screen up to 120.

Decrement as follows. Place out 12 bundles. *How many bundles are there? ... and how many sticks?* Screen the 12 bundles. Then remove one bundle and show it. *Now how many sticks are under there?* Continue removing one or two bundles at a time, down to zero. (*DNK*, p. 84, italics in original)

Similar tasks can be found in:

- *EN*, p. 94
- *TNC*, p. 144
- *LFIN*, p. 57.

As teachers present these tasks to students, they will want to make note of how much of the sequence students are able to say. The teacher may also want to give the student a specific quantity of bundles and ask the student to count the number of sticks or ask the student to give the teacher a specific number of sticks.

If a student is not successful with these tasks, a teacher might wonder:

- Is the student able to complete the task when the sticks are visible?
- Is the student able to complete the task with a different model, such as full 10-frames, 10-dot strips, stacks of 10 Unifix cubes, 10 beads on a 100-bead string?

Task Group A5.3: Incrementing and Decrementing by Tens off the Decuple

Materials: A screen and bundling sticks, including 12 bundles.

What to do and say: Increment as follows. Place three sticks. *How many sticks are there?* Screen the three sticks. Show one bundle and then place it under the screen. *Now how many sticks under there (altogether)?* Continue, adding one or two bundles at a time under the screen, up to 123.

Decrement as follows. Place out 12 bundles and eight sticks. *How many sticks are there?* Screen the bundles and sticks. Then remove one bundle and show it. *Now how many sticks are under there?* Continue removing one or two bundles at a time, down to eight. (*DNK*, p. 85)

Similar tasks can be found in:

- *EN*, p. 94
- *TNC*, p. 144
- *LFIN*, p. 57.

In presenting this task, teachers will want to observe how the student is determining the new total. Is the student counting by ones or is the student able to add ten (or a multiple of ten) to the previous total? Some students may be more successful when the new total is written down for them, so they do not need to hold so many numbers in their head.

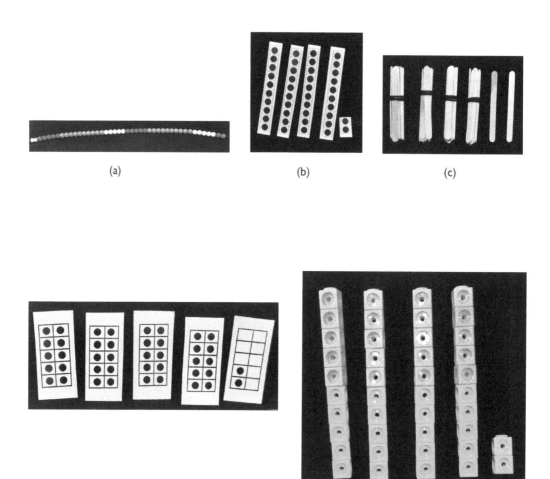

Figure 5.4   Models for base ten

If students are not successful with the task, teachers may wonder:

- Does the student know the sequence for counting by tens, off the decuple?
- Is the student able to complete the task when the sticks and bundles are unscreened?
- Is the student able to complete the task if the bundles of ten are placed to the left of the single sticks?
- Is the student able to complete the task with a different model, such as 10-frames, dot strips, connecting cubes, 100-bead string? (See Figure 5.4.)

Multiplication and Division

As students develop multiplication concepts, we want to make sure they understand that multiplication involves working with equal groups. Can students use what they know about skip counting to determine the total quantity? Do they understand the vocabulary of multiplication: number of groups, number of items in each group, and the total number of items? What do students need to be able to see in order to solve multiplication and division problems? For further discussion of this topic, refer to:

- *EN*, pp. 119–120
- *TNC*, pp. 178–184
- *DNK*, pp. 135–147.

The following tasks represent two visual models for multiplication, equal groups and arrays.

Task Group A7.1: Multiplication with Repeated Equal Groups

Materials: Eight cards, each containing two dots, a large card to screen all eight cards…

What to do and say: Place the eight cards in a row with all but the first face-down. Screen all eight cards. Briefly display, and then screen, the two dots on the face-up card. *This card has two dots.* Turn the first card face down and screen all eight cards. *Under this screen there are eight cards in all, each with two dots, like the first card. How many dots are there altogether?* (*DNK*, p. 157)

Similar tasks can be found in:

- *EN*, p. 132
- *TNC*, p. 186
- *LFIN*, p. 65.

If students are not able to complete the task as presented, teachers should remove the top screen, so the student can see the cards, representing the eight groups.

- Is the student able to determine the total number of dots?
- Does the student use skip counting or does the student count by ones, to determine the total number of dots?

If students are not able to determine the total number of dots when the dots are hidden, teachers should turn the cards over, so the dots are visible.

- Is the student able to determine the total number of dots?
- Does the student use skip counting or does the student count by ones, to determine the total number of dots?
- Is the student able to determine the total number of dots if presented with fewer groups of two dots?

Task Group A7.4: Multiplication with an Array

Materials: A 5 x 6 array (5 columns and 6 rows), a screen...

What to do and say: Screen all but the top row of five dots. *Here is one row of the array. This row has five dots.* Now screen the whole array. *There are six rows altogether. How many dots are there altogether?* (*DNK*, p. 157–158)

Similar tasks can be found in:

- *EN*, pp. 133–134
- *TNC*, pp. 188–189
- *LFIN*, p. 66.

As students are attempting this task, teachers should notice:

- Is the student skip counting or counting by ones?
- Does the student know when to stop counting the groups?
- How does the student keep track of the number of groups?

If a student is not able to complete the task, a teacher might wonder:

- Is the student able to complete the task with a smaller array? For example, can the student complete the task with an array of 3 columns and 4 rows?
- Is the student able to complete the task when the screen is removed?
  - How does the student count the dots?
  - Does the student do any skip counting?
  - Given an unscreened array, is the student able to say how many rows are in the array?
  - Is the student able to say how many dots are in each row?
  - Is the student able to use counters to make an array, with a specified number of rows and columns?
  - Is the student able to select an array that is described? For example, *find an array that has 5 rows with 4 dots in each row.*

Vignette

Yasim is a seventh-grade student who is visually impaired. He lived in a refugee camp for several years and had received inconsistent schooling. His teacher was curious about Yasim's understanding of mathematics. Yasim had demonstrated the ability to say the Forward and Backward Number Word Sequences by ones as well as various skip-counting sequences, including counting by threes. As part of the assessment, Yasim was given a stack of three connecting cubes. The connecting cubes had holes in them so Yasim was able to feel each cube. He determined that there were three cubes in the stack. The assessor asked, 'If you had five stacks of cubes, just like that one, how many cubes would you have?' Yasim responded that he did not know. He was then given five stacks of cubes with three cubes in each stack. To determine the total number of cubes, he counted each cube by ones. After he gave the cubes back to the assessor, Yasim was asked, 'Do you know the answer to 5 times 3?' 'Yes,' he said, 'that's fifteen.' Yasim knew the answer to the multiplication fact, but he had not demonstrated an understanding of multiplication.

Fractions

Fractions are an important topic in elementary school mathematics. Our goal is for students to interact with materials to demonstrate their understanding of fractions.

Task Group A4.1: Equal Sharing of Single Items

Materials: A variety of rectangles made from cardboard, with multiple copies of the same size; writing utensil for making marks; scissors for cutting bars.

What to do and say: Ask the students to share one of the rectangles (it can represent a granola bar or a healthy cake) equally among some number of people. Ask the students to justify their result: How do they know they have made equal shares? Can they justify in more than one way? Do the students think any of the parts are an equal share for that number of people, and how do students know? (*DFK*, p. 50)

This task assesses the student's understanding of several concepts. The teacher will want to notice whether the student is able to fragment the bar into the correct number of pieces, whether the pieces are approximately the same size, whether the student uses the entire bar when making the equal pieces, and whether the student has a way to verify that the pieces are the same size. If the student determines that the pieces are not of equal size, is the student able to make adjustments and try again?

If the student is not able to complete the task, the teacher might wonder:

- Given a collection of bars cut into equal pieces (for example, a bar cut into two equal pieces, a bar cut into three equal pieces, and a bar cut into four equal pieces), is the student able to select the bar which can be shared with a specified number of people?
- Given a bar cut or marked into equal-size pieces, is the student able to say how many people can share the bar?
- Given a collection of bars cut into a specified number of pieces (for example, a collection of bars, each cut into four pieces), is the student able to determine which bar is cut into equal- or same-size pieces? Is the student able to demonstrate that the pieces are the same size?

Task Group A5.1: Parts Within the Whole

Materials: Fraction strips and writing utensils; the fraction strips should all be the same length but also be marked into various numbers of equal parts between 3 and 9…

What to do and say: Give each student a fraction strip and ask them to shade in two parts. Then ask them what fraction of the whole strip is shaded. (DFK, p. 64)

Some students may have difficulty completing this task because of fine motor issues. A possible accommodation might be to partition the fraction strips into sections that can be covered by a cube that is more easily manipulated by the student. Students can be told to 'use the cubes to cover two parts of the fraction strip.' (See Figure 5.5.) Alternatively, the teacher might shade in parts of the fraction strip and say to the student, 'Tell me to stop when I have shaded in two parts of this strip.'

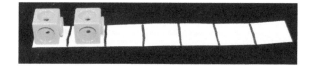

Figure 5.5   Using cubes to cover two parts of the fraction strip

If the student is visually impaired, the parts will need to be delineated in a way that can be perceived tactilely, perhaps a thin line of glue to create raised surfaces that mark the equal sections. Visually impaired students can mark the two sections by placing blocks rather than shading in the sections.

Some students may not understand the direction 'shade in two parts,' or know the language for naming fractions. If the student is not able to complete this task, a teacher might wonder:

- Given a collection of fraction strips, all the same size with various numbers of equal parts shaded, is the student able to recognize which fraction strip has two parts shaded? (See Figure 5.6.)

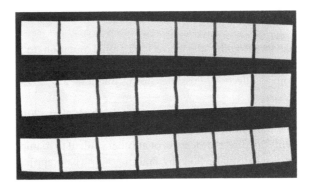

Figure 5.6 Which fraction strip shows two parts shaded?

- Given a collection of fraction strips marked into various equal parts, all having two parts shaded, is the student able to recognize the strip that shows two of seven parts or two-sevenths shaded? (See Figure 5.7.)

Figure 5.7 Which fraction strip shows two of seven parts shaded?

Task Group A5.2: Parts out of the Whole

Materials: Fraction strips both marked and unmarked, writing utensils and scissors; the marked fractions strips should all be the same length but also be marked into various numbers of equal parts.

What to do and say: Give students an unmarked and a marked fraction strip. Building off of A5.1 ask them to cut off two parts from the unmarked strip and name the fraction that amount is of the whole. (DFK, pp. 64–65)

This task requires that the student is successful with the previous task and can label the fractional amount when the piece is removed from the whole. Some students may need assistance with cutting off the two parts because of fine motor difficulties. See the previous task for accommodations for students who are visually impaired.

If a student is not successful with this task, a teacher might wonder:

• Is the student able to recognize the correct fractional notation to identify the fractional amount? For example, after the student cuts off two pieces, is the student able to select the correct notation from a collection? Possible choices might be 2, 7, 2/7, 2/5.

The next series of tasks require that students iterate (Hackenberg et al., 2016, pp. 18–19) the fractional piece to determine the whole. Manipulating the rods may be difficult for students with fine motor difficulties. Students can direct the teacher or another student to manipulate the rods. Another option is the use of the app Cuisinaire Rods by Brainingcamp (paid app), or Relational Rods+ by mathies (free app).

Task Group A6.3: Producing the Whole from Unit Fractions

Materials: Fraction rods (also known as 'Cuisenaire rods').

What to do and say: Show the student a red rod (two units long) and tell them that it is one-third of the whole. Ask them to identify which rod is the whole. Similar questions include the following: 'If the red rod is one-fifth of the whole, find the whole'; 'If the white rod is one seventh of the whole, find the whole'. (*DFK*, p. 79)

To provide the student with the experience of **iterating**, the student can be given a block that can be manipulated and a collection of objects or paper strips of various sizes. Ask the student, 'Which one of these is three blocks long?' Although the task does not mention fractions, it will give the teacher the opportunity to observe the student's ability to iterate a unit of measure. When the student has demonstrated the ability to iterate, the teacher might say, 'This red rod is one-fifth of the whole, can you tell me when I've found the whole?' If a student has difficulty manipulating the materials, the teacher can attempt the task. The student's task is to indicate when the correct rod has been found. The teacher can further assess the student's understanding of iterating by performing the task incorrectly, leaving gaps or overlapping, to see if the student gives corrective feedback.

If a student is not successful with this task, a teacher might wonder:

• Does the student understand that the whole will be three times larger than the one-third?

Materials needed: Connecting cubes – a single connecting cube and three stacks of connecting cubes of various lengths, for example, a stack of 3, a stack of 4, and a stack of 5.

What to do and say: Show the student the single connecting cube and have stacks of 3, 4, and 5 connecting cubes available as choices for the student. Say, 'This cube is one-third of the whole, which one is the whole?' (See Figure 5.8.)

Figure 5.8 The single cube is one-third of the whole. Which one is the whole?

Conclusion

The assessment tasks, accommodations, and modifications presented in this chapter are representative of the types of activities that can help teachers uncover the current understanding of their students. Teachers need to discover what students can do by making tasks more accessible, adapting presentation and/or response options. Chapter 6 will discuss the use of assessment information to write goals and objectives for IEPs. Chapter 10 will explore accommodations and modifications of instructional activities to engender the development of numeracy skills, knowledge, and understanding.

6

Using the Learning Framework in Number to Write Individualized Education Programs

In this chapter, we will look at connections between writing Individualized Education Programs (IEPs), the Learning Framework in Number, and the Teaching and Learning Cycle. We will consider how the Learning Framework in Number and the Teaching and Learning Cycle can inform the writing of IEPs to help ensure that students are receiving an appropriate education that will advance their understanding of mathematics and prepare them for life beyond their school years. The information in this chapter will be helpful for teachers of students with disabilities, instructional coaches and supervisors who support teachers of students with disabilities, and interventionists who want to consider how they can more closely monitor the progress of students.

Individualized Education Programs, the Learning Framework in Number, and the Teaching and Learning Cycle

Individualized Education Programs (IEPs) are documents used in many countries to outline the specialized services needed for students with disabilities to participate and make progress in educational programming. An overview of IEPs in six countries is available in Alkahtani and Kheiralla (2016). This chapter will focus on the specific process and regulations common in the United States. In the United States, the IEP must include the student's current performance, annual goals, special education and related services, the dates and locations of specialized services, how students will participate with non-disabled peers, participation in state and district-wide testing, transition service needs, how progress will be measured, and how parents/guardians will be informed of the student's progress (US Department of Education, 2019). Three of these components can be connected to components of the Teaching and Learning Cycle (see Figure 2.1).

We will begin the IEP process with 'Where are they now?' from the Teaching and Learning Cycle. IEPs must include information on the student's current performance and this information must include strengths of the student. Since instruction begins with what the student knows and is able to do, this information should be available for each student based on our initial and ongoing assessment (see Guiding Principle 2 in Chapter 3). For example, based on an assessment of the student's knowledge of the various aspects of structuring numbers presented in previous books in the Math Recovery series (*EN*, pp. 25–27; *TNC*, pp. 71–75: *LFIN*, pp. 79–81), a teacher can determine what the student is able to do and what the next steps for instruction might include. The statement concerning the student's current level of performance should be written so that it can be understood by other educators, parents/guardians, and the student. Here is a sample of a student's strengths in structuring numbers:

> The student is able to show 1–10 fingers without counting each finger. When using visual supports such as fingers, ten-frames, a math rack, or connecting cubes, the student is able to solve addition and subtraction problems in the range of 1–10, without counting each object one by one.

The student's current level of performance might also include information on the student's abilities in the areas of Forward and Backward Number Word Sequences, numeral identification, addition and subtraction strategies, conceptual place value, multiplication and division, and fractions.

After the IEP team has determined where the student is now, the next step in the Teaching and Learning Cycle is 'Where do I want them to be?' When writing an IEP, knowing where we want the student to be informs the goals and objectives written for the student. The annual goals written for a student should enable the student to be involved and make progress in the general education curriculum. Since the Learning Framework in Number presents a structure and developmental sequence for all students, using the framework as a guide for the next steps in learning assures that learning for all students aligns with the general education curriculum. Most states also require IEPs to include objectives or benchmarks for each annual goal. These objectives or benchmarks might specify a subset of skills that will move the student toward the annual goal or establish a timeline for achieving progress toward the goal. Depending on the needs of the student and the local practices for writing IEP goals and objectives, a student may have a broad goal of increasing numeracy with objectives written for different aspects of the Learning Framework in Number, or a goal might focus on one aspect of the Learning Framework in Number with objectives or benchmarks for achieving the goal. For the remainder of this chapter, 'goal' will be used to indicate a goal or objective. Based on the current level of performance presented above, the IEP team might determine that the next steps in structuring, for this student, can be summarized in the following statement:

The student needs to able to solve addition problems, and related subtraction problems, with sums in the range of 1–10, without using visuals or counting by ones.

The above statement indicates what the student should learn next, but it is not written in the form of a goal or objective for an IEP. A goal or objective needs to be measurable, which leads us to another element in the Teaching and Learning Cycle, 'How will I know when they get there?'

A measurable goal or objective should include the following components:

- A target or observable behavior, for example, solving addition and related subtraction problems, with sums in the range of 1–10.
- Conditions under which the behavior will be measured. This might include if the student will be working independently, in a small group, or in the general education classroom, or what educational strategies will be employed. The conditions can also specify how the prompt will be presented to students. Will problems be presented verbally or in a written format?
- The criteria for successful goal completion. The criteria should include a specific level, perhaps a percentage, and a specific length of time, such as two consecutive weeks or three out of five trials.

Based on the next steps presented above, a measurable goal might read:

Given ten addition and subtraction problems, with sums in the range of 1–10, written vertically or horizontally, the student will solve the problems, without using visuals or counting by ones, with 100% accuracy on three consecutive trials by (date).

The IEP team may decide to break this goal down into smaller benchmarks or objectives. The examples below represent a possible sequence for instruction. IEP teams should adjust the outcomes and criteria based on the needs of the student and local practices. When objectives focus on aspects of structuring with fewer than ten combinations, the orientation of the problem presentations can be varied to achieve ten different opportunities for students to respond.

Sample Benchmarks or Objectives

Given ten addition problems, with sums in the range of 1–10, written vertically or horizontally, the student will solve the problems, without using visuals or counting by ones, with 100% accuracy on three consecutive trials by (date).

Given ten, 5 + addition problems, with sums in the range of 5–10, written vertically or horizontally, the student will solve the problems, without using visuals or counting by ones, with 100% accuracy on three consecutive trials by (date).

Given ten addition problems, using doubles with sums in the range of 2–10, written vertically or horizontally, the student will solve the problems, without using visuals or counting by ones, with 100% accuracy on three consecutive trials by (date).

Given ten subtraction problems, subtracting from 10 or less, written vertically or horizontally, the student will solve the problems, without using visuals or counting by ones, with 100% accuracy on three consecutive trials by (date). (See Table 6.1.)

Table 6.1 Sample goals based on domains of the Learning Framework in Number

Forward Number Word Sequence:

- Current performance – The student is able to count to 10 and say the number after a given number in the range of 1–10.
- Needs statement – In order to develop basic computation skills, the student needs to be able to count to 30 and say the number after a given number in the range of 1–30, without dropping back.
- Objective – When asked to count, the student will count from 1–30 with 100% accuracy on three consecutive trials, by...
- Objective – Given a number in the range of 1–29, the student will correctly answer the question, 'What number comes after ___?' with 100% accuracy on three consecutive trials by...

Backward Number Word Sequence:

- Current performance – The student is able to say numbers when asked to count from 10 to 1, but the student does not say the numbers in the correct order.
- Needs statement – The student needs to be able to say numbers in order when asked to count from 10 to 1.
- Objective – When asked to count backward from 10, the student will count from 10 to 1 with 100% accuracy on three consecutive trials, by...

Numeral Identification:

- Current performance – The student is able to correctly identify numerals in the range of 0 to 20.
- Needs statement – The student needs to be able to correctly identify numerals 0–100.
- Objective – When shown a collection of ten numerals in the range of 0 to 100, the student will indicate the correct numeral when asked, 'Show me the ____,' with 100% accuracy on three consecutive trials by...
- Objective – When shown ten numerals in the range of 0 to 100, in random order, one at a time, the student will identify each numeral correctly with 100% accuracy on three consecutive trials by...

Strategies for Addition and Subtraction:

- Current performance (Select the appropriate current performance statement, depending on the abilities of the student.)
    - The student is able to say the correct sequence of numerals but does not match the number words with the objects when counting collections.
    - The student is able to match words with objects when counting collections but does not know the correct sequence of number words. (Refer to 'Development of Forward Number Word Sequence'.)
    - The student does not demonstrate the understanding that the last number said when counting a collection of items can be used to state how many items are in the collection.
- Needs statements – The *student* needs to be able to determine a quantity of a collection.
    - When asked for a specified quantity of items, the student needs to accurately count out the correct amount from a collection.
    - When asked 'How many?' the student needs to demonstrate an understanding that the last number used when counting a set can be used to quantify the set.

- Objective – Given a collection of ___–___ items, the student will correctly count the objects and use the correct number word or symbol to state how many items have been counted, with 100% accuracy on three consecutive trials by…
- Objective – Given a collection of objects, the student will correctly count out a requested quantity of ___–___ items with 100% accuracy on three consecutive trials by…

Conceptual Place Value:

- Current performance – The student is able to count visible items and solve single-digit addition and subtraction problems. When counting items presented as units of ten and single units, the strategy used by the student involves counting by ones and the student does not recognize ten as a unit that can be used to count objects or solve problems
- Needs statements – The student needs to develop more efficient strategies for adding and subtracting two-digit numbers. As part of this process, the student needs to demonstrate an understanding that a bundle, or other representation of ten ones, can be counted as one unit of ten.
- Objective – When given a collection of items representing units of ten and single units (such as bundles of ten popsicle sticks and single sticks), the student will correctly determine the quantity of objects by counting tens and ones, with 100% accuracy on ten consecutive trials by…

Strategies for Multiplication and Division:

- Current performance – When given pictures of objects arranged in equal groups, the student is able to use known skip-counting sequences to correctly count the number of objects in the picture. If the needed skip-counting sequence is not known, the student will indicate by pointing or by using rhythmic counting by ones, that the group structure is being used to count the objects.
- Needs statement – To promote an understanding of multiplication and division, the student needs to be able to determine the quantity of a collection, arranged in equal groups, when only the number of groups is visible, not the individual items.
- Objective – Given ten pictures depicting equal groups of objects, with the groups visible but the objects hidden, the student will determine the quantity of objects with 100% accuracy on three consecutive trials by…
- Objective – Given ten pictures depicting equal groups of objects with the groups visible but the objects hidden and told the total number of objects represented by the picture, the student will determine the number of hidden objects in each group, with 100% accuracy on three consecutive trials by…

Development of Fractions Concepts:

- Current performance (Select the statements that describe the current abilities of the student.)

  o The student is able to break a physical unit, such as a rectangular piece of paper, into a specified number of smaller units but cannot make all of the smaller units the same size.
  o The student is able to use fragments of a unit, such as a rectangular piece of paper, to reassemble a whole unit.
  o The student is able to break a physical unit, such as a rectangular piece of paper, into equal-size pieces but has difficulty using all of the original unit.

- Needs statements – The student needs to be able to break a physical unit, such as a rectangular piece of paper, into a specified number of pieces that are equal in size.
- Objective – Given a rectangular piece of paper and scissors, the student will partition the paper into three to five pieces of equal size and be able to justify that the pieces are of equal size, two out of three trials on four different days, by…

Using the Learning Framework in Number to write IEP goals can help teachers focus on the numeracy knowledge that will help students make continued progress in mathematics. We believe that the addition and subtraction, conceptual place value, and multiplication and division aspects of the Learning Framework in Number, and the development of fractions knowledge, are developmental milestones. While teachers can present problems to students that will engender movement from one construct to the next, when the student is cognitively ready, we do not believe that students should be pushed to demonstrate progress in these areas. It may take neurotypical students more than a year to move from some constructs to the next and IEP goals should be written with this in mind. We do not advocate writing a goal indicating the movement from one construct to the next, rather goals/objectives should be written about specific skills and behaviors that will indicate increased understanding. Writing goals based on parts of the Learning Framework in Number that indicate conceptual understanding may lead to teachers rushing students or eliciting specific behaviors, such as counting on, rather than waiting for understanding and the use of specific strategies to be developed by students (see problematic teacher behaviors in Chapter 3). For this reason, we encourage teachers to focus on writing goals and objectives based on number word sequences, numeral ID, and structuring. IEPs are **behaviorist** by nature, since they focus on observed behavior and measurable outcomes (Frankl, 2005). Learning number word sequences, numeral identification, and structuring numbers are more conducive to behaviorist strategies than the other aspects of the Learning Framework in Number in which growth should be engendered through constructivist teaching. Further discussion of teaching from a constructivist and behaviorist perspective can be found in Chapter 11.

In addition to using the Learning Framework in Number to guide the progression of goals for students, teachers may consider using dimensions of progressive mathematization for writing goals. Students who have demonstrated the ability to add and subtract could have goals that address the ability to solve more complex problems, such as solving problems with three or four addends, solving problems that extend the range of numbers, solving problems presented in varied orientations, for example, missing addend or missing subtrahend, and demonstrating the ability to use one problem to help solve a different problem, for example, using a doubles fact to solve doubles plus one. More information on the dimensions of progressive mathematization can be found in Chapter 3.

An important part of writing goals and objectives for an IEP is developing a plan for collecting data that will show students have achieved their goals. As goals are being written, teachers should develop a plan for how the data will be collected. If data collection will be difficult, perhaps the goal needs to be rewritten to include targets or behavior that can be observed and measured more easily. Data collection can be in the form of charts (paper or digital), collected work samples, photographs, or videos. With advancements in technology, the opportunities and methods for collecting data will likely increase in the future. A sample data collection form is shown in Figure 6.1.

Students should be given the opportunity to participate in the IEP process whenever possible:

Children, who are capable of forming views, have a right to receive and make known information, to express an opinion, and to have that opinion taken into account in any matters affecting them. The views of the child should be given due weight according to the age, maturity and capability of the child. (Special Educational Needs Code of Practice, 2001, p. 27)

Combination to 5, With Materials

Use fingers, 5-frames, or Unifix cubes
Show (Amount shown) and ask 'How many more to make (Target amount)?'
The student is expected to say the target amount without counting
Scoring : + correct, - incorrect, c counted

Amount shown	Target amount	Date								
0	5									
1	5									
2	5									
3	5									
4	5									
5	5									
0	4									
1	4									
2	4									
3	4									
4	4									
0	3									
1	3									
2	3									
3	3									
0	2									
1	2									
2	2									
		/	/	/	/	/	/	/	/	
		%	%	%	%	%	%	%	%	

Figure 6.1 Sample data collection form

Students may benefit from having simplified versions of their IEP current levels, goals, and objectives written as 'I can...' or 'I will be able to...' statements. The current level for the student described above might read:

I can show different finger patterns without counting. When I have tools to help me, I can solve addition and subtraction problems to 10, without counting.

A student-friendly version of the goal might read:

> I will be able to solve addition and subtraction problems using the numbers 1-10. I'll prove I can do this by solving 10 problems without making mistakes, three different times.

Directing to check is a Key Element of Instruction discussed in Chapter 3. Teachers can use this Key Element to include students in collecting data to show student progress. Students who have a goal of solving addition and subtraction problems to ten can be given a collection of ten-frames to check their work. This practice gives students the opportunity to connect visual representations to bare number problems and share responsibility for documenting their progress. Students can also be involved in setting the criteria for success. Asking students how they will know if they have achieved the intended goal can promote reflection and intrinsic satisfaction (see Guiding Principles 8 and 9 in Chapter 3).

Our process for writing IEPs skipped one component of the Teaching and Learning Cycle, 'How will they get there?' Planning instruction is not a formal part of the IEP process, but it is important to determine what types of instructional activities will help students achieve their goals. Instruction should be based on the Instructional Framework for Early Number presented in Wright et al. (*TN*, pp. 19–21) or the Classroom Instructional Framework for Early Number presented in Wright et al. (*TNC*, pp. 10–11). Both of these instructional frameworks can be linked to the Learning Framework in Number, which provides a scope and sequence for numeracy instruction. The instructional activities should be based on the Guiding Principles of Instruction and Key Elements of Teaching discussed in Chapter 3. We encourage teachers to write goals for themselves concerning the instructional moves they will implement to help students achieve their IEP goals. For example, to facilitate the learning of the student mentioned above who will be working to learn addition and subtraction facts to ten, a teacher might commit to a specified number of minutes each week for working with the student on learning combinations to ten, the development of independent activities that will be available to the student, and a plan for the student to participate in instructional activities or games with other students who can model the desired learning for the student. Committing to instructional plans will ensure that students have opportunities to make steady progress toward their goals.

Conclusion

Although the primary focus of this chapter has been writing IEP goals for students with disabilities, this process can be helpful for setting goals and tracking the progress of any student. Setting goals and planning to monitor the progress of students receiving intervention will help teachers focus instruction and plan for ways students can demonstrate their achievement. Although it might not be practical for classroom teachers to develop specific numeracy goals for each student, selecting a few students representing a cross-section of achievement in the classroom can help teachers monitor the effectiveness of their instruction.

This chapter examined the connections between IEPs, the Learning Framework in Number, and the Teaching and Learning Cycle. Our goal has been to help teachers see how these three tools can be used to help teachers provide more effective numeracy instruction for all students.

7

Brain Research: Implications for Teaching and Learning Mathematics

Anderson Norton
Virginia Tech

Several popular works summarize neuroscience research and its educational implications. Here, we focus on implications that are unique to mathematical development. Mathematics is based in action – mental actions like unitizing, partitioning, and iterating. When challenged by new mathematical tasks, children have to reorganize their existing mental actions. This effortful activity places demands on working memory. Over time, these cognitive demands are offloaded by new mathematical objects, freeing working memory to engage in evermore challenging tasks. We see evidence of this development in neuroscience studies that indicate a general frontal-to-parietal shift as learners progress from novice to expert. This chapter will elaborate on such findings from neuroscience – findings that have unique implications for the teaching and learning of mathematics. These implications include a neural basis for the Dimensions of Mathematizing that frame Math Recovery interventions and implications for particular challenges faced by students with special needs.

Introduction

Mathematics is different than other subjects. In mathematics, students do not study something that is 'out there,' like plants or planets. Rather, they study something within themselves – their own mental actions. These mental actions arise from students' coordinations of their own **sensorimotor activity** (bodily activity that teachers can observe). Once internalized as mental actions, these actions can be coordinated with other mental actions to build mathematical objects.

Consider the mental action of partitioning a whole into five equal parts. This mental action is a crucial building block for fractions. It arises from a coordination of simpler actions. As adults, we might take this coordination for granted; we might see a rectangular bar like the one shown in Figure 7.1 and immediately imagine five equal parts within it. However, for many of our students, the task requires effortful activity. This effortful activity is also productive because it is the origin of mathematics itself (Piaget, 1970).

Figure 7.1 Partitioning a whole

When attempting to partition a whole into five equal parts, three competing goals are at play (Steffe & Olive, 2010):

1. The student needs to create five parts.
2. The parts must be equal in size.
3. The whole must be exhausted, with nothing left over.

Meeting all three goals at once poses quite a challenge for many students. At first, a student might meet only one or two of the goals. For example, the student might produce five little parts, all the same size, but because the parts are too small, there is a leftover part that the student just ignores or throws away.

As we have seen in Chapter 3, teachers have strategies to help students address the **cognitive demand** of such tasks so that, over time, students might learn to satisfy all three goals by coordinating related activities. For instance, a teacher might ask the student whether the leftover part also should be used, or the teacher might ask how the student would adjust the size of the parts if the student were to try again. Having manipulatives available (for example, construction paper and scissors) provides the student with material to act upon – a medium on which students can carry out activity that has not yet been coordinated as a single mental action, like partitioning.

Just as mental actions arise from students' coordinated sensorimotor activity, mathematical objects, like fractions, arise from students' coordination of mental actions. Thus, mathematics should feel personally empowering for students. As teachers, we honor students' mathematics by recognizing it, through formative assessment, and supporting its development, by posing appropriately challenging instructional tasks (see Chapter 9 on differentiating instruction). We find evidence of this development in neuroscience – evidence for the psychological development of **mathematical objects** from coordinated mental actions. This chapter will illuminate such evidence and highlight related implications for teaching students with special needs.

We begin with a description of the neural anatomy of the brain, focusing on the outer layer of the brain, called the **neocortex**. The neocortex largely serves the purpose of coordinating sensori-motor activity and mental actions – the foundation for mathematical development. We will see that mathematical development corresponds to a frontal-to-parietal shift wherein functions of the frontal lobe, like working memory, are offloaded with the development of mathematical objects that correspond to cognitive structures in the parietal lobe, which support **spatial–numerical reasoning**. Because many students with disabilities exhibit reduced working memory (see Chapter 12), this shift will have important implications for addressing their needs.

The Neural Anatomy of the Neocortex

The neocortex is the outer layer of the brain, wrinkled with peaks and valleys. It is the cortex (or region) of the brain unique to mammals; 'neo' refers to its relatively recent appearance in evolution. This region is responsible for high-level functions, such as working memory and spatial transforma-tions. The **sensorimotor cortex** plays a central role in these functions and appropriately appears in the center of the neocortex (see Figure 7.2).

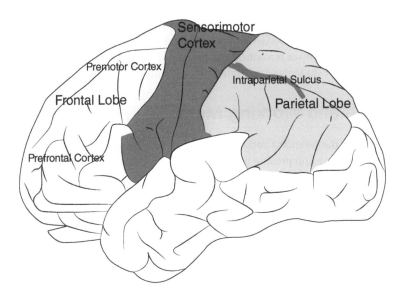

Figure 7.2   Neocortex

The Sensorimotor Cortex

We have argued that mathematical objects arise from coordinations of mental actions, and that men-tal actions arise from coordinations of sensorimotor activity. Then the sensorimotor cortex would be the primary engine for all mathematical development. Indeed, findings from cognitive psychology support this perspective. Sensorimotor actions involving the fingers play a particularly important role in mathematical development.

Whenever you make any voluntary movement, whether with your hands, feet, or eyes, an electrical signal is sent from your sensorimotor cortex to the muscles in that part of the body. In turn, the nerves in those muscles return a signal, back to the brain, providing your sensorimotor cortex with a sense of movement. The sensorimotor cortex contains a map of your entire body so that various locations within it (up and down the red area in Figure 7.2) control various parts of your body. Importantly, the location adjacent to the purple segment in Figure 7.2 corresponds to the sensorimotor area that controls the hands and fingers.

Studies of child development demonstrate that, beginning in infancy, a host of sensorimotor activities predict later mathematical achievement, including crawling (Bell & Fox, 1997; Kermoian & Campos, 1988) and gesturing (Ehrlich, Levine, & Goldin-Meadow, 2006). Sensorimotor activity involving the hands and fingers has a particularly strong and lasting effect on mathematical development (for a full summary of related research see Norton, Ulrich, Bell, & Cate, 2018).

Fingers serve as one of our first mathematical manipulatives. This fundamental connection is encoded in our base-ten number system (ten fingers) and our use of the term 'digits' to refer to numbers. Long after we stop counting on our fingers, the connection still appears in our neural pathways (Fayol, Barrouillet, & Marinthe, 1998; Noël, 2005; Rusconi, Walsh, & Butterworth, 2005). For example, even when we, as adults, solve simple mathematical tasks, such as determining whether a given number is odd or even, our brains send electrical signals to our fingers (Sato, Cattaneo, Rizzolatti, & Gallese, 2007). More generally, we will see that manual manipulation, whether with fingers or tools, serves as the primary evolutionary and neurological basis for mathematics. Thus, frequent and appropriate use of manipulatives is a critical component of mathematical instruction (Sowell, 1989) and accommodations for students with limited motor ability are an important consideration.

The Frontal Lobe and Working Memory

As the name suggests, the **premotor cortex** of the **frontal lobe** sits just in front of the sensorimotor cortex. It serves to imagine and prepare motor activity. Likewise, a major function of the prefrontal cortex is to control activity, either motor (physical) or imagined (mental), and to put multiple actions in sequence. For example, if you wanted to partition the stick shown in Figure 7.1 into fifteen equal pieces, you might plan to partition the stick into five equal pieces and then partition each of those pieces into three equal pieces. This two-part plan is possible for you if you have already formed partitioning as a mental action that you can compose with other mental actions (for example, partitioning a whole into five equal parts and then partitioning each of those parts into three equal parts).

Planning sequences of actions, whether physical or mental, is the domain of executive function – a primary function of the **prefrontal cortex** and the central component of working memory (Kane & Engle, 2002). The **central executive** allows us to devise plans to meet new goals, such as solving new mathematical tasks. Unlike familiar tasks for which we might have an automatic response (for example, remembering that 8 times 7 is 56), new tasks require cognitive effort. This cognitive effort consists of finding ways to use our available mental actions, or to perform sensorimotor actions, to meet the new goal. Returning to the initial task using Figure 7.1, consider the cognitive demands of partitioning a stick into five equal pieces if that were not already available to you as a single mental action. Figure 7.3 illustrates the role **executive function** would play in meeting that demand.

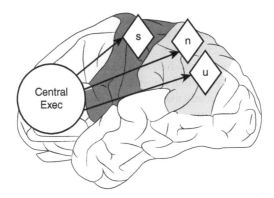

Figure 7.3 The role of executive function in problem solving

In order to solve the task of partitioning a stick into five equal parts, students might need to coordinate three different actions: the mental action of unitizing a segment length (u); the motor action of moving that segment length along the length of the whole stick, **segmenting** the whole into equal pieces (s); and the mental action of counting, using their number sequence to keep track of the number of segments created (n). The students' central executive would call upon all three actions in sequence while monitoring their coordination so as to ensure that the whole is exhausted after five segments. If part of the stick remains, or if the fifth segment goes past the end of the whole stick, the students would then need to consciously reflect on their activity and adjust the size of the unit segment. Thus, we see that the mental action of partitioning, which might constitute a single action for you and me, can be cognitively demanding for our students. However, as we will see, this cognitive demand is important to maintain because it induces students' construction of their own mental action of partitioning.

The Parietal Lobe and Spatial–Numerical Reasoning

Figure 7.3 places the motor action of segmenting in the sensorimotor cortex and the mental actions of unitizing and counting (a student's number sequence) in the parietal lobe. The reason for the placement of these latter two is that mental actions no longer need to be carried out through sensorimotor activity; they largely fall in the domain of the parietal lobe, especially when acting on spatial or numerical objects (Buccino et al., 2001; Hubbard, Piazza, Pinel, & Dehaene, 2005). Recall that the area just in front of the sensorimotor cortex – the premotor cortex – is involved in planning or preparing to carry out a motor action. The **parietal lobe** is situated just behind the sensorimotor cortex and is involved in anticipating the spatial–numerical effects of actions on objects. For example, when you mentally rotate a three-dimensional figure, such as a cube, your parietal lobe does much of the work (Cohen et al., 1996).

The **intraparietal sulcus** (the purple segment in Figure 7.2) is a particularly important area within the parietal lobe. It aligns with the motor area associated with the hand and is involved in grasping objects with the hand, as well as a vast range of mathematical activity (Butterworth & Walsh, 2011; Rosenberg-Lee, Lovett, & Anderson, 2009). This alignment reinforces the idea that actions with the hand play an important role in mathematical development. Some researchers argue that manual dexterity, which evolved primarily for tool use, has provided humans with a neural foundation for mathematical development (Penner-Wilger & Anderson, 2013).

We have noted that fingers provide children with readily available manipulatives, hence the close connection between fingers and counting. Other kinds of manipulatives afford different kinds of actions that may be important for mathematical development. For example, by cutting off strips of construction paper and fitting them into a whole sheet, students can physically carry out the kinds of activity that lead to the mental action of partitioning. Along the way, they might establish the reciprocal relationship between the size of a piece and the number of times it fits into the whole. Such activities provide experience with the kinds of **spatial–numerical transformations** that constitute mathematics. Thus, in using manipulatives with our students, we take advantage of a primordial connection between mathematics and tool use.

Frontal-to-Parietal Shift

We have seen that a primary role of the frontal lobe is the effortful coordination of available actions into novel sequences of activity (see Figure 7.3). We have also discussed the role of the parietal lobe in imagining mental actions that no longer need to be carried out through sensorimotor activity. As students develop mathematically, more and more of their effortful coordinations of simpler actions become available as singular mental actions (such as partitioning). Those mental actions can then be coordinated with other actions through executive function. Thus, mathematics builds on itself through a neurological shift from the frontal lobe to the parietal lobe.

The frontal-to-parietal shift essentially offloads demands on working memory so that effortful tasks, which place high demand on working memory, become more and more automatized through cognitive structures in the parietal lobe. Evidence of the shift can be found in studies that compare more novice students to more expert students on a variety of mathematical tasks (Ansari & Dhital, 2006; Rivera, Reiss, Eckert, & Menon, 2005). For example, Ansari and Dhital (2006) conducted a neuroscience study of 10 year olds to 20 year olds who were asked to compare two collections of dots, where each collection had between 1 and 9 dots in it. In solving the tasks, the 10 year olds exhibited relatively greater frontal lobe activity, whereas the 20 year olds exhibited relatively greater parietal lobe activity.

While the frontal-to-parietal shift offloads demands on working memory, that same cognitive demand induces the shift to begin. Thus, it is important for us, as teachers, to maintain cognitive demand in the tasks we pose, to support the shift. On the other hand, working memory is limited, so we need to ensure that executive functioning focuses on the coordinations of actions essential to mathematical development. Moreover, we need to assess whether those actions are available for the student. In the next section, we turn to related implications for assessment and instruction.

Supporting Mathematical Development

Neuroscience suggests three distinct and important roles for the neocortex in mathematical development. It all starts in the sensorimotor cortex – the center of sensorimotor activity. The frontal lobe governs planning and sequencing of that activity, as well as mental actions that can be carried out in imagination. As students progress in their mathematical development, more and more activities and sequences of actions become available as singular mental actions, or spatial–numerical transformations, structured within the parietal lobe. In this section, we will consider specific implications of these roles, with supporting examples.

Engaging students in activity

First and foremost, students need to engage in meaningful activity in order to construct mathematical objects, whether those objects are whole numbers, fractions, or triangles. Until students have developed all relevant mental actions they will need to engage in sensorimotor activity. At this stage, they might rely on their fingers and other manipulatives that enable them to carry out the desired activity. Here, we provide examples of tasks for assessing and supporting students' development of two important mental actions: iterating and partitioning. We also suggest accommodations for students with limited motor coordination.

Iterating

The mental action of iterating involves taking an item or a length as a unit and making identical copies of that unit to make a composite unit – a new unit made up of smaller units. To assess whether a student can iterate a unit, we need to know whether the student can use it to build collections of units where: (1) the collection becomes a composite unit; and (2) any of the constituent units in the **composite unit** can be taken as identical with the others and used to rebuild the collection. Here, we focus on iterable units of 1, but for more advanced tasks, students will also need to learn to iterate composite units (for example, iterating units of 7 to produce 56 as a new composite unit) and unit fractions (for example, iterating 1/6 to produce 11/6 as a fractional number).

To assess whether a student has iterating available as a mental action, you might ask the student questions like the following: 'How much is seven 1s?' If the student immediately responds that there are seven 1s in 7, this is a good indicator that 1 is an iterable unit for that student. It indicates that the student can build up 7 as a composite unit – a unit composed of units of 1. To follow up, you might ask, 'What number has five more 1s than 7?' This will be a confusing question for students who do not think about numbers like 7 and 5 as numbers composed of iterated units of 1. However, for students who do, the question is the same as asking, 'What's 7 plus 5?'

For students who do not yet mentally iterate units of 1, even the first question might be challenging. Students might respond by counting on their fingers to 'seven' and then counting each finger, as a 1, to determine that there are seven 1s in 7. This activity would indicate that 1 is not yet an iterable unit for the students because they need to carry out the sensorimotor activity of counting to 7 on their fingers and then counting each finger, rather than anticipating that the mental action of iterating a unit of 1 seven times is what produces 7. To support the development of iterating as a mental action, students need opportunities to coordinate and anticipate their sensorimotor activity of counting.

Note that the assessment questions exemplified above do not include opportunities for sensorimotor activity. This is because we are assessing students' available mental actions – actions they can perform in imagination without manipulatives. However, when we are trying to support the development of those mental actions, manipulatives become critical. The tasks in Figure 7.4 are designed to support students' development of the mental action of iterating units of 1 through coordinated sensorimotor activity using manipulatives.

Figure 7.4 illustrates two instructional tasks. The first task (Figure 7.4a) involves collections of chips that the student can count out. Counting involves a coordination of sensorimotor actions of reciting number words and shifting attention (for example, pointing) to different but similar items, maintaining a one-to-one correspondence between number words and attentional shifts. This is not yet iterating, but related activity can support the development of that mental action. For example, Steffe (1992) has used activities involving two collections of items, with one or both collections covered, to support that development. The first task relies on that approach.

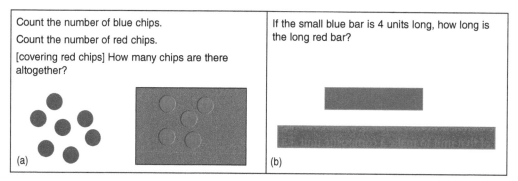

Figure 7.4 Instructional tasks for supporting iterating

To solve the first task, students need to internalize the results of their counting activity. They might count on from 7 by imagining figural patterns, such as the pattern for 5 on a die, in order to keep track of the five extra counts: '8, 9, 10, 11, 12.' This would be a significant step toward iterating. The task can be scaled up or down by using larger or smaller numbers, respectively, and it can be modified to tasks like the following: 'I want a total of 20 blue chips, so how many more blue chips do I need [with the counted blue chips covered or uncovered]?'

The second task (Figure 7.4b) involves continuous units of length, rather than discrete units, and the unit of 1 is not shown. To solve the task, students would need to imagine the four units of length 1 that would comprise the length of 4. Moreover, they might put together two blue bars to make two units of 4 and notice that the red bar contains an extra unit of 1. Tasks like this second task are more challenging than those like the first task, but they can further support students' internalization of units of 1 and their iterations: the blue bar as four iterations of 1; and the red bar as nine iterations of that same unit of 1.

Partitioning

As shared in examples throughout the chapter, the mental action of partitioning involves a coordination of multiple activities (see Figure 7.3) to satisfy competing goals of (1) creating n equally sized pieces and (2) exhausting the whole with those pieces. We use the term fragmenting to describe the more general activity of breaking a whole into parts (Steffe & Olive, 2010). Students progress through levels of fragmenting as they learn to coordinate their activity to resolve those competing goals and develop a mental action of partitioning. The task in Figure 7.5 is designed to assess and support students' progress through those levels. Similar tasks can be found in Chapter 9 of DFK (Hackenberg et al., 2016).

Suppose five friends want to share this candy bar equally.

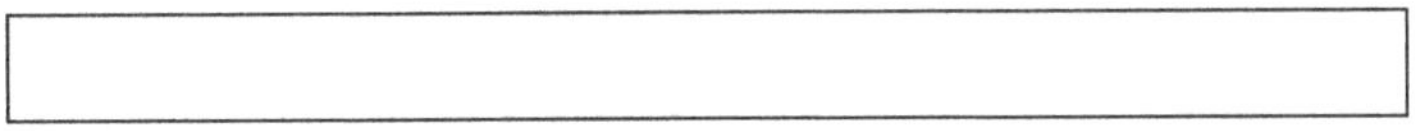

Make a single mark to determine how much one person would get. How can you check whether it's the right size?

Figure 7.5 Instructional tasks for supporting partitioning

At lower levels of fragmenting, students focus on only one goal: either making the right number of parts, or making sure they are equal. In responding to the task in Figure 7.5, a student might focus on creating five parts. Asking the student to check whether the marked part is the right size might prompt the student to fit it into the whole five times, segmenting the whole into five equal pieces. If the part is too short, there will be a leftover piece in the whole, so the marked part might need to be adjusted. Students should be allowed to engage in trial and error activities to make such adjustments: should the marked part be longer or shorter? This kind of activity can help them to progress toward higher levels of fragmenting where they explicitly attend to the two competing goals (cf. Hunt, Tzur, & Westenskow, 2016).

Accommodations for Students with Limited Sensorimotor Ability

As discussed in Chapters 9 and 10, students with special needs will need teachers to adjust tasks to accommodate those needs while preserving the tasks' instructional benefits. In supporting students' development of mental actions, such as iterating and partitioning, instructional benefits include the opportunity to coordinate sensorimotor activity. However, some students with special needs have constraints on their sensory or motor ability. Thus, we need to consider the motor activity and manipulatives with which the student can engage and find ways to leverage those resources.

For example, if a student has a visual impairment, the student might need a more tactile manipulative, so fraction rods might be used for the partitioning task shown in Figure 7.5. Giving the student a long rod and a box full of other rods, the teacher can ask, 'Which of the rods in this box would be a fair share if five people wanted to share the candy bar [long rod]?' Likewise, if a student has limited use of the hands and fingers, the teacher might use larger blocks as manipulatives. Some students might not be able to use manipulatives at all, but then teachers can rely on attentional shifts in the students' eyes – this too is sensorimotor activity – as they visually iterate one length within another.

In supporting students' development of mental actions, the key is to elicit students' available sensorimotor activity and prompt them to coordinate that activity in new ways. The specific sensorimotor activity might vary across students, rendering different manipulatives more or less appropriate for different students. It is the coordination of those available activities, in meeting goals, that induces the development of mental actions.

Maintaining Cognitive Demand

In coordinating sensorimotor activity, the prefrontal cortex of the frontal lobe functions as the central executive, which sequences actions (sensorimotor and mental) in service of meeting new goals (see Figure 7.3). Recall that the central executive is the central component of working memory. While working memory is limited, it is also the driver of mathematical development, so students need to be challenged with tasks that require them to coordinate existing mental actions in new ways, to develop new mathematical objects. Sustained cognitive demand can induce a frontal-to-parietal shift in neural activity that corresponds to offloading demands on working memory through the development of new structures – structures that correspond to neural activity in the parietal lobe, which allow students to make sense of a task or find its solution with little or no conscious effort.

For example, consider the case of a student who has developed mental actions of partitioning and iterating. In other words, the student can readily partition a whole into a specified number of equal parts and can iterate units of 1 to produce composite numbers. Even if this student had learned nothing about fractions before, the student's available mental actions would provide a power to construct fractions as measures. To support this construction, a teacher might pose tasks like those illustrated in Figure 7.6.

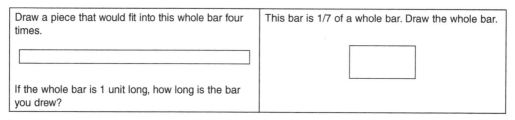

Figure 7.6   Instructional tasks promoting fractions as measures

To solve the task on the left side of Figure 7.6, students might draw a small part and iterate its length across the length of the whole bar, possibly using their fingers to measure the length of the small part and keep track of its iterations. If the small part fits in more than four times, the students might realize they need a longer part, or, at that point, they might realize that they can just partition the whole bar into four equal parts. Regardless, this kind of effortful activity is productive because it serves to coordinate the student's available actions of iterating and partitioning. Those coordinations lead to a 1-to-4 relationship between the part and the whole, which the student might symbolize by the fraction ¼. Thus, unit fractions like ¼ become mathematical objects available for measuring non-unit fractions, like ¾.

Note that teachers might need to help students use appropriate (conventional) symbols, such as ¼. However, we should not try to circumvent the effortful activity that defines unit factions as mathematical objects and gives their symbols meaning. Likewise, for the task on the right side of Figure 7.6, students might need help interpreting the symbol, 1/7, but, nevertheless, the student should be allowed to struggle in coordinating the iterating and partitioning activities that relate 1 and 7 in that 1-to-7 (or 7-to-1) relationship. We characterize this kind of struggle as 'productive struggle' because it leads to mathematical development (Lynch, Hunt, & Lewis, 2018).

Increasing Cognitive Demand

As students progress in coordinating their mental actions, they can be given more and more challenging tasks – increasing cognitive demand or, rather, maintaining demand for students as they
develop. For example, if students can solve tasks like those shown in Figure 7.6, they might engage in
games like the one illustrated in Figure 7.7 from *DFK* (Hackenberg et al., 2016). Such games require
the student to do more than coordinate a unit fraction with the whole; they also require the student
to construct non-unit fractions as iterations of a unit fraction.

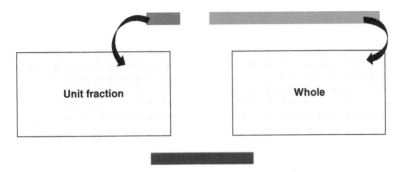

Figure 7.7   Guess my fraction

The game works with pairs of students using fractions rods. One student chooses a rod to represent the whole, then finds a rod that represents a unit fraction of that whole, and then chooses a
rod that is some number of iterations of that unit fraction. For the example shown in Figure 7.7, the
orange rod is the whole, the red rod is 1/5 of that whole, and the brown rod is three iterations of the
red rod – so 3/5 of the whole. The student hides the whole rod and the unit fraction (1/5 rod) and
shows the other student the non-unit fraction (the 3/5 rod): 'this is 3/5.' The other student has to
determine which rod represents 1/5 and which one represents the whole, choosing them from the
box of fractions rods.

Note that this game requires students to reverse the mental action of iterating 1/5 three times to produce 3/5, instead partitioning 3/5 to produce 1/5. It also requires students to become explicitly aware
of relationships between the three kinds of units: the whole, the unit fraction, and the non-unit fraction. These coordinations are cognitively demanding, but they are precisely the coordinations students
need to perform and internalize in order to understand fractions as mathematical objects.

Accommodations for Students with Limited Working Memory

Many students with special needs in mathematics have to contend with reduced working memory
resources (Bull & Scerif, 2001). For some students, this reduction is due to a specific cognitive factor, as it might be for students on the autism spectrum (Steele, Minshew, Luna, & Sweeney, 2007).

For other students, this reduction is a consequence of managing affective issues, such as math anxiety, which compete for the limited resource (Eysenck & Calvo, 1992). There are at least two ways that teachers can support students' productive use of working memory. First, teachers can support the student by reducing non-salient demands on working memory. Second, teachers can provide students with figurative materials (for example, encouraging students to draw pictures) to coordinate actions in new ways.

Teachers can provide modifications that enable students to engage in activity while maintaining cognitive demand, rather than modifications that circumvent these critical drivers of mathematical development. In particular, math anxiety places demands on working memory as students attempt to control or inhibit negative feelings associated with solving mathematical tasks (Eysenck & Calvo, 1992; Morsanyi, Busdraghi, & Primi, 2014; also see Chapter 12). At least one neuroscience study suggests that these negative feelings can be so strong that they activate the brain's pain network (Lyons & Beilock, 2012). Teachers can help students reduce this unnecessary burden by providing students with extra time (removing time pressure) and making sure the student has a comfortable working environment (Furner & Berman, 2003). In contrast, teachers often feel compelled to reduce the demands of the task itself by telling the student, step by step, what to do. Instead of limiting the unnecessary demand of anxiety, this would limit the productive activity of solving the task.

When the task itself is too demanding, teachers can support students by encouraging them to use figurative materials, such as manipulatives or drawings, to work through the various coordinations involved in solving the task. The 'disappearing sequences' tasks, in Chapter 3 of *DNK* (Wright et al., 2012) and here in Chapter 10, illustrate the strategy for students learning to produce a number word sequence. In those tasks, students can rely on a written-out number sequence, such as '2, 4, 6, 8,…,' to recite the sequence, but after each recital a number is erased so that students rely less and less on the figurative material each time.

In learning fractions, figurative materials such as fractions rods can help students carry out coordinations through activity. Working with the rods offers support for limited working memory while maintaining the demand that students carry out the coordinations. Likewise, drawings could help students lay out the various units and actions between units (for example, drawing a whole bar split into seven equal parts) involved in solving a fractions task. Also, when the purpose of the task is to promote a new concept rather than to practice computation, it may be appropriate to use smaller numbers in the task. Note that the tasks illustrated in Figures 7.4–7.6 all use small numbers so that the student can concentrate on coordinating their activity and mental actions, rather than expending effort on computing sums or products. On the other hand, those tasks require students to partition the whole into parts like fifths and sevenths (not just halves and fourths) to support a more general concept of partitioning and fractions.

Developing New Structures and Addressing Dyscalculia

Constructing new mathematical objects involves the coordination of mental actions. In the case of fractions, mental actions of partitioning and iterating are coordinated as inverses of one another: partitioning a whole into five equal parts yields parts that, when iterated five times, reproduce the whole. Thus, understanding mathematical objects like fractions requires students to know them forward and backward, literally. With whole numbers, too, students need to learn to coordinate their mental actions within reversible structures, such as when they learn to make and break apart tens.

Constructing mathematical objects, like unit fractions and ten, as **reversible structures** poses a critical challenge to mathematics educators. The challenge is compounded when working with students with special needs.

As outlined in this chapter, neuroscience studies of mathematical development suggest that **automated structures** correspond with neurological activity in the parietal lobe. Specifically, mathematical objects rely on neural activity in and around the intraparietal sulcus. But neuroimaging studies have shown reduced gray matter in and around the intraparietal sulcus of students diagnosed with **dyscalculia** (for example, Rykhlevskaia, Uddin, Kondos, & Menon, 2009). Such studies indicate a neurological basis for those students' difficulties in constructing mathematical objects, like fractions.

Students with dyscalculia – about 5% of students – have special needs specific to mathematics (Kaufmann, 2008). In line with other findings presented here linking fingers, numbers, and the intraparietal sulcus, these special needs manifest themselves in challenges related to both finger counting and number processing. One suggestion is that students be allowed to use their fingers, or other manipulatives, to perform numerical computations until no longer needed. Prematurely restricting students' access to manipulatives, including their fingers, could hinder their mathematical development.

Students with dyscalculia may need prolonged opportunities to engage in activities like the one illustrated in Figure 7.8, relying on manipulatives and sensorimotor activity when needed. Such tasks promote **reversible reasoning** (Hackenberg, 2010) by encouraging students to carry out actions forward and backward. At that same time, they can support students in constructing numbers as mathematical objects, which are defined by their structured relationships with other numbers, or units. For example, understanding 3 as a composite unit means being able to build other numbers, like 18, as iterations of that unit; recognizing 18 as six measures of 3, a student can reverse that reasoning to reproduce the unit of 3 by partitioning 18 into six equal parts.

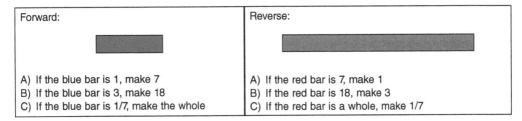

Forward:	Reverse:
A) If the blue bar is 1, make 7	A) If the red bar is 7, make 1
B) If the blue bar is 3, make 18	B) If the red bar is 18, make 3
C) If the blue bar is 1/7, make the whole	C) If the red bar is a whole, make 1/7

Figure 7.8 Reversible reasoning tasks

Across all students, regardless of special need, we need to begin with the question introduced in Chapter 5: 'What can the student do?' These actions, whether sensorimotor or mental, are the building blocks for mathematics. To circumvent students' available actions and necessary ways of acting is to circumvent students' mathematics and relegate their thinking to something that will remain foreign. Note that this view lies in opposition to a deficit view of special needs and mathematical development. Rather, in line with Hunt and Tzur (2017), special needs refer to the need for special considerations in teacher–student interactions. Here, we have considered implications from neuroscience for promoting productive interactions, including productive struggle. In closing, we note how those implications also promote many of the Dimensions of Mathematizing that undergird Math Recovery at large.

Dimensions of Mathematizing

Many of the neuroscience findings summarized here support Dimensions of Mathematizing used throughout Math Recovery (also see Chapter 10). These dimensions include **unitizing**, structuring numbers, distancing the instructional setting, grounded habituation, complexifying, extending the range of numbers, notating, and formalizing. We have already mentioned the role of unitizing as a mental action that is fundamental to students' understanding of number and measurement. As students continue to develop mathematically, the structures that coordinate their mental actions also *structure numbers* so that composite units and unit fractions can be taken as units for measuring other numbers.

Distancing the instructional setting relates to the idea that, over time, students' coordinated sensorimotor activities should become internalized as mental actions. Teachers can support this shift by gradually distancing students from the figurative material on which they learn to coordinate their sensorimotor activity. However, we also need to make sure students have manipulatives and other figurative supports available when they need them. Teachers might strike a balance by hiding manipulatives from students but keeping them present for reference when needed. For example, in the example shown in Figure 7.4(a), covering counters can encourage a student to carry out the activity of counting on, in imagination. Disappearing numbers tasks provide similar examples.

Grounded habituation occurs as actions become internalized and as coordinations of actions become automatized. This habituation corresponds to the frontal-to-parietal shift that characterizes mathematical development and explains the construction of new mathematical objects, such as unit fractions. The shift, from effortful to automatized activity, frees working memory to take on ever more complex tasks.

Extending the range of numbers enables teachers to maintain cognitive demand as students develop. We have noted that the example tasks shared here use fairly small numbers so that students can focus their attention on coordinating mental actions rather than performing computations. However, as students develop new coordinations, these coordinations can be strengthened by including larger numbers, or even shifting to different classes of numbers, as in the tasks in Figure 7.8, which progress from a unit of 1 to composite units, to unit fractions.

Even the most talented mathematicians experience limitations in working memory. Professional mathematicians regularly work on tasks so complex that they could not hope to solve them without relying on outside resources to offload working memory. Whether professional or amateur, mathematicians of all ages rely on **notating**, and eventually **formalizing**, to offload working memory. For young students, notations often include drawings that help them keep track of units and their relations to one another. At more advanced stages, students learn about formal notation, such as algebraic equations, that can support evermore complex problems.

Conclusion

When working with students with special needs, we are working with young mathematicians. Although we need to address their special needs, the goal of our interactions is the same as it is when professional mathematicians interact – to meet challenges rather than circumvent them and to solve problems rather than avoid them. Neuroscience informs us that mathematical development occurs through challenge, productive struggle, and effortful activity – cognitive demands that induce a frontal-to-parietal shift in neurological activity. On the one hand, working memory is limited for all of us. On the other hand, we need to place appropriate demands on that limited resource in order for mathematical development to occur.

8

Dyscalculia

Dyscalculia is a specific learning disability affecting approximately 5% of students. Using a narrow definition of dyscalculia, as discussed in this chapter, we will explore specific interventions that have been found to be successful in remediating the difficulties experienced by students with dyscalculia.

Definitions and Theories

In Chapter 7 we read that dyscalculia has a neurological basis and affects approximately 5% of students. The first difficulty in discussing dyscalculia is finding a definition or checklist of characteristics that is used universally. The term dyscalculia is used by some to refer to any mathematical disability regardless of the specific type of difficulty experienced by the student. This use of the term is exemplified by the potential warning signs for dyscalculia cited by Raja and Kumar (2012):

> slowness in giving answers to mathematics questions in comparison with other learners, difficulties in mental calculations, using fingers to count simple totals, mistakes in interpreting word problems, difficulty to remember basic mathematics facts, losing track when counting or saying multiplication tables, difficulty in remembering the steps in a multistage process, difficulties with position and spatial organization.

Are these warning signs of a specific disability labeled dyscalculia or just indications of math difficulties in general? Could some of these difficulties be prevented by teaching for understanding rather than requiring memorization of facts and procedures?

Some authors question whether dyscalculia is a distinct disability or merely part of the continuum of ability or attainment in mathematics (Dowker, 2009; Szűcs & Goswami, 2013). Other researchers suggest that teachers should view students' difficulties as a delay rather than as a deficit (Butterworth, Varma, & Laurillard, 2011). Perhaps it would be best to not use the term dyscalculia at all since a diagnosis of dyscalculia implies that there is something wrong with the student and can make teachers feel that they are not responsible for the student's progress (Gillum, 2012; Munn & Reason, 2007).

There are several terms used interchangeably with dyscalculia, including math learning disability, learning disorder, developmental dyscalculia (as opposed to acquired dyscalculia or **acalculia**), mathematical disorder, arithmetic difficulties, and arithmetic disorder (Kumar & Raja, 2009; Monei & Pedro, 2017; Ta'ir, Brezner, & Ariel, 1997). A review of additional articles will reveal several more terms used to describe learners who have difficulty with mathematics. Are there specific characteristics that lead to a diagnosis of dyscalculia or is the term dyscalculia just another term used to indicate any difficulty in learning mathematics?

A review of the literature shows no universal agreement exists on how dyscalculia is manifested in students. The Department for Education and Skills (UK) defines dyscalculia as:

> a condition that affects the ability to acquire arithmetical skills. Dyscalculic learners may have difficulty understanding simple number concept, lack an intuitive grasp of numbers, and have problems learning number facts and procedures. Even if they produce a correct answer, or use a correct method, they may do so mechanically and without confidence. (Dowker, 2009)

As indicated by this statement, some researchers consider dyscalculia to be a broad term referring to any type of severe difficulties in mathematics (Kumar & Raja, 2009). The general consensus is that students with dyscalculia have difficulty achieving the same level of mathematics as their grade-level peers, and this lack of achievement in mathematics is not commensurate with their achievement in other academic areas. In an attempt to find 'pure' cases of dyscalculia, Gifford and Rockliffe found the only agreed-upon definition was 'long term incapacity to learn number facts' (2007, p. 21). Some authors reserve the term dyscalculia to refer to a specific, core deficit that can cause further difficulties for students, such as a difficulty learning number facts. These specific deficits will be outlined later in this chapter. The term dyscalculia is also used to describe the difficulty with mathematics experienced by people with various syndromes such as Turner syndrome, fragile x syndrome, Gerstmann syndrome, and velocardiofacial syndrome (Ta'ir et al., 1997; Wilson et al., 2006). It should also be noted that while we are referring to 'students' in this chapter, dyscalculia is considered to be a disability that lasts into adulthood.

Ta'ir et al. (1997) propose two types of dyscalculia: profound dyscalculia, to signify an impaired ability to quantify and seriate (order objects or collections by a defined criteria); and secondary dyscalulia, to refer to mathematics difficulties caused by other disabilities such as language, working memory, attention difficulties, etc. Other authors have proposed three sub-types of dyscalculia:

> (1) a specific and isolated disorder of mathematics; (2) a mathematics impairment in the context of deficiencies in other non-numerical cognition (e.g. a general learning disability); and (3) dyscalculia with comorbid disorders (e.g. attention-deficit hyperactivity disorder [ADHD] and dyslexia). (Furlong, McLoughlin, McGilloway, & Butterworth, 2015, p. 1)

Examples of impairments that might lead to the second sub-type of dyscalculia are poor teaching, low socioeconomic status, general cognitive deficits, attention problems, and poor short-term, long-term, and working memory (Price & Ansari, 2013). In order to focus on interventions that will build the foundational skills of students, the remainder of this chapter will focus on the first sub-type, 'a specific and isolated disorder of mathematics' (Furlong et al., 2015, p. 1), although it can be difficult to find a student who has dyscalculia and is not also impacted by **dyslexia**, **dysgraphia**, **ADHD**, or a myriad of other learning difficulties, the third sub-type of dyscalculia mentioned above (Gifford & Rockliffe, 2007; Wilson et al., 2006).

There are various theories on how this specific and isolated disorder manifests itself and the implications for learning mathematics. One theory is that people with dyscalculia are not able to subitize (Babtie & Emerson, 2015; Gillum, 2012; Michaelson, 2007; Schleifer & Landerl, 2011), but not everyone agrees that subitizing is at the core of dyscalculia (Bugden & Ansari, 2016; Desoete, Ceulemans, Roeyers, & Huylebroeck, 2009). Other researchers say that the core deficit of people with dyscalculia is an inability to determine the quantity of a collection, either by sub-itizing or by counting each object (Butterworth et al., 2011). Combining these two theories is the observation that students with dyscalculia count small quantities, which other students are able to subitize, and make errors when counting larger quantities (Sella et al., 2013). These observa-tions align with the theory that dyscalculia may be a blockage at the perceptual and figurative stages of the Learning Framework in Number (Munn & Reason, 2007). The inability to reason quantitatively will not only impact students' abilities to add, subtract, multiply, and divide, but also impact their ability to reason about time, money, direction, and space (Michaelson, 2007). Some researchers question whether students are experiencing difficulty determining a quantity, or if the difficulty occurs when the students attempt to represent the quantity ver-bally or symbolically. In other words, the student is able to determine the quantity but has difficulty communicating about the quantity (Butterworth et al., 2011; Mazzocco, Feigenson, & Halberda, 2011; Piazza et al., 2010; Witzel & Mize, 2018). It is interesting to note that stu-dents with dyscalculia, who have difficulty matching quantities to written or spoken numerals, do not have difficulty matching letters with letter sounds (Raja & Kumar, 2012). Another core deficit observed by researchers is the inability to compare quantities (Butterworth et al., 2011; Michaelson, 2007; Sella et al., 2013). When shown two collections, students cannot indicate which collection contains more or less than the other. Students who experience this difficulty will be more successful if there is a larger difference between the two collections. These stu-dents also have difficulty putting collections in order, such as putting a collection of connecting cube towers in order from least to greatest (Ta'ir et al., 1997). These difficulties with compar-ing quantities and seriation may be connected to another core deficit experienced by students with dyscalculia, the lack of a **mental number line** (Kucian et al., 2001; Link, Moeller, Huber, & Fischer, 2013; Siegler & Ramani, 2008; von Aster & Shalev, 2007). The lack of a mental number line impacts students' ability to learn addition and subtraction (Link et al., 2013).

In summary, the specific difficulties that have been associated with dyscalculia are determining quantity, either by subitizing or counting, communicating about quantity, comparing quantities, and the development of a mental number line. It is not clear how these deficits might impact each other, but when considering the progression of skills and understanding presented in the Learning Framework in Number, it seems apparent that having any one of these deficits will impact the devel-opment of conceptual understanding in mathematics. In the next section of this chapter we will look at each of these specific deficits, how they fit into the Learning Framework in Number, and how teaching strategies presented in the previous books in this series will help students overcome these difficulties and make progress in mathematics.

Subitizing

Subitizing involves the ability to determine the quantity of a small collection without the need to count each item. Students who are not able to subitize need to count each object, even to determine the quantity of a small collection. The inability to subitize will lead to further difficulties in mathematics. First, students who need to count each object by ones will be slower and are more prone to make errors in determining the quantity (Schleifer & Landerl, 2011). Second, students who need to count each object are not demonstrating the ability to unitize, which is one the elements of progressive mathematization discussed in Chapter 3. The inability to unitize will affect students' ability to learn addition and subtraction facts with understanding. This may explain why students with dyscalculia are observed to rely on counting their fingers to solve addition and subtraction problems (Piazza et al., 2010; Raja & Kumar, 2012). While the use of fingers is expected as a way for students to keep track of their counts as they are developing addition and subtraction strategies, we anticipate that the use of fingers will diminish as more sophisticated strategies are developed. These more sophisticated strategies rely on the ability to unitize. The inability to unitize will also impact students' abilities to understand and work with the base-ten system because they will not have the basic understanding that a group of ten ones can also be seen and understood as one group of ten. Students who are not able to unitize will also have difficulty understanding and working with the operations of multiplication and division, which require seeing and thinking about groups of objects. Multiplication and division as well as fractions require students not only to unitize but also to coordinate different kinds of units. (See Chapter 7 for more information on units coordination.)

The ability to subitize improves into adulthood and, with practice, students can improve their ability to subitize (Desoete et al., 2009; Fischer, Gebhardt, & Hartnegg, 2008). Instructional strategies to improve students' abilities to subitize are included in the previous books in this series. Subitizing of spatial patterns is included in Part C of the Learning Framework in Number presented in *TN*, p. 13, as part of Early Structuring in the Learning Framework in Number presented in *LFIN*, pp. 79 and 111, and in Chapter 1 of this book. *TNC*, pp. 82–90, presents a variety of activities for students to develop and practice subitizing skills. The general trajectory of skills moves from regular spatial patterns to irregular spatial patterns, and then moves to five-frames and ten-frames. Students should have the opportunity to build patterns, determine quantities when the patterns are fully visible, and finally say the quantity after the pattern is flashed (shown quickly). The purpose of flashing the pattern is to dissuade the student from counting, and to promote quantitative visual imagery (Thomas & Tabor, 2012). Based on the finding that students with dyscalculia are more successful determining the difference between quantities when the differences are larger, it may be beneficial for students to first learn the regular patterns for one and six and then add other patterns. It has been our experience that students enjoy subitizing activities when they can be successful. It is as if they feel they have discovered a magic power.

Subitizing and Comparing Quantities

Students who are still learning to subitize regular spatial patterns and are learning to compare quantities can play a game known by various names such as Face Off, Top It, Compare, Number Battle, or War.

Intended learning: Subitizing regular spatial patterns, labeling quantities with a number word, and comparing quantities.

Materials: A deck of teacher-made cards with regular spatial patterns, available at https://study.sage-pub.com/system/files/Dice%20numeral%20cardsThese.pdf. Cards used and the size of the deck can be adjusted based on the needs of the students.

Description: This game is recommended for two players. Divide the cards evenly between the players. Players put their cards in front of them, face-down, in a single pile. Each player turns over the top card in their pile. The player with the larger quantity takes both cards and puts them in a separate pile. If players turn over cards with the same quantity, they continue to turn over cards until one player has a card with more dots. Play continues until cards in the original piles are exhausted. The player with the largest pile of cards is the winner. The winner can be determined by counting the cards, comparing the stacks of cards, or laying the cards side by side to determine which player has more.

Notes:

- Play the game with a total of ten cards, five for each player, to reduce the time needed to play the game and the number of cards that need to be counted at the end.
- It is not necessary to include all of the spatial patterns. Students with emerging subitizing and comparison skills can play with cards representing the quantities one, three, and six.

Chapter 4 of this text includes additional suggestions for working with students who are not yet able to subitize.

Vignette

Mathias was able to name the quantity of each domino pattern for 1–6 but he had a difficult time counting objects with one-to-one correspondence. He knew the correct verbal sequence to use, but he either said the sequence faster than he touched the objects, or touched the objects faster than he said the sequence. At other times he became distracted and failed to count all the objects or counted some objects twice. His teacher noticed that when the objects to be counted were placed in a domino pattern, Mathias knew how many objects there were. Knowing the total helped him slow down and focus on the objects to be counted. After the objects were counted in the domino pattern, they could be moved to different configurations to give Mathias more practice counting with one-to-one correspondence.

Counting and Comparing Quantities

As illustrated in the vignette above, the ability to recognize the quantity of spatial patterns may assist students in counting collections. Providing students with blank five- or ten-frames may help students organize larger collections, enabling them to be more accurate in determining the quantity of collections. Using the trajectory of subitizing skills and the visual models presented in the existing books in this series will enable students to develop the skill of subitizing and build on that skill to develop strategies for addition, subtraction, multiplication, and division.

Inaccuracy in counting larger collections is another difficulty that has been observed in students with dyscalculia. It is not clear if the students have difficulty counting collections because they do not know the correct sequence of numbers or because they do not have one-to-one correspondence between the number words and the objects being counted. If one-to-one correspondence is the source of the difficulty, are students not matching a number word to each object, or are they having difficulty keeping track of which objects have been counted, making sure to count each object once and only once? The ability to count visible objects or perceptual counting is a Stage of Early Arithmetical Learning (SEAL), presented in *TN*, p. 9, and *LFIN*, p. 75. Students who are not able to determine the quantity of visible objects are considered emergent in the Stages of Early Arithmetical Learning. In addition to the concept of one-to-one correspondence, matching a number word to each object, students must know the correct order of number words. The ability to say the sequence of numbers is referred to as Forward Number Word Sequence in the Learning Framework in Number (see Chapter 1). Chapter 5 of *TN* includes a variety of activities for teaching the Forward Number Word Sequence and Perceptual Counting to students.

Diffy, from *TNC*, pp. 61–62, is a game that will give students practice with counting and comparing quantities. Difficulty comparing quantities is another problem experienced by students with dyscalculia. In addition, students who play with dot dice will have repeated exposure to the regular spatial patterns, which will help develop the skill of subitizing.

ACTIVITY IA4.1: Diffy Game

Intended learning: To use counting to compare two quantities and find which is more.

Materials: Interlocking cubes, dice or spinner and counters.

Description: In pairs, the first child throws a 1–6 die and counts out that number of interlocking cubes and makes a tower. The second child rolls the die and counts and makes another tower of cubes. They compare the towers and decide which tower has more cubes. The child with the higher tower takes a counter to keep a score. If there is no difference in the towers no one takes a counter. The activity continues until one child has collected five/ten counters.

Notes

- Discuss the difference. Whose tower is higher? How much higher?
- Change the setting of cubes to counters and arrange the counters in a line, horizontally or vertically. (*TNC*, pp. 61–62)

Additional considerations for the Diffy game:

- Students can begin playing with a die that only has the dot patterns for 1, 2, and 3.

- Using a five- or ten-frame will help students organize the counters they collect for building the tower with the most cubes or the largest collection.
- When playing with counters instead of interlocking cubes, arrange the counters in a random arrangement as opposed to a vertical or horizontal line.
- Using a numeral die will allow students to match a numeral with a quantity.
- Students who are developing the ability to count larger quantities can use a die with larger numerals or use two dot dice.

Labeling a Quantity with a Number Word or Numeral

The Learning Framework in Number, presented in Chapter 1, includes the domain of number words and numerals. The previous books in this series, specifically *EN*, *TN*, *TNC*, and *DNK*, contain assessment tasks which isolate the skills of numeral identification from saying number words and number word sequences. These assessment tasks allow teachers to determine which specific skills are causing difficulties for students. 'The rudimentary knowledge of Number Word Sequences and numerals without a context of quantities is an important domain in the development of students' number knowledge, and it requires explicit instruction' (*DNK*, p. 25). After students have developed fluency with reading numerals and saying sequences of numbers, instructional tasks presented in *TN*, *TNC*, and *DNK* give students opportunities to integrate these number words and numerals skills, with their developing understanding about quantity and operations.

Development of a Mental Number Line

The mental number line describes a spatial representation of number magnitude along an analog number line which is assumed to be activated automatically whenever we encounter a number. (Link et al., 2013, p. 75)

The ability to correctly place numerals on an empty number line, with only endpoints given, improves with age and experience. First-grade students' ability to estimate the location of numerals on an empty number line is positively correlated with their current understanding of addition and with their ability to solve unknown addition problems (Booth & Siegler, 2008). The authors also found that 'exposure to accurate visual representations of numerical magnitude improved children's arithmetic learning' (Booth & Siegler, 2008, p. 1028). The previous books in this series present two instructional tools that provide accurate visual representations of a number line: the numeral roll and the **numeral track** (see Figure 10.1, the Glossary, and this book's cover photo). A variety of activities for both of these tools are presented in *TN*, *TNC*, and *DNK*. These tools are primarily used to develop knowledge of number word sequences and numeral identification. As students are developing these skills, they are exposed to the left-to-right representation of the magnitude of numbers. The numeral track is well suited for students to practice estimating the location of specific numerals on an empty number line as the closed doors hide the numerals while scaffolding the location of the numerals. The 100-bead string is another instructional tool that presents a linear model of number (see Figure 8.1).

Figure 8.1   A 100-bead string presents a linear model of number

Students are able to represent quantities, add, and subtract using the 100-bead string to represent their thinking (Miller, Gabrielson, Scholla, & Jobin, 2016). This quantitative model of a number line lays the foundation for the use of an empty number line to notate addition and subtraction strategies. Information on using the empty number line for notating addition and subtraction, conceptual place value, multiplication, and structuring numbers can be found in *DNK.*

Playing linear, numerical board games has also been shown to help students develop numeracy skills (Siegler & Ramani, 2008). Although this study was conducted with low-income pre-school students, the authors (Kucian et al., 2001) feel that the intervention has implications for students who need to develop a mental number line. When students play a linear board game, they experience the order of numbers and the magnitude of numbers:

> When a child moves a token in such a game, the greater the number that the token reaches, the greater: (a) the distance that the child has moved the token, (b) the number of discrete moves the child has made, (c) the number of number names the child has spoken and heard, and (d) the amount of time the moves have taken. Thus, such board games provide a physical realization of the linear ruler or mental number line. (Siegler & Ramani, 2008, p. 656)

Teachers can develop linear board games using a portion of a numeral roll, perhaps just the numerals 1–10, or a numeral track. A numeral roll provides the support of the printed numerals for students who are learning number word sequences, while the numeral track allows students to practice saying the number word sequences and check the result of their counting by lifting a flap to reveal the number underneath. The numeral track can be used with some numerals revealed to provide additional support. Students can play the games with a dot or numeral die, and the quantities on the die can be adjusted to meet the needs of the students.

Teddy Bear Walk is a linear board game from *TNC.* Although this game is originally presented as a setting that engenders the addition and subtraction strategies of counting on and counting back, our intended focus is on seeing and saying the sequence of numerals and developing the mental number line.

ACTIVITY IA3.10: Teddy Bear Walk

Intended learning: To use counting-on and counting-back or more advanced strategies in addition and subtraction.

Materials: Teddy Bear Walk board (https://study.sagepub.com/system/files/Teddy%20Bear%20 Walk_1.pdf) and a teddy bear or counter for each player.

Description: Players take turns to: (a) roll a die; (b) predict which square their teddy bear will walk to by taking the number of steps indicated on the die; (c) move their teddy bear the number of steps and check whether or not their calculation was correct. The game ends when one teddy bear reaches the end of the walk.

Notes

- Typically the die (or spinner) has the numerals 1, 2, and 3. When appropriate, a die with 1 and 2 only could be used.
- To include subtraction activities, when a teddy bear lands on a shaded square the next roll will be a subtraction task and the teddy bear will need to retrace steps.
- Observe the strategies used to solve the addition and subtraction tasks. (*TNC*, p. 49)

Additional considerations for Teddy Bear Walk:

- Teachers may want to change the name of the game to reflect the age and interests of the students.
- The length of the game board can be adjusted based on the needs of the students and the amount of time available to play the game.
- Students can practice the backward sequence of numbers by playing the game in reverse. The left to right for forward sequence of numbers, and the right to left for backward sequences, should be maintained to reinforce students' understanding of forward and backward sequences and number before and number after.

In addition to playing linear board games, studies have shown the benefits of whole-body movement in helping students develop a mental number line (Link et al., 2013). Students can be asked to move left or right along a number line, or perhaps squares of paper taped to the floor or to the wall. Given a starting number, students can move to the left or right to indicate where other numerals will be located. If the numerals are hidden under the squares, students can lift the square to reveal the correct numeral. In the intervention proposed by Link et al. (2013), students moved in a right or left direction rather than a forward or backward direction to indicate the position of the new number. Moving right or left maintains the orientation that students typically experience when they look at a number line.

Stand in Line from *TNC*, p. 45 is an example of an activity that focuses on the development of number word sequence and incorporates whole-body movement.

ACTIVITY IA3.6: Secret Numbers

Intended learning: To order non-sequential numerals.

Materials: Large numeral cards, sets of smaller cards (for working in pairs).

Description: Provide six non-sequential numerals on cards, for example 17, 23, 28, 31, 36, 42. Select two children. Give the largest number (42) to one child and the smallest (17) to another. Place the two children with their cards about three metres apart. Select a third child to choose one of the remaining numbers. They must keep their number secret and decide where to stand in between 17 and 42. Ask: *What could the number be?*

Establish that it must be more than 17 and less than 42. Ask the child to reveal their secret number. Continue with a second secret number, then a third and fourth until all the cards are in the correct order.

- Vary by using other sets of cards.
- Vary the range of numbers used.

Notes

- Suitable for whole class or small groups.
- Adapt for pairs by providing sets of cards for children to order and record. (*TNC*, p. 46)

Additional considerations for Secret Numbers:

- Conduct the activity using sequential numeral cards.
- Place markers can be used to indicate where students might stand.
- After the sequence is constructed, a student can move to the right and left, along the line, saying the sequence of numbers.
- Students who are still developing their knowledge of the number word sequence can be given cards that are immediately before or after numbers that are visible.

Conclusion

Successful interventions for students with dyscalculia are based on one-on-one assessments to determine students' current abilities and teaching based on students' needs. These needs are determined by questioning, observing, and listening to students (Babtie & Emerson, 2015; Messenger, Emerson, & Bird, 2007). The activities cited in this chapter illustrate how instruction guided by the Learning Framework in Number can address the core difficulties experienced by students with dyscalculia. Since the skills addressed are embedded in the Learning Framework in Number, teachers can use the framework to guide instruction and build on these developing skills.

9

Differentiating Instruction

Amy J. Hackenberg
Indiana University

In this chapter we provide information about how to differentiate mathematics instruction for students' diverse ways of thinking. We consider a framework for understanding students' diverse ways of thinking that undergirds the Math Recovery program and a set of teaching practices for differentiating instruction for that thinking. Then we show two examples from classrooms. The first example demonstrates a lower prep strategy – parallel tasks – and the second demonstrates a higher prep strategy – tiering instruction. We note that Universal Design for Learning (CAST, 2018) is a recent initiative in some schools and districts, and we view UDL as one way to differentiate instruction.

Differentiating instruction is a popular initiative in schools and districts. Teachers are often charged to do it without much guidance. How much change in one's teaching is required to differentiate instruction well? Some teachers think differentiating instruction is about using some new strategies – and it is partly about that; other teachers think it requires more significant renovation of their teaching (Brighton & Hertberg, 2004; Tomlinson, 1995). Understandably, teachers are concerned about several issues, including increased workload (Tobin & Tippett, 2014), management of the classroom environment when students are engaged in different activities (Tomlinson, 1995), fairness of different work and support for students (Hockett, 2010), and management of formative assessment data and varied student assignments (Simpson, 1997).

However, differentiating instruction has been found to have positive effects on elementary and middle school students' achievement in science and reading (for example, Mastropieri et al., 2006; Reis et al., 2011), and it has influenced elementary school students to demonstrate increased respect for students with disabilities and more positive cross-cultural student interactions (Santamaria, 2009). There have been few studies on differentiating *mathematics* instruction. But in one study, Gearhart and Saxe's Learning Mathematics through Representations (LMR) project, the authors designed a sequence of 19 lessons for fourth- and fifth-grade students focused on developing students' understanding of number lines as a core representation for learning fractions and integers. Each lesson featured key aspects of **differentiation**, such as problems that were accessible to a range of students; a variety of individual, small-group, and whole-classroom instruction; and ongoing formative assessment (Gearhart & Saxe, 2014). In an efficacy study with a well-matched comparison group, the authors found that students in LMR classrooms showed significantly greater learning gains than students in comparison classrooms (Saxe, Diakow, & Gearhart, 2013).

Why Differentiate?

In fact, teachers, schools, and districts have always had to determine how to handle diverse ways of thinking in classrooms, as well as other aspects of student diversity, including diagnosed disabilities, languages, cultures, races, and genders. For decades many middle and high schools in the US and UK have handled diverse ways of thinking by tracking or streaming, respectively, where students are slotted into different pathways of courses so that students who think similarly might be taught together. The main rationale is that it will be easier to teach students together who have developed similar ideas.

There are at least three problems with this approach. First, all teachers know that even students in the same tracked class (for example, 'regular' sixth-grade math) are quite diverse in their thinking. Second, low-achieving students are often placed in classes that emphasize rote learning and do not allow movement to classes with high-achieving peers (Boaler, Wiliam, & Brown, 2000; Stiff, Johnson, & Akos, 2011). Third, and most pernicious, recommendations for class placements have been found to be **biased** against promoting students of color to advanced classes (Flores, 2007; Rubin, 2006; Stiff et al., 2011), creating significant opportunity gaps (Flores, 2007). In response to such issues, the National Council of Teachers of Mathematics (NCTM, 2018) recently recommended that high schools discontinue tracking in mathematics.

Yet simply placing students with diverse ways of thinking in the same classroom does not address the significant issues students may experience due to different learning needs (Gamoran & Hannigan, 2000). Teaching diverse students in one classroom must be done with great skill and care in order to fulfill a promise of being more humane than tracking (Mevarech & Kramarski, 1997; Rubin, 2008) and to close opportunity gaps. Differentiating instruction is a pedagogical approach to manage classroom diversity in which teachers proactively adapt curricula, teaching methods, and products of learning to address individual students' needs in an effort to maximize learning for all (Tomlinson, 2005). So, differentiating instruction involves systematic forethought rather than only reactive adaptation. In this sense, differentiating instruction is similar to Universal Design for Learning (CAST, 2018). That is, UDL is one way to differentiate instruction for all students based on data by providing multiple means of engagement, representation, and expression (CAST, 2018). We use the broader term, differentiating instruction, because it includes UDL and other ways to differentiate. In this book, we also focus differentiating instruction specifically on mathematics, as we explain next.

Differentiating for Students' Diverse Ways of Thinking

Teachers can differentiate for many characteristics of their students, including students' interests and learning preferences (Tomlinson, 2005). In a five-year research project, Hackenberg and colleagues (Hackenberg, Creager, & Eker, 2020) studied how to differentiate mathematics instruction for middle school students' diverse ways of thinking; we explain what we mean by 'diverse ways of thinking' shortly.

Definition. One outcome of the project was a definition for differentiating mathematics instruction: 'proactively tailoring instruction to students' mathematical thinking while developing a cohesive classroom community' (cf. Tomlinson, 2005). Here, 'tailoring instruction' requires planning ahead for different thinkers, as well as questioning and prompting in a responsive way (Jacobs & Empson, 2016). It also means that not all students will experience the same tasks at the same time. A 'classroom community' is one where students regularly discuss ideas (Lampert, 2001), often have different ideas (O'Connor, 2001), and value diversity (Bielaczyc, Kapur, & Collins, 2013). In classrooms where differentiating instruction is practiced, community members do not just respect differences but celebrate them (Laud, 2011), and fairness is redefined as everyone getting what they need in order to grow (Tomlinson, 2005).

Units coordination stages. To understand and respond to students' diverse ways of thinking, Hackenberg and colleagues (2020) used a framework about how students structure number and quantity that also undergirds the Math Recovery program. The power of this way of thinking about differentiation is that similar principles can be used at different age levels and mathematical topics because the framework impacts how students reason with whole numbers (Steffe, 1994; Ulrich, 2015, 2016), fractions (Steffe & Olive, 2010), measurement (Steffe, 2013), and even algebra (Hackenberg & Lee, 2015). We now briefly portray features of this framework, which is described more completely in *DNK* (Wright et al., 2012) and *DFK* (Hackenberg et al., 2016).

Humans are not born with abstract ideas of number. Initially children are pre-numerical, which basically means that they engage in counting, but the result of their counting does not have an amountness meaning (Steffe, von Glasersfeld, Richards, & Cobb, 1983). A strong behavioral sign of becoming numerical is counting on, which means that when faced with a problem of adding 9 + 5, children will start with the 9 and count on by 1s – and they will initiate this reasoning. Once students have become numerical, they demonstrate three different, relatively stable ways of organizing number and quantity into units. These ways of thinking are called stages of units coordination (Hackenberg et al., 2016) because transitioning between them requires significant learning that can take a couple of years (Steffe, 2017). Before we describe the stages, we have to explain what we mean by units.

Units are discrete 1s; they also refer to measurement units like centimeters or non-standard units (Ulrich, 2015). Children organize units into larger units as they construct number and quantity, and the nature of their units changes (Steffe et al., 1983). For example, early counters learn to think of 4 as both a single unit (one 4) and as four individual units (four 1s). Children who think of 4 as a single unit of four units have constructed a *composite unit (a unit of units)*. Similarly, early measurers learn to think of 1 foot as both a single length and as made of twelve equal-sized parts called inches. In doing so they create 1 foot as a composite unit. Creating composite units is an example of coordinating units.

Students at stages 1–3 of units coordination have all constructed composite units, but the nature of their composite units is not the same. To understand these differences, consider the Jump Rope Problem: 'We need a jump rope that measures nine chopstick lengths. There are four toothpick lengths in a chopstick length; how many toothpick lengths will measure the jump rope?'

Students at stage 1 of units coordination can track multiple instances of 4 as they solve the Jump Rope Problem (Steffe, 1992; Ulrich, 2015). So, these students can engage in multiplicative reasoning of the most basic kind (Steffe, 1992). However, for them there is not a multiplicative relationship between a unit of 1 and their composite unit, 36. This means that they can solve the problem of finding the number of toothpick lengths in the rope's length, but they do not create a unit consisting of nine 4s as they solve the problem (Ulrich, 2015). Instead, it is like they have two number sequences running side by side, one on which to accumulate the total number of toothpick lengths and one to keep track of the number of chopstick lengths.

Students at stage 2 of units coordination do create a unit consisting of nine 4s as they solve the Jump Rope Problem (Figure 9.1, top). These students have created three levels of units in their activity of solving the problem: The length is a unit of nine units of four units of 1. However, in further activity the length becomes a unit of 36 units of 1 for these students (Figure 9.1, bottom); they do not maintain the three levels of units as they continue to solve problems.

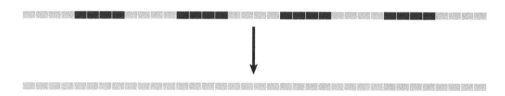

Figure 9.1   Three levels of units become a unit of units for students at stage 2

In contrast, students at stage 3 of units coordination maintain the three levels of units. In solving the Jump Rope Problem they can treat the 36 simultaneously as a unit of nine units of four units of 1 and as a unit of 36 units of 1. In addition, they can switch to view the 36 toothpick lengths as a unit of four units of nine units of 1 (Figure 9.2). Making these switches in structure is essential for constructing many ideas about fractions (Hackenberg & Tillema, 2009; Steffe & Olive, 2010). The different ways students at each stage tend to solve the Jump Rope Problem are described in Table 9.1. Estimates of the percentages of students by stage in the United States are shown in Table 9.2.

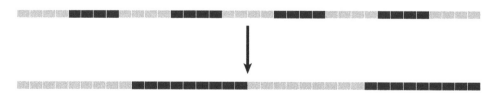

Figure 9.2   Students at stage 3 can switch between three levels of units structures

Table 9.1 Solutions to the Jump Rope Problem by units coordination stage

Stage	Typical solution for the Jump Rope Problem	Typical view of the result, 36 toothpick lengths
1	Count on by 1s past known skip-counting patterns for 4s	No multiplicative relationship between 1 toothpick length and the 36
2	Use additive strategies to accumulate the nine 4s, e.g., 4 + 4 = 8; 8 + 8 = 16; 16 + 16 = 16 + 10 + 6 = 26; 26 + 6 = 26 + 4 + 2 = 30 + 2 = 32; 32 + 4 = 36	1 toothpick length × 36
3	Use multiplicative strategies, e.g., 5 × 4 + 4 × 4	1 toothpick length × 36 and 4 toothpick lengths × 9

Table 9.2 Percentage of students by stage

Stage	First grade	Third grade	Fifth grade	Sixth grade
Pre-numerical or 'just' numerical	45	5	0	0
1	35 to 45	35 to 40	35	30
2	10 to 15	45 to 50	40	30
3	0 to 5	0 to 10	25	40

Source: Steffe (2017)

Five Teaching Practices to Differentiate Instruction

Hackenberg and colleagues (Hackenberg et al., 2020) identified five teaching practices that supported differentiating instruction (Figure 9.3). They found that Practices 3–5 could also impede differentiating instruction at times. Math Recovery teachers already regularly engage in Practices 1 and 3, and likely some of the others as well. We provide brief descriptions of each practice and then focus on Practice 2 with two examples.

(1) Using research-based knowledge of students' mathematical thinking
(2) Providing purposeful choices and different pathways
(3) Inquiring responsively during group work
(4) Attending to small-group functioning
(5) Conducting whole-class discussions across different thinkers

Figure 9.3 Five practices for differentiating mathematics instruction

Practice 1: Using research-based knowledge of students' mathematical thinking. This practice is about using current research as a guide in charting pathways for students' thinking during a segment of instruction. Math Recovery teachers already engage in this practice by using the research-based Math Recovery Program in their work. For example, Guiding Principle 4 (Chapter 3) requires Practice 1. However, even when using an existing framework, a critical feature of this practice is inquiring into the framework as one interacts with students. Teachers who use their interactions with students to deepen their understanding of the framework can ultimately make the framework their own so that it becomes a generative tool (Franke, Carpenter, Levi, L., & Fennema, 2001; Steinberg, Empson, & Carpenter, 2004). In other words, the framework 'comes to life' so that a teacher uses it to guide interaction but also has deep enough understanding of the framework and students together to adapt and extend the framework. As noted in Chapter 3 of this book, this practice recognizes and respects the professionalism of teachers.

Practice 2: Providing purposeful choices and different pathways. This practice is about developing choices of problems or activities that fit with students' ways of thinking – choices for which the teacher can provide a rationale. It is also about providing different pathways of problems for different groups of students in the same class that address the 'same' mathematical idea. Practice 2 is informed by Practice 1, the teacher's use of research-based knowledge, and Practice 3, the teacher's responsive inquiry into students' thinking in groups (discussed next). We describe Practice 2 before Practice 3 because, in implementing a lesson, this practice would come prior to Practice 3, and we examine Practice 2 in more detail later in the chapter.

Practice 3: Inquiring responsively during group work. This practice is about listening, observing, and asking questions in order to gather information about students' mathematical thinking and how they are progressing on problems and ideas. It is about trying to understand how students are understanding problems (Jacobs & Empson, 2016), making conjectures about their thinking, and posing questions to test out these conjectures (Dyer & Sherin, 2016). It is also about posing questions, adaptations of problems, or follow-up problems to help students stay active as thinkers, particularly if they seem to be stuck, are responding in surprising ways, or have appeared to find the problems easy. Finally, this practice is also about determining which student ideas are important to bring up in whole-class discussion for the potential learning benefit of everyone. As with Practice 1, Math Recovery teachers already engage in this practice regularly. Guiding Principles 2, 3, 5, 6, 7, and 8 (Chapter 3), as well as Key Elements 10–23, are aspects of Practice 3.

Practice 4: Attending to small-group functioning. This practice is about helping students engage in small-group interactions productively so that they can do mathematical work. Teachers can promote productive small-group interaction in several ways. One way is to have class discussions about the purposes of working in groups and ways to talk about mathematical ideas so that everyone learns more (Lampert, 2001). Another option is to provide students with group roles to support mathematical interaction (Featherstone et al., 2011). These roles come with specific responsibilities and sample comments of what it sounds like to enact that role; teachers hold frequent discussions with students about the roles and how well students are using them as they work together. Ultimately this practice is about helping groups develop autonomy so that they can function without direct teacher supervision (Hackenberg et al., 2020). Here, group autonomy means being able, as a small group, to work independently but together with other groups in the classroom, taking responsibility for tasks and making some judgments about solutions and processes without appeal to another authority, such as the teacher or a textbook (cf. Yackel & Cobb, 1996).

Practice 5: Conducting whole-class discussions across different thinkers. This practice involves holding a common whole-class discussion even though students have often worked on different (but related) problems as per Practice 2. So, the teacher has to bring out different ways of thinking explicitly at opportune moments, even though students may find it challenging to interpret the thinking of others. The purpose of doing so is to help everyone develop their own mathematical thinking, but a pressing question is how that is done across students who are thinking quite differently. So, this practice brings up the issue of what students have the potential to learn from each other. Practice 5 is important for building community. However, it can also threaten the development of community when students have difficulty understanding each other, or if some students are seen as knowing more and others knowing less (Hackenberg et al., 2020). At these times teachers can pose a question that is challenging for everyone, indicating that everyone has something to learn; emphasize that learning important ideas takes time, thereby giving space to all; and vary groups (Hackenberg et al., 2020).

The interplay between Practices 1 and 3 is at the heart of differentiating instruction, because to differentiate instruction for students' diverse ways of thinking one has to get to know that thinking – otherwise there is no reason to differentiate (Hackenberg et al., 2020). To get to know students' thinking requires interacting responsively (Practice 3). However, that practice is not done in a vacuum – a teacher has to have some understanding about big ideas in the domain, including what has been found important in prior research (Practice 1), in order to guide responsive inquiry into students' thinking. This interplay between Practices 1 and 3 is regularly enacted by Math Recovery teachers, so they are well poised to differentiate instruction!

More about Practice 2: Providing Purposeful Choices and Different Pathways

Because Math Recovery teachers have expertise in the foundation of differentiating instruction, namely, the interplay between Practices 1 and 3, the rest of this chapter will focus on the less well-known Practice 2, providing purposeful choices and different pathways. Math Recovery teachers already engage in this practice when they make plans to progressively mathematize or fold back (Chapter 3). The rationale for this practice involves at least three issues. First, students may feel some empowerment or motivation if they can choose what to work on (Heacox, 2002). Second, students may choose a problem that is a good challenge to them, if they know that the teacher is posing problems that are accessible to different thinkers in the class. Students might not always make the choice the teacher would make for them, but, third, student choices themselves are a useful formative assessment for the teacher. Because student choices are informative in this way, typically teachers provide purposeful choices in earlier lessons and may follow up in later lessons with different pathways designed for different groups of students (Tomlinson, 2005).

Two strategies to provide purposeful choices to students are **choice problems** (Land, 2017; Land et al., 2014) and **parallel tasks** (Small & Lin, 2010). Choice problems involve posing the same problem to all students but with a choice of number, where the choices are differentiated for different ways of thinking. For example:

> **Brownie Problem:** Starr is selling brownies at the bake sale, and she has 3/4 of a tray left. A customer comes and orders (1/3, 1/5, 5/6) of what is left. Draw a picture of the customer's order and determine how much of the tray the customer is buying.

In this problem, the easiest choice is 1/3, because the tray has three 1/4 parts. So, 1/3 of the 3/4 is one of those 1/4 parts. Note that 1/5 is a choice of medium difficulty because it requires taking 1/5 of each 1/4 – distributive reasoning that can be challenging (Hackenberg et al., 2016; Hackenberg & Tillema, 2009). Finally, 5/6 is a harder choice because it requires taking a proper fraction of each 1/4; an even harder choice would be an improper fraction like 7/5.

Parallel tasks (Small & Lin, 2010) are a set of two or three different problems designed to target different levels of thinking yet address closely related mathematical ideas. We give an example in the next section.

The follow-up strategy of **tiering instruction** involves designing different sequences of problems and activities for different groups of students based on conjectures about what will best support students' learning needs (Pierce & Adams, 2005; Tomlinson, 2005). Tiering often occurs after teachers have gotten to know students' thinking in a domain; they see a variety of thinking that will not be supported well with a 'one-size-fits-all' approach; and they have ideas about problems that may be helpful for different groups. We give an example of this strategy as well, from a study with first-grade students (Tabor, 2008).

We note that these strategies for Practice 2 range from those requiring lower levels preparation, or *lower prep*, to those requiring higher levels of preparation, or *higher prep* (Tomlinson, 2005). For example, changing a problem to include some number choices is relatively low prep compared to designing different pathways of activities and problems for students in a tiered lesson. However, to explore and justify what number choices are useful for different thinkers and why is not trivial – it too involves the interplay between Practices 1 and 3. We now give an example a lower prep strategy, using parallel tasks, and then an example of a higher prep strategy, tiering instruction, from Tabor's (2008) study.

An Example of Using Parallel Tasks

Set-up. This example comes from an after-school math class taught by Hackenberg (Hackenberg, et al., 2020), which took place twice per week for an hour for a total of eighteen class meetings. Nine middle school students participated, three at stage 3 of units coordination, and six at stage 2 of units coordination. The class focused on relationships between rational number knowledge and algebraic reasoning. One topic that we addressed was developing distributive reasoning to support students' understanding of fractions and algebra. Toward that end, we worked on this set of parallel tasks (Figure 9.4).

In these two tasks, task I is more challenging and task II more basic for several reasons. First, task II is stated in terms of sharing language, which is more basic than fractions language (Hackenberg et al., 2016). Second, task II does not ask students to explicitly represent unknowns with notation. Third, task II involves a more basic quantity (length) than task I (weight). Note that, in this case, we put the

---

Weights and Lengths of Candy Bars

Read each problem below (I and II).

Then **choose which you want to work on, I OR II.**

I.   *Weight of Candy Bars Problem.* Ming has five identical candy bars. Each bar weighs *h* ounces. Draw a picture of what 1/7 of all candy looks like. How much does 1/7 of all candy weigh? Explain your drawing and your answer.

II. *Sharing Candy Bars Equally Problem.* Ben has three identical candy bars. Each bar has the same unknown length. How can you share these bars equally with five people? Show how to make the equal shares. Draw out the share for one person and tell how much of a candy bar one person gets. How much of all the candy does one person get? Explain your answers.

- After you choose I or II, **start work individually** with the appropriate paper (showing 5 bars or 3 bars). <u>Get some ideas down yourself before you start work with your group.</u>

- Once you have some ideas down, talk to group members about your ideas. <u>You can transition to using JavaBars if you'd like.</u> **Also, please do show more than one solution** if you have more than one idea in your groups.

Figure 9.4 Parallel tasks for equal sharing and taking fractions of unknowns

more challenging choice first – it is important to vary the position of this choice so students do not always assume that it comes last (Small & Lin, 2010). This comment applies to choice problems as well. However, both tasks I and II involve some similar ways of thinking. In particular, to solve them in efficient ways requires distributive reasoning. For example, to share three bars among five people involves sharing each bar among five people so that each person gets three one-fifth parts of a bar, one from each bar. Solving task II can lead to thinking that is notated in this way: 1/5 of 3 is 1/5 of $(1 + 1 + 1) = 1/5 + 1/5 + 1/5 = 3/5$. Similarly, to take 1/7 of five weights requires taking 1/7 of each weight, or 1/7 of one weight five times. So, solving task I can lead to thinking that is notated in this way: 1/7 of 5*h* is 1/7 of $(h + h + h + h + h) = 1/7h + 1/7h + 1/7h + 1/7h + 1/7h = 5/7h$.

We expected students at stage 2 to choose task II and students at stage 3 to perhaps choose task I. Our expectations were mostly met, with just one student at stage 3 choosing task II. So, the two students at stage 3 who chose task I worked together on it, and the other seven students worked in groups of two and three on task II.

Students' work. The two students at stage 3 showed evidence of distributive reasoning in their work on task I. At first they estimated that 1/7 of 5*h* was about 2/3 of *h*. But then they made a more precise response by drawing a picture in a computer environment called JavaBars (Biddlecomb & Olive, 2000), where they took 1/7 of each of 5 bars (Figure 9.5). So, they had 1/7 of *h* five times, or 5/7 of *h*. They explained this work to the class in the next class meeting.

Students at stage 2 demonstrated a central challenge in their work on task II (Figure 9.4) and other problems like it. They found it hard to name the share in two ways, in relation to one bar and in relation to all the bars (Hackenberg & Lee, 2016; Liss, 2015). For example, one pair of these students

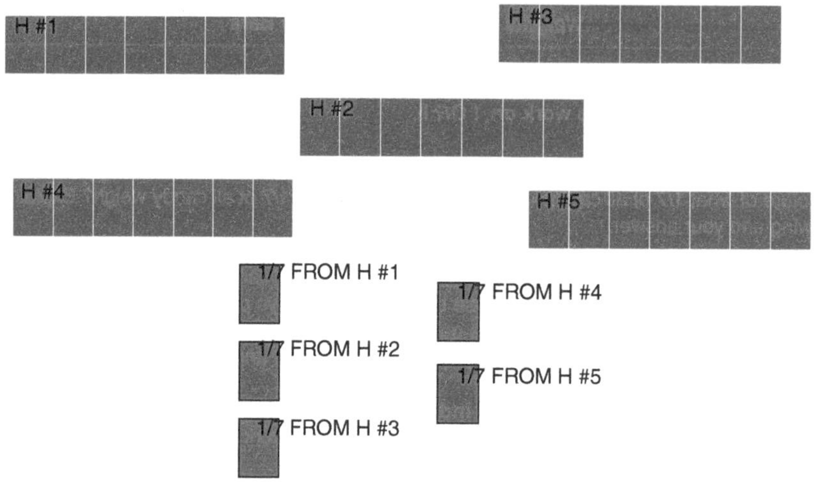
H #1
H #3
H #2
H #4
H #5
1/7 FROM H #1
1/7 FROM H #4
1/7 FROM H #2
1/7 FROM H #5
1/7 FROM H #3

Figure 9.5 Work on task I by students at stage 3

consistently named the result of equal sharing in relation to all of the bars (Figure 9.6). This drawing and explanation show that the students saw the share as 3/15 of all the candy, which was 1/5. However, they did not see the share as 3/5 in relation to one bar without considerable questioning support. With other similar problems over the next three class meetings, this pair of students consistently named the result in relation to all of the candy, not in relation to one bar. During this time we had three class discussions about students' work, including a spirited debate about whether, when two bars were shared equally among three people, the share for one person was 1/3 or 2/3.

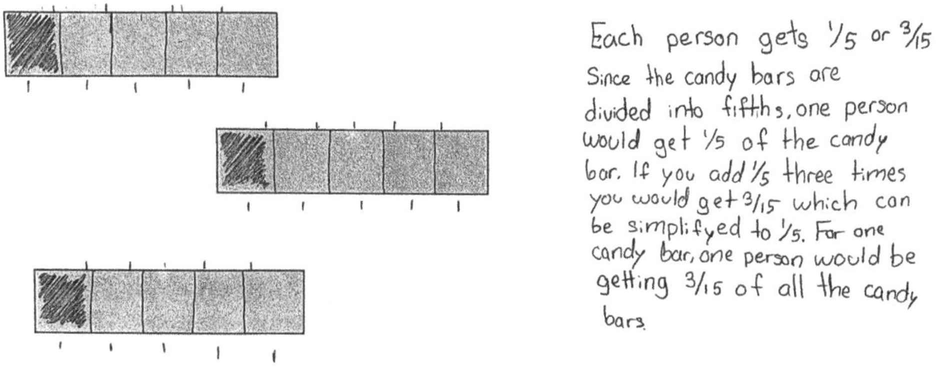
Each person gets 1/5 or 3/15
Since the candy bars are divided into fifths, one person would get 1/5 of the candy bar. If you add 1/5 three times you would get 3/15 which can be simplifyed to 1/5. For one candy bar, one person would be getting 3/15 of all the candy bars.

Figure 9.6 Work on task II by a student at stage 2

What we as teachers learned. What we learned as teachers from this segment of the class was that the parallel tasks seemed appropriate. Students at stage 2 were considerably challenged by working on the problems without notating unknowns because they had to coordinate several units in order to name shares in two ways. In addition, the problems supported all students to make shares distributively and thereby engage in distributive reasoning, which is valuable for many aspects of mathematics in middle and high school, such as proportional reasoning (Aydeniz, 2018; Liss, 2015). Finally, the different tasks were closely related, so we were able to hold engaging whole-class discussions across them.

An Example of Tiering Instruction

Set-up. This example comes from two first-grade classrooms in which Tabor (2008) investigated the influence of particular manipulatives on the emergence of the specific conceptual place value strategies of jump and split (Wright et al., 2012). There were three units in the study, which occurred from January to May, interspersed with other classroom units. Tabor designed and documented instructional sequences, conducted all student interviews, and led the whole-class discussions for all lessons in the three units. In January, 17 of the 41 students across both classrooms (42%) were unable to count on to add during the baseline assessment, which indicates that at the start of the study they were pre-numerical (Steffe et al., 1983). According to the information in Table 9.2, these classes would be considered within expectations for first grade. In order for pre-numerical students to participate in situations of adding and subtracting with students who were numerical and at different stages of units coordination, it was imperative to differentiate instruction, which occurred during all three units.

By the third unit, the Interstate Driving Scenario, which occurred in May, only 5 students were pre-numerical (12%). Tabor (2008) introduced the interstate driving context because it made use of the structure of exit numbering in the interstate system in most states in the United States. The exit numbers correspond to the number of miles driven north of the state line. For example, Exit 89 is 89 miles north of the state line. Students spent 11 days on this unit. Due to knowing students' thinking well at this point in the year, as well as observing considerable differences in that thinking, classroom teachers and Tabor (2008) tiered instruction.

Lesson 1. On the first day of the unit Tabor introduced the context to students during a whole-class discussion by asking how many of the students had ever ridden in a car on the interstate. Every student in both classes indicated they had done so. The class discussed the names of the local exits, and Tabor recorded the exit names and numbers on chart paper (Figure 9.7).

Then Tabor introduced the idea that exit numbers indicate the number of miles the exit is away from the state line. She posed a few problems involving the local exit numbers such as, 'If I got on the interstate at Exit 67 and got off at Exit 89, how far would I have driven on the interstate?' Students were given about a minute to mentally solve the problem and prepare to share their solution. Tabor used an empty number line to notate their solutions as they were proposed (Figure 9.8).

After the introduction of the context, students in both classrooms spent the remainder of the class playing math games that were tiered based on their individual assessed need. The pre-numerical children played a game involving adding the result of tossing a 4–9 numeral cube and 1–2 dot cube to advance on their gameboard. The rest of the children were playing 'Add or Subtract 12.' Some students were given base-ten manipulatives or whiteboards and markers for using the empty number line to show their reasoning.

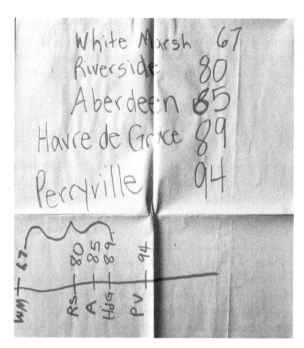

Figure 9.7   Names of local exits with numbers, as discussed in class

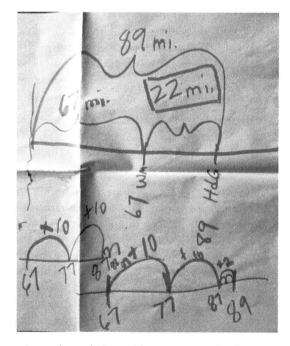

Figure 9.8   Teacher notating student solutions with an empty number line

Lesson 2. The next day, the entire grade level went on their annual field trip to the zoo. During this trip, the buses drove on the interstate discussed during class in Lesson 1. This experience appeared to be highly motivating for the students because of that discussion, and they were keen to share their interstate driving observations during Lesson 2.

After students had discussed the actual interstate exits nearby, the teacher introduced fictitious exit numbers on other interstates so as to carefully select exit numbers that would be appropriate for all students in the class. Then she grouped together students who were thinking similarly. There were three tiers as follows:

1. The students who were pre-numerical worked in a group and were given small exit numbers. They worked with problems that involved driving only one or two miles, such as entering the interstate at Exit 6 and driving two miles north. Students determined at what exit the car left the interstate. Thus, they solved problems in which the initial exit number and number of miles driven were both known.
2. Students just beginning to develop ten as a composite unit were given scenarios with the same structure, but with bigger numbers and number of miles that were multiples of ten. For example, the car entered the interstate at Exit 54 and drove 10 or 20 miles north. Again, students determined at what exit the car left the interstate.
3. Students who demonstrated that they thought of 10 as a composite unit worked with more complex numbers and problem structures. For example, in the problem structure discussed so far, the car entered at Exit 67 and drove 24 miles north; at what exit did it leave the interstate? These students also worked on missing addend problems, where the entering and leaving Exit numbers were known, and they were to determine the distance traveled. For example, the car entered at Exit 47 and exited at Exit 63; how many miles did the car drive on the interstate? Finally, these students also worked on subtractive scenarios. For example, the car entered at Exit 89 and drove south fourteen miles; at what exit did the car leave the interstate? Or, the car entered at Exit 74 and left at Exit 58; how many miles did the car drive?

Within these three tiers, some students were encouraged to use base-ten materials to solve their problems. Other students were prompted to think about materials they had previously used to support their problem solving. In this way, the students were encouraged to use mental imagery to solve the problems. And students were encouraged to use the empty number line to demonstrate their thinking to their peers and teachers.

Lessons 3–11. As the unit progressed, the tasks that students explored became increasingly more sophisticated, and the interstate driving context served as background for differentiated games involving different sets of dice or spinners to generate addition and subtraction problems. For example, one group used a 1–30 numeral die, a 4–9 numeral cube, and a +/– cube. Another group used two 1–30 numeral dice and a +/– cube. The third group used a 1–6 numeral cube and a 1–3 dot cube with all additive problems. All of the gameboards used on a given day looked similar and had similar names and game play objectives to minimize obvious differences between the games. As students demonstrated the development of new, more sophisticated strategies, they flexibly moved into other groups using more complex numbers. Thus, the unit exemplified the flexible use of groups, an important hallmark of differentiation (Tomlinson, 2005), as well as the norm of not overly emphasizing differences (Laud, 2011).

During whole-class discussions about students' solutions, the teacher purposefully selected students to share who were using different strategies. She typically sequenced student solutions from less sophisticated to more sophisticated strategies. And she modeled solutions using the empty number line or other appropriate models, privileging more efficient strategies in order to open opportunities for students to make advances in their strategies.

What students learned. By the end of the unit all but four students had become numerical. Students in the classroom increased their facility to make combinations of ten and to state number word sequences for incrementing and decrementing by ten (forward and backward). For example, only 7 students were initially facile with making combinations of ten in January, while 28 were in May. Similarly, only 4 were facile with the number word sequence for incrementing and decrementing by ten in January, and 30 were in May. In addition, 28 students developed at least one of the mental advanced ten strategies (jump or split), and 11 of those students demonstrated both jump and split strategies to mentally solve two-digit addition and subtraction problems.

What the classroom teachers learned. The classroom teachers learned about the planning that is required to tier instruction, including the need for ongoing formative assessment to track students' ways of thinking about number. Planning also requires knowledge of developmental progressions for typical learners and the kinds of thinking involved in developing jump and split strategies, which Tabor brought to the study. This learning is in the province of the interplay between Practices 1 and 3 (Figure 9.3), inquiring responsively into students' thinking in the context of research-based knowledge on that thinking.

In addition, classroom teachers learned about Practice 5, holding classroom discussions across different thinkers. One of the teachers reported that she had not understood wait-time until she saw Tabor wait to make space for students' thinking and articulation. Both teachers noted that they learned about the purposes of classroom discussion across different thinkers and problems. The purpose was not to show every single strategy, but to select and sequence (Stein, Engle, Smith, & Hughes, 2008) students' strategies in an increasingly sophisticated manner so that students had opportunities to make sense of the thinking of their classmates, and so that students considered what might make a strategy more efficient – for example, completing a problem by jumping by several tens at once, rather than by each ten one at a time.

Recommendations about Differentiating Instruction

The examples from these two studies lead to some recommendations about providing choices and different pathways, Practice 2.

Number choices. We are reluctant to say that a specific number choice always works for students with a particular concept of number or at particular stage of units coordination. We do recommend that teachers get to know their students' thinking, trying out different number choices and observing the outcomes (Land et al., 2014). Math Recovery materials contain many tools that teachers can use to get to know students' thinking, such as the Learning Framework in Number and domain overviews in *DNK* (Wright et al., 2012) and students' units coordination stages in *DFK* (Hackenberg et al., 2016).

For example, in Tabor's (2008) study, it might stand to reason that pre-numerical students should work with smaller numbers, and probably not many numbers larger than 20. Since these students have yet to construct an amountness meaning for number, keeping track of larger counts is an unnecessary cognitive load. However, once students become numerical, they still are likely to need relatively small numbers because they will not yet have constructed composite units. For many of these students, adding on ten to a number is still a relatively large challenge, especially repeatedly. Students who are at stage 1 of units coordination can engage in adding on ten repeatedly and track the number of tens they have added. Yet it is not until stage 2 of units coordination that students are able to engage more fluidly in additive reasoning that involves breaking numbers apart strategically.

Hackenberg's project with the middle school students has yielded recommendations about number choices for middle school students that focus on fractions, decimals, and percents (Figure 9.9). These are likely helpful to keep in mind with upper elementary students as well. For example, with percents, well-known 'benchmark' percents like 50% and 25% are easier because students often have some ideas about them from everyday life and the use of money. In addition, these percents are common unit fractions. For example, if students know that 25% is 1/4, they can find 25% of a quantity by dividing by 4. In contrast, percents that are less than 1% or larger than 100% are harder to conceptualize.

Notes about Number Choices for Middle School Students	• **Whole numbers:** Almost any whole numbers are fair game; larger numbers will sometimes be harder to conceptualize, e.g., a rate of 12 gallons per minute v. a rate of 250 gallons per hour
	• **Fractions:**
	○ *Easiest:* ½, ¼, ¾, mixed numbers with ½, like 4½
	○ *Harder:* other <u>proper</u> fractions
	○ *Hardest:* <u>improper</u> fractions like 7/5 ← for some, 7/5 and 1 2/5 are NOT the same number
	• **Decimals:**
	○ *Easiest:* decimals with 0.5 like 2.5; decimals to tenths where the number is greater than 0.1, like 0.8, 4.3, etc.
	○ *Harder:* decimals to the hundredths, like 0.12, 5.78, etc.
	○ *Hardest:* decimals that go beyond hundredths and have 0s in some of the places, e. g., 13.075
	• **Percents:**
	○ *Easiest:* well-known percents like 25%, 50%, 75%, 10%, 5%
	○ *Harder:* other whole number percents between 0 and 100%
	○ *Hardest:* percents smaller than 1%, percents with fractions or decimal amounts (e.g., 33 1/3%, 57.5%), or percents larger than 100%

Figure 9.9   Number choices for middle school students

Other choices. Of course, number choices are not the only choices to make. Orienting students to particular ways of thinking via language requires understanding where students are likely to struggle and what counts as more basic and more advanced ways of thinking. In the example of parallel tasks, sharing language was more basic than fraction language, and leaving unknowns implicit was more basic than explicitly notating them. However, that did not mean Hackenberg did not want all students to grapple with fraction language and notating unknowns – they all did so eventually. Designing parallel tasks can be a good foundation for tiering instruction, because the parallel tasks may be the start of different pathways for students to work on, via follow-up tasks.

Similarly, in Tabor's (2008) study, designing different pathways for students involved not just number choices but also the structure of problems in terms of what was known and unknown. Generally speaking, missing addend problems and other subtractive situations are more accessible to students once they are at least at stage 1 of units coordination (Steffe, Cobb, & von Glasersfeld, 1988).

Conclusion

In conclusion, the main goal in this kind of differentiating instruction is to provide each student with challenges that are sensible to them, so they are working at the edges of their current reasoning. This instruction contrasts with a 'one-size-fits-all' approach that overwhelms some students and under-challenges others. Teachers well versed in the Math Recovery program already engage in the foundation of differentiating mathematics instruction. It is important for them to recognize what they already do to differentiate; we hope that the teaching practices for differentiating instruction can help them to do that, as well as to frame a larger vision for differentiation.

10

Teaching Students with Disabilities

In this chapter we present a variety of activities that have been designed to build conceptual understanding for all students. Accommodations and modifications are provided as well as suggestions for involving students with different learning needs in the same activity.

Chapter 3, 'Good Instruction for All Students,' outlined the Guiding Principles for Instruction, the Key Elements of Math Recovery Teaching, and Dimensions of Progressive Mathematization. These overarching principles and teacher actions can guide instruction based on district curriculum, intervention programs, and teacher-created materials. There are additional practices used in Math Recovery teaching as well as teaching strategies found successful in working with students with disabilities that can help students build their skills and knowledge and construct new conceptual understanding.

Teachers engaged in reflective practice and who want the opportunity to closely observe students may record lessons for later review (Ellemor-Collins & Wright, 2008). While the original purpose for the video is for teacher review, the recording can also be used as part of student instruction. Students can watch video of themselves to witness the successful use of a new skill or strategy such as saying a number word sequence correctly or counting on for the first time. Using video in this manner is similar to the strategy of Video Self-Modeling used as an intervention for students with autism spectrum disorders (Tsui & Rutherford, 2014). Watching video might also be used to draw a student's attention to errors or to have students evaluate the correctness of their answer.

Vignette

Lisa used a counting-on strategy (as opposed to counting from one) to solve an addition problem, for the first time. She used the strategy consistently during the rest of the lesson, but her teacher was concerned that since this was a new behavior for Lisa, she might revert to the less efficient strategy at the next lesson. During the next lesson, the teacher had Lisa watch the portion of the previous lesson's video in which she used the counting-on strategy to solve problems. Lisa was asked to talk about what she saw in the video and was praised for thinking of the new strategy.

Vignette

Watching video might also be used to draw a student's attention to errors. Evan is inconsistent in saying the backward sequence of numbers, often skipping the decuple or saying the incorrect decuple such as '33, 32, 31, 29, 28' or '33, 32, 31, 20, 29.' Each day, Evan's teacher has him watch the previous day's video and asks him to determine if each sequence was said correctly. A numeral roll is available so Evan can check the verbal sequence with it (see Figure 10.1).

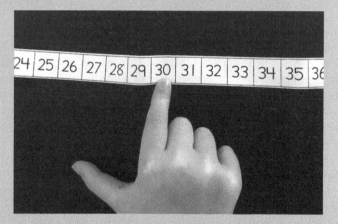

Figure 10.1   A numeral roll can be used to check verbal sequences

Acknowledgements to Kate Anderson. Used with permission.

Figure 10.2   Examples of work box tasks

Source: Provided by Lia Ess, Independent School District 196

Students need opportunities to construct new understanding and **rehearse** skills, knowledge, and understanding they have already acquired. Both goals can be accomplished by working on appropriate activities with an adult, with other students, and independently. One way to provide independent practice is through the use of work boxes and structured teaching (Hume & Carnatan, 2008). Work box tasks should be tasks that can be completed independently by the student. In addition to practicing math skills, students are learning to follow a schedule and work independently.

Students can rehearse and habituate numeral identification, number word sequences, counting, addition/subtraction, and multiplication/division strategies through the use of games. Games provide opportunities for repeated practice in an intrinsically motivating environment. Games can be played with an adult who will ask guiding questions to advance the students' strategies. Playing games with peers allows students to see classmates using more sophisticated strategies and gives students opportunities to practice newly acquired strategies. In addition to learning and practicing math skills, playing games gives students the opportunity to practice social skills such as taking turns, participating in conversations, practicing self-control, showing respect, resolving conflicts, and learning to be good winners and losers. Students who need more experience with social skills may benefit from playing games in which the mathematics is easier for them so they can focus on social skills. Learning to participate in games with other students ensures that learning continues, even when the teacher is not available to work with students. Playing games can also be used in lieu of traditional homework, giving parents and guardians a chance to have positive interactions with their child involving mathematics.

The other books in the Math Recovery series provide exemplary instructional tasks to teach the skills, knowledge, and conceptual understanding outlined in the Learning Framework in Number. In this chapter, we will present representative tasks from the other books along with modifications for students with disabilities. We will also illustrate how the needs of various students can be met during a single activity. Students with disabilities, and other students who may need intervention, will benefit from one-to-one or small-group instruction to accelerate their progress. Even with a small-group size, it is likely that students in the same group will have differing needs. Teachers will need to differentiate tasks and assign roles to keep all students engaged and working to advance their skills. It is not our intention that all options presented below are utilized in a single lesson; rather the different roles are presented as opportunities for students with different instructional needs to be involved in a single activity.

When planning for the differentiation of instructional tasks, teachers should utilize the considerations for assessment accommodations introduced in Chapter 5.

Considerations for Assessment Accommodations and Modifications

When accommodations or modifications are needed, teachers should ask:

- What is the essential element of the task that must be preserved?
- What aspect of the task might make it inaccessible to the student?
- What presentation accommodations or modifications can I make to lend accessibility and yet preserve the intent of the task?

  - Does the student need the task to be more perceptual?
  - How can I use different materials to help the student be more successful?
  - Does the student have the prerequisite vocabulary to complete the task?
  - Will the student be successful with smaller/simpler quantities?

- What supports are needed to enable the student to demonstrate content mastery?

  - What response options will be helpful for the student?

    - Verbal?
    - Written?
    - Demonstrating with manipulatives?

  - Is the student able to generate a response independently or will it be helpful to provide choices?

- How will we use information gained from these modified tasks to provoke the student to build new and more sophisticated knowledge and understanding?

Additional considerations exist for instructional tasks that will be used to advance the students' skills and conceptual understanding.

Considerations for Instructional Accommodations and Modifications

- What are the barriers to this student's learning this content, and how can they be overcome?
- What skills does the student possess that might compensate for inabilities or weaknesses?
- How might this content be broken down into more manageable portions?
- What additional scaffolds might be needed?
- How will scaffolds be faded/distanced?
- What questions can I ask to promote student thinking and reflection?

(See Chapter 9 for more strategies on differentiation.)

Number Words and Numerals

ACTIVITY IA3.1: Arrow Cards Draw for Numeral Identification

Intended learning: To identify numerals.

Instructional mode: Shorter, rehearsal mode for partners.

Materials: One set of arrow cards for each group

Description: Place all tens and ones arrow cards numerals face-down on the table top. Each student draws one of each color arrow card, a tens card and a ones card. Students build the number with the arrow cards. Each student reads his or her number. Students 'expand' the arrow cards to verify the numeral identification. (*DNK*, pp. 38–39)

Adaptations

- As students become more adept at reading multi-digit numerals, they can transition to sets of **arrow cards** that are all printed on the same color.
- When students are able to read two-digit numerals, the range can be extended to three-, four-, five-,... digit whole numerals and then to numerals that include decimals.
- Students who are working to identify single-digit numerals can be responsible for reading those numerals before they are combined to form the two-digit numeral.
- A student can be responsible for writing the numerals and adding <, >, or = symbols to indicate the relationship between the numerals.
- The activity can be gamified by having students compare their numerals to see who built the largest, or smallest, numeral. The student who is determined to be the winner of that round can place a chip on an empty five- or ten-frame. The first person to fill their frame is the winner. A student can be responsible for announcing the score and how many more chips a student needs to win.
- A student can be responsible for building each corresponding number with base-ten materials. See 'Conceptual Place Value,' below.

- A student working on multi-digit addition or subtraction can be responsible for determining the sum or difference of the numerals.

ACTIVITY IA3.6: Disappearing Sequences

Intended learning: To build facility with any forward or backward number word sequence.

Instructional mode: Shorter rehearsal mode of individuals, partners, or whole group.

Materials: Scrap paper and pencil or white board and marker.

Description: This activity is a means of automatizing and number sequence. On a piece of paper or a white board, write out the first twelve terms in the desired sequence in order in a straight line left to right. Make sure that the sequence is accurate. For example, if working on the multiples of three, students would write: 3, 6, 9, 12, 15, 18, 21, 24, 27, 30, 33, 36. Have the students recite the sequence as you touch each numeral until they can say the sequence with facility. After students have recited the sequence several times, ask for a volunteer to select a number to be covered. Cover the numeral with a sticky note, or scratch it out, such that it cannot be read but its place in the sequence is still marked. Have students recite the sequence again as you point to each numeral, including the covered number. This facilitates students visualizing the sequence. Continue to ask for volunteers to select a term to cover and then have the whole group recite the full sequence. That is, have students recite the full 'disappearing' sequence each time a numeral is removed. Repeat the process until all twelve numerals have 'disappeared'. Recite one final time, touching the spots in which each numeral used to be. (*DNK*, pp. 41–42)

Adaptations

- Using numeral cards, students work together to put numerals in the correct sequence.
- The teacher can keep one card out of the sequence and ask students which numeral is missing.
- All students recite the sequence when the numerals are visible.
- A student working on Numeral ID can select the numeral to be covered.
- A student working on Numeral Recognition can cover the card selected or turn it face-down.
- A student looking at a visible sequence can be responsible for making sure the sequence is recited correctly as cards are turned over.
- Combine 'Count Around' *TNC*, p. 42, with 'Disappearing Sequences.'
- Combine 'Numbers on the Line' *TNC*, pp. 42–43, with 'Disappearing Sequences.'

Counting, Addition, and Subtraction Strategies

ACTIVITY IA4.4: Addition Spinners

Materials

- Spinner 1 – numerals 3, 4, 5, 6, 7, 8 (or other numerals chosen by the teacher).

Figure 10.3   Counting by three's with 'Disappearing Sequences'

- Spinner 2 – numerals 2, 2, 3, 3, 4, 5.
- Dice may be substituted for the spinners.

Description

The teacher:

- Spins the first spinner and counts out this number of counters (e.g. six) then screens them under a card (a regular or modified die could be used in place of the spinner).
- Spins the second spinner with numerals 2, 2, 3, 3, 4, 5 (or other suitable numerals) and places this number of counters (e.g. three next to the screen).
- Says: There are six counters under here and three counters here. How many counters are there altogether?
- Allows time for the children to solve the task and might re-pose it, or briefly display the counters under the card.
- Continues the activity using different numbers generated by the spinners. (*TNC*, pp. 63–64)

Adaptations

- Rolling a die may be easier than spinning a spinner for some students.
- Students who are learning about cause and effect can be responsible for activating a random selection device. This enables the student to be part of a group activity and learn from the actions of the other students.
- Students working on numeral identification can be responsible for reading the spinner or die.
- Larger objects such as connecting cubes or blocks can be used for easier manipulation.
- Baskets or dishpans can be used to screen larger objects.
- Students who are learning to count perceived items can be responsible for counting the items to be screened and/or counting to check the total.
- A numeral roll, with spaces for students to place the counters, will help students learn numeral identification, the forward sequence of numbers and one-to-one correspondence.
- The game can be played without screening the objects.
- The game can be played screening both sets of objects.
- After a student has determined the total amount of screened items, one screen can be removed and a student who is more successful counting partially screened items can verify the total.
- A student can be responsible for writing the addition sentence.

Structuring: Non-count-by-one Strategies

ACTIVITY 7.5.3 Partitioning and Recording Using Flashed Ten frames

- Flash a ten-frame showing a five-wise 8. How many dots did you see? Tell me two numbers that make 8. Write the two numbers.
- Flash the ten-frame again. Write another two numbers that make 8.

- Try to write all of the ways we can make 8.
- Similarly for other numbers in the range 2 to 10 using both pair-wise and five-wise patterns. (*TN*, p. 146)

Adaptations

- Flash cards based on the needs of the student (regular or irregular dot patterns, five-, ten-, or twenty-frames).
- Given a collection of ten-frames, a student can be asked to select the ten-frame that matches the frame that was flashed.
- Students may be able to answer questions based on a description of the card. For example, the teacher might say, 'I'm looking at a ten-frame with five dots on the top row and three dots on the bottom row. How many empty spaces are there?' or 'I'm looking at a ten-frame with five dots on the top row and three dots on the bottom row. How many dots are there altogether?'
- Students can use blank frames and counters to build the frame described by the teacher. If the frame is built behind a screen, the frame can be revealed and compared to the original screen after other students have responded to questions about the frames.
- Students can take turns describing frames to the rest of the group.
- The same card can be flashed to a second student to verify the answer given by the first student.
- A third student, who needs a longer amount of time to look at the frame or perhaps needs to count the dots, can verify the answer given by the previous students.
- A student working on numeral identification can be responsible for finding the numeral to match the number of dots on the frame.
- A student can be responsible for writing all of the possible addition and subtraction sentences represented by the frame. (See Figure 10.4.)

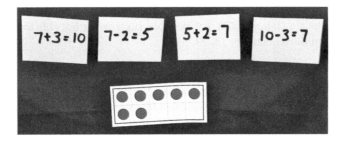

Figure 10.4   How can this ten-frame be used to illustrate each equation?

Conceptual Place Value, Addition, and Subtraction to 100

After students have mastered basic addition and subtraction facts (within 20), teachers will usually have students learn to solve two-digit addition and subtraction problems. The two-digit problems generally progress from problems that do not require regrouping, when using the traditional algorithm, to problems that do require regrouping formerly known as borrowing and carrying. Teachers may determine that students are making steady progress until they encounter problems that require regrouping. Students might puzzlingly and persistently respond to problems such as those shown in Figure 10.5.

$$
\begin{array}{r} 24 \\ +18 \\ \hline 312 \end{array}
\qquad
\begin{array}{r} 1\!\!7 \\ -\ 9 \\ \hline 8 \end{array}
\qquad
\begin{array}{r} 24 \\ -16 \\ \hline 12 \end{array}
$$

Figure 10.5 Student misconceptions using a traditional algorithm

As teachers investigate to find the sources of student confusions, they may discover that:

- All learning to this point has relied upon memorization of basic facts and procedures.
- The students do not have a concept of the quantity the numerals represent.
- The students have not developed an understanding of how addition and subtraction work or how to solve problems for which they do not immediately know the answer.
- The students have not constructed the strategy of counting on or counting back to solve addition and subtraction problems. They are not able to use the strategy of counting on to solve a missing addend problem. It should be noted that: 'Simply mimicking the strategies of others to count-on to add does not appear to be sufficient… Children need opportunities to construct a meaningful understanding of addition from which the strategy of counting-on to add is a natural development' (Tabor, 2008, pp. 81–82).
- The students don't know combinations and partitions of numbers to 10 (Tabor, 2008).
- The students do not know the number word sequences needed for incrementing and decrementing by ten (Tabor, 2008). For example, students are not able to continue the pattern of adding ten in the sequence 3, 13, 23, 33,… .

Students who have not acquired these prerequisite skills and understandings will not make steady progress with multi-digit addition and subtraction.

Students developing conceptual place value will benefit from exposure to and experience with a variety of base-ten models and representations of multi-digit numerals such as:

- Popsicle sticks, bundles of ten, and individual sticks
- Connecting cubes, trains of ten, and individual cubes
- One-hundred bead string with alternating colors of beads marking tens
- One-hundred bead math rack
- Mini ten-frames, full ten-frames, and partially filled ten-frames
- Numeral cards
- Place value/arrow cards

- Numeral roll
- Hundreds chart
- Base-ten blocks
- Dimes (10-cent coin) and pennies (1-cent coin)

See Figure 5.4 for examples of base-ten settings.

An activity can be designed in which students rotate to different spaces to interact with a variety of materials, or students can stay with the set of materials that best meets their needs.

The activity begins with a student drawing a numeral card and reading the numeral to the rest of the group. The numeral should remain hidden from the rest of the group until the end of the activity. This job can be assigned to a student who is working on numeral identification. Students stationed at the hundreds chart or numeral roll are responsible for putting a marker on the numeral announced by the student. The students at the hundreds chart and numeral roll might be students who are working on numeral recognition. Another student might be responsible for writing the numeral on a dry erase board. A student can be responsible for building the numeral with arrow cards. The rest of the students build the number with their base-ten materials. After the number has been built, the student with the numeral card reveals the numeral. Does the numeral on the card match the numerals on the hundreds chart, numeral roll, white board, and built with arrow cards? Did students correctly represent the numeral with the base-ten materials? The teacher can ask questions that will help students notice similarities and differences between the representations. The teacher can also ask questions to extend the thinking of students. These questions can be differentiated based on the needs of the students and the materials they are using. For example:

- Ask the student with arrow cards, 'How many tens are in the number?' 'How many ones are in the number?' 'Can you see proof or evidence of that many tens and ones when the arrow cards are expanded to show all the cards?' 'What is the value of that many tens?'
- Ask the student with the popsicle sticks, 'What is ten more (or less) than the number?'
- Ask the student with the hundreds chart, 'Can you find the new number (ten more or ten less) on the hundreds chart? What do you notice?'
- Ask the student with the mini ten-frames or 100-bead string, 'What is the next decuple?' 'How many to get to the next decuple?'
- Ask the student with the 100-bead math rack, 'How many more to get to one hundred?'
- Ask the student with the dimes and pennies, 'How much money do you have?'

When students have demonstrated the prerequisite skills and understanding mentioned previously and are able to use the materials presented above to show their understanding of two-digit numerals and the related quantities, they are ready to learn higher decade addition and subtraction. It is important that students are given the opportunity to develop this understanding before they are taught the procedures of traditional algorithms. Premature introduction of the traditional algorithms impedes further development of conceptual understanding (Hunt & Silva, 2020).

Rather than jump from adding and subtracting single-digit numbers to adding and subtracting two-digit numbers, *DNK* suggests a sequence of tasks for adding and subtracting a one-digit number to a two-digit number:

- Adding and subtracting within a decade, for example, 35 + 2 or 46 − 3.
- Adding on to a decuple number, for example, 60 + 5.
- Subtracting to a decuple number, for example, 76 − 6.
- Adding to get to the next decuple, for example, 27 + ? = 30.
- Subtracting from a decuple, for example, 90 − 6.
- Adding or subtracting across a decuple, for example, 38 + 4 or 36 − 7.

Each type of problem should be introduced with base-ten materials, then connected to written expressions, and finally presented as bare number problems. If students stumble with the bare number problems, they can be prompted to think about how they would solve the problems if they had the base-ten materials. This promotes the students' figurative visualization. Students can gain facility with the different types of problems by playing games that will provide repeated practice. For further discussion of the higher decade addition and subtraction problem types, refer to *DNK*, pp. 111–113. A collection of games and instructional activities can be found in *DNK*, pp. 124–134.

When students are ready to begin solving multi-digit addition and subtraction problems, it is important to ensure that they have a solid conceptual understanding of ten as a unit in the base-ten system. This understanding will be developed through experience with composing and decomposing

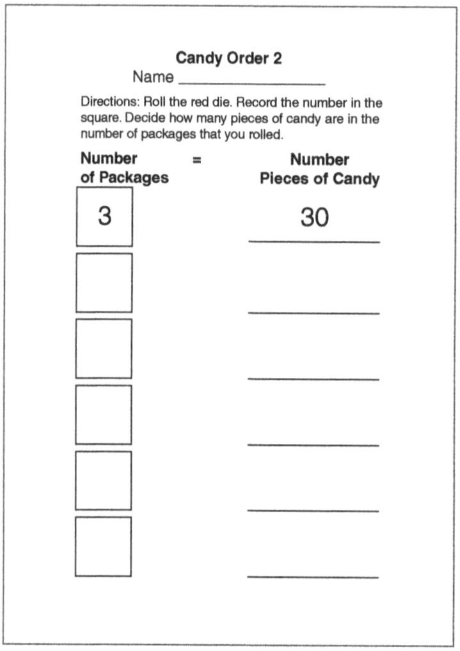

Candy Order 2

Name _____

Directions: Roll the red die. Record the number in the square. Decide how many pieces of candy are in the number of packages that you rolled.

Number of Packages	=	Number Pieces of Candy
3		30
		_____
		_____
		_____
		_____
		_____

Figure 10.6   Determining how many items are in multiple groups of ten

Source: Tabor (2008, p. 236)

collections of ten. The use of groupable items such as trains of connecting cubes, bundles of sticks, or counters arranged in ten-frames, allows students to decompose a group of ten into a collection of ten ones as opposed to pre-grouped collections, such as base-ten blocks which require students to physically trade a rod of ten for a collection of ten ones (Tabor, 2008). The manipulation of groupable items may assist students in constructing a conceptual understanding of multi-digit addition and subtraction. Teachers may be tempted to rush or even skip student experiences with materials and begin to teach the procedure for solving multi-digit problems using the standard algorithm. In their position paper 'Procedural Fluency in Mathematics', the National Council of Teachers of Mathematics states that: 'once students have memorized and practiced procedures that they do not understand, they have less motivation to understand their meaning or the reasoning behind them' (National Council of Teachers of Mathematics, 2014b). One possible sequence of instruction involves a collection of activities based on the scenario of a candy factory (Tabor, 2008) modified from Cobb, Boufi, McClain, and Whitenack (1997). The tasks include hands-on experiences with making groups of ten, determining the number of items in multiple groups of ten (see Figure 10.6), determining how many packages of ten can be made from a given number of items (see Figure 10.7), determining how many items are needed to fill a package of ten (see Figure 10.8), adding multiples of ten to a two-digit number (see Figure 10.9), and adding a single-digit to a multi-digit number (see Figure 10.10). Although the scenario presented is a candy factory, it can be changed to packaging anything that is interesting to the student. The manipulatives and models can be adapted to meet the needs of the students. Tasks can be adapted by using a variety of dice or spinners to generate numbers. Many students will benefit from experiences with a variety of representations for tens and ones.

Candy Inventory 1

Name _____

Directions: Roll the yellow decahedron decade die. Record the number in the square. Decide how many packages of candy can be made from the number of pieces that you rolled.

Number of Candies	=	Number of Packages
30		3

Figure 10.7 Determining how many tens can be made from a given number of items

Source: Tabor (2008, p. 235)

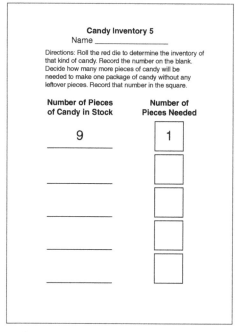

Figure 10.8 Filling a package of ten

Source: Tabor (2008, p. 239)

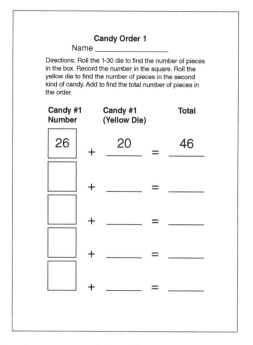

Figure 10.9 Adding multiples of ten to a two-digit number

Source: Tabor (2008, p. 240)

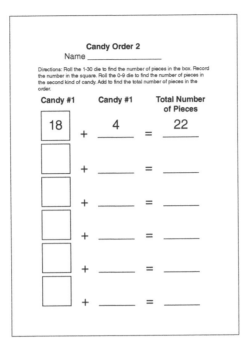

Figure 10.10 Adding a single-digit to a multi-digit number

Source: Tabor (2008, p. 241)

Vignette

Enrique is developing his math and language skills. His significant hearing loss was not discovered until he was in kindergarten. He speaks Spanish at home and English at school, but both languages are delayed because of several years of undetected hearing loss. It is sometimes difficult to tell if his misunderstandings are mathematics, language, or both. When Enrique was introduced to the Candy Factory scenario, he often confused the number of pieces with the number of packages even though he had previously demonstrated a good understanding of tens and ones using bundles of popsicle sticks and single sticks. Since the instructor was using empty ten-frames to represent the packages and round counters to represent the candy, she showed Enrique pictures of rectangular boxes of chocolates. They discussed the number of pieces of candy in the various boxes and an empty ten-frame was presented as a box for packaging candy. Enrique stated that the box would hold ten pieces of candy. As the sequence of activities began, Enrique indicated that he did not need to see the boxes or pieces of candy to complete the first three tasks (Characteristic of Children's Problem Solving: Curtailment and Asserting Autonomy, see Chapter 3). As Enrique progressed through the tasks, the ten-frames and counters were available to help him solve the various problems.

Multiplication and Division

ACTIVITY IA7.2 Snack Time

Intended learning: To develop initial strategies for multiplication.

Instructional mode: Shorter rehearsal mode for pairs.

Materials: Snack time record sheet (see Figure 10.11), 6 paper bowls, unit cubes or blocks to model snacks, one 1–6 digit cube, and one decahedron with the numerals 0–9 for each pair.

Description: This activity allows students to repeatedly create equal groups of a specified number. Introduce the activity. You are going to be fixing the snack orders for a group of children at the zoo. We need to make sure that all of the snacks are equal. Today the snack will be grapes. Roll the dot cube to see how many servings you will need to prepare to fill the order. Roll the 0–9 decahedron to determine the number of grapes you will need for each bowl. Finally, calculate the total number of grapes you will need in order to prepare the snack. You may use the blocks and bowls to help you. Your partner's job is to make sure you have the snack order correct. Record your snack order on your record sheet and then exchange jobs with your partner. (*DNK*, pp.163–164)

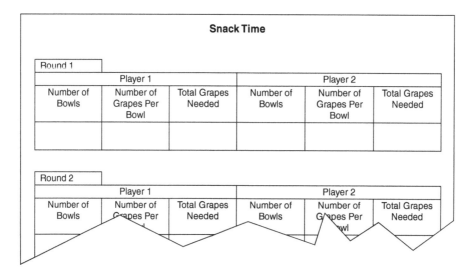

Figure 10.11 Snack time record sheet

Source: Wright et al. (2012)

Adaptations

- Make custom dice or spinners with numbers to meet the needs of students. For example, both dice can have numerals 2, 2, 3, 3, 4, 4. Numerals on each die can be written in different colors, one color representing the number of servings and the other color representing the number of grapes in each serving. The numerals on one or both dice can be increased as students become more competent with the task.

- Students who are learning about cause and effect can be responsible for activating a random selection device. This enables the student to be part of a group activity and learn from the actions of the other students.
- Students working on numeral identification can be responsible for reading the spinner or die.
- Students who are learning to count perceived items can be responsible for counting the bowls and objects to be placed in each bowl.
- The game can be played putting the 'grapes' on plates so the equal groups will be visible to the students.
- After the bowls of grapes have been assembled, a cloth can be placed over the bowls to screen the number of groups and the number of objects in each group.
- A student can be responsible for determining which skip-counting sequence can be used to determine the total number of grapes. Given a selection of written sequences, is the student able to select the correct sequence?
- A student can be responsible for writing a multiplication sentence to match the visual model.
- A variation of the game can be played to work on division and making equal groups. Students draw a card that presents a scenario for sharing the grapes. *There are 18 grapes and 3 bowls. How many grapes can be put in each bowl so that all the snacks are equal?* Tasks can be assigned as above with different students reading the problem, counting and sharing the grapes, and writing number sentences.

Fractions

Many students, children and adults, find fractions and especially arithmetic operations with fractions challenging. There are a variety of rules and procedures that can be memorized, but they rarely lead to a deep conceptual understanding of how fractions work. If the previous statements are true for typically developing students, imagine how much more challenging fractions are for students with disabilities. As with the previous topics discussed in this chapter and as indicated in Chapter 7 'Brain Research: Implications for Teaching and Learning Mathematics,' students need hands-on experiences with materials to develop a conceptual understanding of fractions. The following tasks from *DFK* (Hackenberg et al., 2016) provide examples of the types of tasks that will be helpful for students. Additional tasks are presented in Chapter 7.

Task Group A4.4: Making Connected Numbers

Materials: A small thin rectangle made from thick cardboard or plastic, paper, writing utensils.

What to do and say: Ask the students to trace the rectangle on the paper and call that 1 length a 1-stick. Ask them if they can create a length that is two times the 1-stick. If they suggest tracing another rectangle, ask them to do that and say that we'll call that length a 2-stick. Ask them if they can make a length that is three times the 1-stick. If they make a length that is three of the rectangles, say that we'll call that a 3-stick. Ask them if they can make a 4-stick, and can they do it in more than one way. They could join a 3-stick and a 1-stick or copy the 2-stick two times. If they repeat the 1-stick four times, that could be a sign of iterating. (*DFK*, pp. 51–52)

Adaptations

- Students with fine motor disabilities may find it difficult to trace the rectangle. Adjusting the size and thickness of the rectangle will be helpful for some students.
- The activity can be gamified by giving each player a die with the numerals 2, 3, 3, 4, 4, and 5 and a thick cardboard or plastic rectangle. Students roll their die behind a screen and use the cardboard or plastic rectangle to draw a stick of the length indicated by the die. Students then compare their drawings to see who has the longest (or shortest stick). The student who is determined to be the winner of that round can place a chip on an empty five-frame. The first person to fill their five-frame is the winner. A student who is not ready for the activity of iterating might benefit from determining which drawing is longer (or shorter) and placing the chips on the five-frame.
- Rather than asking a student to draw a stick of different lengths, the student can be presented with drawn rectangles of different lengths and asked to use a cardboard or plastic rectangle to measure the length of each drawn rectangle. To be successful with this task, students will need to iterate the cardboard or plastic rectangle a number of times to determine the length of each drawn rectangle. A block can be used, instead of a plastic or cardboard piece, for easier manipulation.
- If students have not developed the mental action of iteration, they can be given several copies of the plastic or cardboard pieces (or blocks) to measure the drawn rectangles. This scaffold will provide students with the experience of using objects as a measurement tool. After the students have demonstrated success with using the measurement tools, the teacher can tell the students that all but one of the measurement tools are missing. Can the students find a way to use the remaining rectangle to measure the drawn rectangles?

The Common Core State Standards indicate that students in Grade 5 should:

Use equivalent fractions as a strategy to add and subtract fractions.

CCSS.MATH.CONTENT.5.NF.A.1

Add and subtract fractions with unlike denominators (including mixed numbers) by replacing given fractions with equivalent fractions in such a way as to produce an equivalent sum or difference of fractions with like denominators. *For example, 2/3 + 5/4 = 8/12 + 15/12 = 23/12. (In general, a/b + c/d = (ad + bc)/bd.)* (CCSSM, 2010b, italics in original)

Research indicates that to accomplish this task with conceptual understanding, students must be able to partition a whole into fractional parts and iterate a unit fraction to build wholes and proper fractions. They should be able to name unit and proper fractions when they are part of a whole and when the fractional pieces are removed (disembedded) from the whole (*DFK*). These mental actions can be engendered through experiences with materials in which students are given opportunities to partition wholes into fractional pieces and use fractional pieces to build wholes. Conceptual understanding of operations with fractions can also be developed through hands-on experiences with materials. While addition and subtraction of fractions with unlike denominators is often taught procedurally, we contend that all students deserve to understand what they are doing when they perform these operations. The first step is for students to create multiple fractions of the same bar and demonstrate an understanding of how the fractions are related.

ACTIVITY IA11.1: Transforming Bars 1

Intended learning: Students will learn how to partition a given partitioned bar in order to show a different fraction in the bar, where the number of parts in the target fraction is a multiple of the number of parts in the given bar.

Instructional mode: Students working in pairs with instruction from the teacher followed by whole-class discussion.

Materials: Multiple copies of a piece of paper with 3/3-bars on it (see Figure 10.12), 4/4-bars, 5/5-bars, etc. Depending on class size you might want each pair of students to get a differently partitioned set of bars or you can have some pairs use the same. Additional materials include colored pencils or markers, and fractions written on small index cards or pieces of paper. The fractions should be out of a number of parts that is a multiple of the number of parts in the bars. For example, if you are using 5/5-bars, you might have 1/10, 1/15, 1/20, 1/25, etc.

Description: Give each pair of students some paper with rectangles that have the same number of parts. Also, slip to each student in the pair a different fraction to make, for example, if a pair of students had the 5/5-bars, then you could give one student 1/10 and the other student 1/15. They should not know each other's fractions initially. Ask each student to transform a bar to show their fraction but without showing it to their partner. Then partners tell each other what their target fraction was and predict what their partner did to make it. Following the predictions, partners can show each other their drawings to check. Finally, they should each color their bars to show the original fraction and state how many of the target fractions are needed to make, or measure, one unit-fraction of the original bar. For example, how many 1/10s are the same size as 1/5? Then they each work with another fraction. Following several rounds, hold a class discussion about how students made their target fractions and what they noticed about how many target fractions made up a unit fraction of the original bar. Here you can also introduce the term 'co-measurement'. (*DFK*, pp. 155–156)

Figure 10.12   Multiple copies of the same rectangle, aligned

Source: DFK

Adaptations

- Use large pieces of paper or long strips of paper to represent the fraction bars. Card stock or tag board will be easier for some students to manipulate. Segment the bars to represent 2/2-bars, 3/3-bars, or 4/4 bars. Starting with fewer segments will make the task more accessible because fewer segments will result in larger segments, giving students more space to draw the lines for their new fractions.
- Have students work in cooperative pairs to determine how the new fraction should be represented. Students with limited fine motor abilities can have their partner draw for them. Students work together to decide if the representation is correct.
- Students can be given different size fraction bars to represent the new fractions. For example, a student given a 2/2-bar can be asked to find the fraction bar that represents 1/4 of the bar. Teachers will need to keep the size of the fraction bars in mind when making the segmented bars to give to students. Another possibility is to make different size strips of cardboard that students can use to determine the new fraction. If all students have the same set of fraction bars, partners can predict which fraction strip their partner used behind a screen to represent the new fraction.

Conclusion

The instructional tasks in this chapter are representative of the kinds of tasks students should experience to develop a conceptual understanding of number and operations. We also provided a sample of possible accommodations and modifications. Each student brings unique needs and abilities to the learning experience, and it is our hope that the examples provided illustrate the possibilities for meeting the needs of all students.

11

The Constructivist as Teacher

This chapter will examine **behaviorism** and **constructivism** and their impacts on mathematics instruction for students with disabilities and their teachers.

The various instructional strategies used when teaching students with disabilities can be categorized according to two basic learning theories: behaviorism and constructivism (Duhaney & Duhaney, 2000; Steele, 2005). These two theories are fundamentally different. The differences in teaching based on the two theories are summarized in Table 11.1.

Table 11.1 Comparison of Behaviorist and Constructivist Perspective

Behaviorist	Constructivist
Teacher-centered	Learner-centered
Teacher as possessor of knowledge	Teacher as member of learning community
Teacher as disseminator of information	Teacher as facilitator and coach
Learning as an individual activity	Learning as a cooperative activity
Emphasis on testing	Emphasis on alternative, authentic, or performance-based assessment
Focus on lectures	Focus on discovering and constructing knowledge
Emphasis on rote memorization	Emphasis on applicable understanding

Source: Duhaney and Duhaney (2000, p. 397)

Current instruction of students with disabilities is primarily from a behaviorist perspective, and mainstream research in special education supports this practice (Gersten et al., 2009). One possible reason for the popularity of research devoted to behaviorist techniques of instruction for students with disabilities is that it is easier to conduct randomized control trial research when you can control for fidelity of implementation and have specific, measurable behaviors as outcomes. Behaviorist instructional strategies such as explicit instruction or direct instruction are often scripted, making it easier to train teachers to deliver the same instruction to all students (Woodward & Tzur, 2017). The objectives special education teachers develop for Individualized Education Programs (IEPs) need to be observable and measurable, which also favors a behaviorist perspective. The need for observable and measurable behavior leads to teaching discrete and observable skills. In summary, reasons for the preponderance of teaching based on behaviorism are that it is easier to train teachers, write instructional materials, and assess students from a behaviorist perspective (Poplin, 1988).

Specific techniques associated with a behaviorist perspective include: explicit instruction; discrete trial; I do, You do, We do (Gradual release); corrective feedback; errorless learning; Applied Behavior Analysis (ABA); precision teaching; and Direct Instruction (DI) (Boyd & Bargerhuff, 2009; Doabler et al., 2015; Gersten et al., 2009; Knight, 2002; Trent, Artiles, & Englert, 1998). Two common threads in these techniques are: (1) teachers are responsible for transferring knowledge to students and (2) success is measured by a change in student behavior.

As indicated by its name, behaviorism teaches behavior, and it is not always clear whether student behavior indicates student understanding. When teachers expect certain behavior, students may give up sense-making to please the teacher (Clements & Battista, 1990). An example of this is recounted by Cobb (1988) who interviewed a second-grade student about her strategies for solving addition problems. When the problems were presented as horizontal sentences, the student used a counting-on strategy to solve the problems. When the same problems were presented vertically, the student attempted to use the algorithm taught in class, adding first the ones column and then the tens. Since she failed to 'carry the 1' she produced incorrect answers to the problems that were written vertically. When the interviewer asked the student about getting two different answers to the same problem $16 + 9 =$, the following conversation took place.

I: So when we count we get 25 and when we do it this way [points to the worksheet] we get 15. Is that okay to get two answers or do you think there should be only 1?

A: [Shrugs her shoulders.]

I: Which one do you think is the best answer?

A: 25.

I: Why?

A: I don't know.

I: If we had 16 cookies and 9 more, would we have 15 altogether?

A: No.

I: Why not?

A: Because if you counted them up together, you would get 25.

I: But is this [points to the answer of 15 on the worksheet] right sometimes or is it always wrong?

A: It's always right. (Cobb, 1988, p. 98)

This conversation indicates the student believed the mathematics she learned at school need not make sense. The important thing was to follow the rules presented by her teacher. The answers on the worksheet might be taken to mean that the student does not understand addition; however, what she really does not understand is the procedure taught to her by her teacher.

From a constructivist perspective, teaching and training are two different things. Constructivist teachers set up situations or present problems to build on what students already know while behaviorist teachers manipulate the environment to change student behavior (Duhaney & Duhaney, 2000). The outcome of teaching is understanding, and the outcome of training is behavior (von Glasersfeld, 1991). 'When defining learning as performance and responding to the teacher's or the researcher's knowledge, the role of children's thinking is downplayed' (Hunt, MacDonald, & Silva, 2019, p. 4). Assessing student understanding can be challenging because teachers cannot see what students understand; they can only make assumptions based on students' words and behaviors. The challenge for teachers of students with disabilities increases when students are non-verbal or have difficulty with expressive language.

Constructivism

Constructivism is a theory of how we learn or make meaning of the world around us. An important aspect of constructivism is that we construct or build new knowledge on the foundation of what we already know. As we encounter new situations, we either assimilate the new experience with what we already know, or need to change our current thinking to accommodate the new information. We need to change our current thinking when we experience **perturbation**, an experience that does not align with our current understanding (Cobb, 2005). New knowledge is created when we reflect on our actions and new ideas are integrated with existing knowledge (Clements & Battista, 1990).

Constructivism in Education

The theory of constructivism may be easy to apply to learning but applying the theory to instruction can be more difficult (Cobb, 1988). Teachers who subscribe to a constructivist view of teaching and learning do not always agree on the specifics of implementing constructivism in the classroom (Davis, Maher, & Noddings, 1990b). However, Poplin outlines principles of the constructivist teaching/learning process:

1. All people are learners, always actively searching for and constructing new meanings, always learning.
2. The best predictor of what and how someone will learn is what they already know.

3. The development of accurate forms follows the emergence of function and meaning.
4. Learning often proceeds from whole to part to whole.
5. Errors are critical to learning. (1988, p. 405)

(1) Everyone is working to make sense of their environment. Even students who we perceive as the most significantly disabled are trying to make sense of their experiences and integrate their experiences with what they already know. When we consider that everyone is learning from the time they are born, we can envision that all students are at a point along their learning journey. As teachers, it is our job to determine where students are on their journey and guide them further along the path. Although teachers who instruct from a constructivist perspective do not transmit knowledge to their students, they are responsible for selecting and presenting problems that will advance students' understanding and for establishing an environment which will open possibilities for more advanced ways of thinking. Teachers are also responsible for providing scaffolds to help students bridge between their current understanding and the understanding needed to solve new tasks (see Key Elements of Instruction, Chapter 3).

(2) Teachers who base mathematics instruction on the theory of constructivism will determine what students currently understand and then work to expand the students' ability to solve a wider variety of problems (see Progressive Mathematization, Chapter 3). The need to determine what students currently understand makes formative assessment an important aspect of constructivist teaching. The goal of assessments based on constructivist approaches is to see what students 'do, can do, and can do with help' (Meltzer & Reid, 1994, p. 339). The initial assessment should be used to 'prescribe more effective teaching, not to predict future learning' (Meltzer & Reid, 1994, p. 342). Constructivist teachers are constantly assessing as they teach. Each interaction becomes an assessment, enabling teachers to determine the next steps for student learning. Teachers who implement the Teaching and Learning Cycle (see Figure 2.1) are engaging in the practices of initial and ongoing assessment to guide instruction.

(3) When teaching from a constructivist perspective, teachers ensure that the mathematical problems students are asked to work on make sense to them, and that new learning will serve as a foundation for building more advanced concepts in the future. 'Learning should not only take us somewhere; it should allow us to go further more easily' (Bruner, 1977, p. 17). As students continue to construct their understanding of mathematics, teachers continue to construct their understanding of how students engage with mathematical ideas:

Each learner has a tool kit of conceptions and skills with which he or she must construct knowledge to solve problems presented by the environment. The role of the community – other learners and teacher – is to provide the setting, pose the challenges, and offer the support that will encourage mathematical construction. (Davis et al, 1990a, p. 3)

This contrasts with the transmission of knowledge from teachers to students. When teachers attempt to transmit knowledge, they are making assumptions that all students bring the same understanding to the words, symbols, and materials used by the teacher. Constructivist teachers wait until after students have developed an understanding of a concept to introduce the socially constructed norms for communicating about mathematics (see Progressive Mathematization: Notating and Formalizing in Table 3.1, Chapter 3).

(4) Students learn best when they are curious about big ideas. For most students, completing worksheets of routine addition, subtraction, multiplication, and division problems does not spark curiosity. However, they may become intrigued by an activity such as Palindromization in *DNK* (Wright et al., 2012, pp. 193–195). The big idea of generating numerical palindromes can entice students to perform multiple, multi-digit calculations. This big idea gives students opportunities to practice a skill that is a small, but important, part of learning mathematics. After students have engaged with this activity, they may be curious about what other patterns they can find when doing various calculations.

(5) Errors are an important part of learning, and understanding the errors made by students is an important aspect of teaching from a constructivist perspective. Mistakes give teachers insight into the current limits of student understanding and guide teachers in deciding what problems or situations will advance student understanding. A wrong answer can indicate how a student is trying to make sense of a problem. For example, a student who knows that if you have twelve eggs and take away four eggs, you will have eight eggs left, might incorrectly solve the problem as

$$
\begin{array}{r}
12 \\
-\ 4 \\
\hline
12
\end{array}
$$
(Ginsburg, 1997)

Instead of just marking the answer as incorrect, a constructivist teacher will want to question the student to find the reason for the incorrect answer. Perhaps the student is attempting to apply a current understanding to subtract the smaller digit, 2, from the larger digit, 4. This common misconception has been referred to as the smaller from larger subtraction bug or pathological splitting (Tabor, 2008). Perhaps the student does not realize that the numeral 12 represents twelve objects. Errors present opportunities for teachers to look at problems from the student's perspective. A behaviorist's job is to transmit knowledge to change behavior; a constructivist's job is to uncover conceptions and misconceptions to increase understanding.

Constructivist Teaching for Students with Disabilities

Many argue that constructivist teaching is not appropriate for students with disabilities for a variety of reasons (Apps & Carter, 2006; Desoete, Roeyers & De Clercq, 2004; Knight, 2002; Kroesbergen & VanLuit, 2005; Mercer, Jordan, & Miller, 1996; Montague, 2003; Xin et al., 2016). Desoete et al., (2004) argue that students with learning disabilities do not have the metacognitive skills needed to learn from instruction based on constructivism. Kroesbergen and VanLuit (2005) found that students with mild mental retardation were able to improve their automated mastery of multiplication facts from both behaviorist (direct instruction) and constructivist (guided instruction) methods but students taught by direct instruction improved more. The study did not investigate whether the students understood the multiplication facts or whether the knowledge was retained. The study also did not mention whether or how the students' previous knowledge was assessed. Teaching from a constructivist perspective is predicated on the use of formative assessments and ongoing assessment to determine the instructional sequence. While instructional strategies such as guided instruction, cooperative learning, student-centered learning, project-based learning, discovery, exploratory, or inquiry learning have been associated with constructivist teaching, if these strategies are implemented without determining and building on students' current understanding, they will not help students construct new meaning.

Studies by Mercer et al. (1996) and Xin et al. (2016) both advocate for instruction that moves students from concrete to representational and then abstract strategies, but both report that students with learning disabilities will benefit from more behaviorist instruction at different points in the learning process to help them keep up with their peers. This is a dilemma for teachers of students with disabilities. Should students with disabilities be taught so that they can keep up with their peers, or should they be taught so they develop understanding?

It seems that students who are taught using strategies to help them keep up with their peers will eventually hit a wall, caused by a lack of understanding and a repeated message that mathematics might not make sense. Apps and Carter (2006) say that it is difficult to determine whether an instructional strategy is constructivist because there is a lack of procedural reliability and that instructional strategies that have been associated with constructivism are impractical because they require small-group instruction. The argument concerning procedural reliability is fair and is probably a reason why there are so few studies on the effectiveness of constructivist teaching. Since students and teachers are continually constructing new knowledge, it is difficult to establish procedures that will work for all students and teachers. In fact, the idea of a procedure for teaching runs counter to constructivism. The movement away from whole-class instruction to a guided math or math workshop model has made small-group instruction, that is, responsive to the needs of students, possible (Hoffer, 2012; Lempp, 2017; Newton, 2017; Sammons, 2010).

Knight (2002) indicates that knowledge can be constructed through explicit instruction and that constructivist teaching methods do not recognize the needs of students with learning disabilities.

Mercer et al. (1996) identified learning characteristics of students with learning disabilities that they believe interfere with constructivist teaching methods. Each characteristic is presented below, followed by our response:

1. Students with learning disabilities don't have adequate prior knowledge.

    Students don't need adequate prior knowledge because a constructivist teacher will build on the knowledge students have.

2. Students with learning disabilities have difficulty sustaining attention.

    It is difficult to determine the reason for this difficulty. Is it because the instruction they are receiving doesn't make sense to them or have any connections to their current experiences? Is it because they are not given opportunities to interact with mathematics and materials that will help them make sense of instruction?

3. Students with learning disabilities lack the cognitive and metacognitive processes needed to solve problems.

    This is related to the first characteristic. A skilled teacher will build on the processes students have in place and will present problems to extend those processes.

4. Students with learning disabilities have acquired learned helplessness.

Learned helplessness is understandable when students have been consistently asked to solve problems that don't make sense to them. Constructivist teachers will present accessible problems and/or provide the scaffolding needed for students to experience success.

5. Students with learning disabilities have social skills deficits.

This can be a challenge when activities require more social interaction than simply listening to a lecture or watching a demonstration. The development of social skills is an important part of being a student and preparing for life beyond school. Some teachers have found success with decreasing the social expectations when students are constructing new mathematical ideas and increasing the social expectations when students are reviewing or reheasing mathematics they already understand. As students develop their social skills and their identities as mathematitions, they can become more engaged in constructing mathematical ideas through group activities.

6. Students with learning disabilities are passive learners.

Do students with learning disabilities appear to be passive learners because they cannot engage with the mathematics that is being presented, or is it because they lack the social skills to participate in classroom activities? Whatever the case, when students are presented with problems that are challenging, yet accessible, they will be more likely to become actively engaged.

Steele identified some key ideas for teaching students with learning disabilities from a behaviorist perspective:

1. Break down tasks into small segments
2. Model, demonstrate, and explain each step in a procedure or new task
3. Include as much extra practice and review as needed for mastery to occur
4. Incorporate structure and predictable routine into lessons
5. Use monitoring and feedback as lesson progresses rather than waiting until conclusion. (2005, p. 4)

Many of these key ideas taken from the behaviorist perspective are already part of constructivist teaching or can easily be incorporated while still allowing students the opportunity to construct their own knowledge:

(1) Since teachers are building on the prior knowledge of students, it follows that tasks given to students will be manageable for students, with scaffolding provided, as needed. If the task is not accessible, teachers will make the adjustments needed to the task or support given (see Key Elements of Instruction, Chapter 3).
(2) Constructivist teachers may demonstrate the use of materials as such as a numeral track or the rules for playing a game (see Key Elements of Instruction 3: introducing a setting and 6: directly demonstrating). Teachers might also model a strategy during student interactions, but the purpose of the modeling is to expose students to a strategy that the teacher determines is accessible to students and will build on what the students already know. Students are not directed to mimic the teacher's strategy.
(3) Students of constructivist teachers are given opportunities to practice existing strategies while working to develop new ones. For example, 'as students establish facile multiplication strategies

for all basic facts within a range, instruction can progress to rehearsing those basic facts toward habituation' (Wright & Ellemor-Collins, 2018, p. 134).

(4) Structure and predictable routines can be incorporated into constructivist lessons. A visual schedule can be made, perhaps using pictures of various settings or pictures of students engaging in activities, so students know what activities to expect during the lesson.

(5) The Key Elements of Instruction (see Chapter 3) indicate several opportunities for teachers to provide feedback: giving encouragement to a partly correct response, directing to check, querying an incorrect response, correcting a response, querying a correct response, affirming, confirming, highlighting, and privileging a correct response (Wright & Ellemor-Collins, 2018).

Montague (2003) acknowledges that constructivist teaching is playing an increasing role in general education classrooms but contends that students with learning disabilities will need explicit instruction to learn the processes and strategies to succeed in constructivist classrooms. This argument seems to miss an important point of constructivist teaching: that students construct knowledge, building on the foundation of what they already know. If students are truly in a constructivist classroom, they will have opportunities to learn the processes and strategies they need to succeed. It is possible that students are in a classroom in which teachers are using student-centered teaching, or one of the many other strategies associated with constructivism, but if the instruction does not build on what the student knows, the instruction is not constructivist for that student.

Behaviorism relies on the use of extrinsic rewards to change student behavior whether it is edible reinforcers, prizes, stickers, or praise from a teacher. These rewards will increase the desired behavior, if it is a behavior the student is capable of performing. However, if we use extrinsic rewards in place of the reward of understanding, then learning will cease when the rewards stop (Bruner, 1977). Teachers need to use a balance of intrinsic and extrinsic rewards and should not neglect the effects of 'interest and curiosity, and the lure of discovery' (Bruner, 1977, p. 30). (See Guiding Principle 9 in Chapter 3.)

Students need tools and building materials with which to construct their knowledge (Noddings, 1990). If we consider previously constructed knowledge to be the foundation for building new knowledge, then conventional knowledge, such as the names of numerals and the forward and backward sequence of numbers, can be considered some of the tools and materials needed for the construction. These pieces of conventional knowledge will not be constructed by students. Here is a situation in which a behaviorist approach can be appropriate for teaching. How we teach depends on what we are teaching. Thus, we believe that the question should not be "which instructional approach is better," but rather, "which instructional approach is best suited to achieving the ends we have in mind?"' (Gresalfi & Lester, 2009, p. 266). The reader is referred to Chapter 1 of this book, 'The Learning Framework in Number for the Classroom', for additional guidance on conventional versus constructed knowledge.

Students with disabilities go through the same stages as typically developing students, and, when given the opportunity, they can construct the same understanding and problem-solving strategies (Behrend, 2003; Eriksson, 2008; Grobecker, 1999; Moscardini, 2010; Woodward & Montague, 2002). If students in general education classes are given the opportunity to construct conceptual understanding and students with disabilities are primarily taught procedures, how will students with disabilities gain access to the general education curriculum? Are we widening the gap between students with disabilities and students without disabilities by not giving everyone access to the same instruction (Boyd & Bargerhuff, 2009)?

Grobecker (1999), feels that a misunderstanding of constructivist principles by people in the field of learning disabilities is one reason for a lack of research on the problem-solving abilities of students with disabilities. In her experience, 'children with LD are capable of adapting their thinking when engaged in problem-solving situations appropriate to their logical orders' (Grobecker, 1999, p. 53). Studies reviewed by Woodward and Montague (2002) indicate that while the strategies used by students with disabilities may be delayed, the development of strategies follows the same trajectory as non-disabled students. While studies cited in this chapter have been focused on students with learning disabilities and mild cognitive disabilities, constructivist teaching can be applied to all students, regardless of their perceived abilities. In fact, it is with perceived abilities that constructivist teaching begins. Eriksson refers to a student's current understanding or perceived abilities as 'the arithmetic of the child' and says this should be the basis of 'the arithmetic for the child' or what can be learned next (2008, p. 9). Every student gives us a place to start, our job is to find it.

Conclusion

The title of this chapter, 'The Constructivist as Teacher', indicates that we are the constructivists. We must build on our current understanding of how students construct their understanding of mathematics, and we must continue to construct our own understanding of mathematics. We must build on our current understanding of what students understand and the next instructional step for each student. This can be accomplished through a three-step process. First, teachers form a hypothesis about how students currently think. This can be accomplished through assessments, interviews, or observing how students interact with problems. Second, teachers test their hypothesis by posing a problem or presenting an activity and observing students' responses. Third, teachers modify their hypothesis based on student responses. The cycle continues as teachers and students construct their understanding of mathematics (Wright, 2000).

Figure 11.1   Student solving a two-digit horizontal expression

(Continued)

For example, presenting two-digit expressions horizontally encourages the use of mental strategies as seen in Figure 11.1. After listening to the student's response, the teacher can determine if he needs more experiences with base-ten settings, needs additional practice using his current strategy, or is ready for more complex problems.

We must also take time to reflect on our teaching practice. What have we learned from a student that will help us in working with future students? How can we adjust our practices to meet the learning needs of each student? 'The Constructivist as Teacher' acknowledges that every student we encounter has something to teach us, and the title embraces that challenge.

12

Supporting Students with Other Special Needs

Outside the realm of IDEA, which mandates educational services for students with disabilities in the United States, many students have special needs that benefit from special consideration. Among these students with other special needs are students who are part of a historically **marginalized population** or **underserved population**, students living in poverty, English learners (ELs), students who suffer from **mathematics anxiety**, students with exceptional abilities and talents in mathematics, and others beyond the scope of this chapter. While these students may not have a legal document called an IEP that governs the scope of special modifications and accommodations impacting their education, they do fall under the US Every Student Succeeds Act of 2015 (ESSA) federal legislation and can benefit from some special consideration during mathematics instruction (Bartell et al., 2017). It should also be noted that students with disabilities may also fall within any of these other groups. This chapter will give an overview of some strategies and perspectives teachers may use to better meet the needs of students with these other types of special needs, as well as some reflections on these issues. The purpose of this chapter is to raise awareness, promote discussion, and point the reader toward additional resources. It is not intended as a thorough integration of all topics included.

Students from Historically Marginalized and Systemically Underserved Groups

Over the last few years, much has been written of equity and affording students from historically marginalized or **underserved groups** access to quality education including rigorous mathematics (Flores, 2007; Gutiérrez, 2008). Equity was a major theme at the 2019 National Council for Teachers of Mathematics (NCTM) Research Conference. Sessions dealt with issues of equity, diversity, culture, **inclusion**, and social justice. These notions have been a focus of NCTM research for some time as evidenced by the Special Equity Issue of the *Journal for Research in Mathematics Education* in January of 2013 (Gutiérrez, 2013). All the articles in the special issue address equity with respect to power and identity.

'The New Teacher Center has identified "systemically underserved students" as: Black, LatinX, [*sic*] and indigenous students; students living in poverty; English language learners; immigrant students; and students with disabilities' (Persyn & Valbrun-Pope, 2020, slide 45). This definition is based on the US Department of Education's definition of 'High-needs students' (US Department of Education, n.d.). During the 2020 Symposium, the New Teacher Center highlighted several disturbing facts:

> Fourth grade students from diverse backgrounds face significant achievement gaps of up to 40% in key content areas... 45% of high-poverty schools receive less state and local funding than was typical for other schools in their district... Underserved students are more likely to not receive high-quality grade-level assignments in their classrooms. (Howard et al., 2020, slide 16)

Kotok (2017), in a longitudinal study of high-achieving ninth-grade students, found Black and Latinx[1] students did not make the same gains in high school as their White and Asian American peers who were achieving the same at baseline. He credits this disparity to an opportunity gap systemic across the country.

One critical factor in this achievement gap may be the implicit bias held by teachers. Copur-Gencturk, Cimpian, Lubienski, and Thacker (2020) report disturbing findings from an experiment conducted with K–12 teachers. The findings reveal teacher bias with respect to race and gender when scoring student work. The researchers asked teachers to rate the appropriateness of student responses. The identical work samples were randomly presented to 390 teachers participating in several different professional development courses, the only difference being the first name visible on the work. The researchers had selected names commonly associated with boys and girls of different ethnicities. While teachers showed no difference in scoring obviously correct or incorrect responses, when responses were partially correct, the teachers' implicit biases were demonstrated. When the work sample had a name typically associated with a White boy, teachers of all ethnicities were significantly more likely to score the sample higher than when the same sample had the name of a student of color or a White girl. Since teacher expectations are associated with student performance, implicit biases held against systemically underserved students likely negatively impact the achievement of those students. Indeed, Ellis (2009) provides a stark reminder that bias and low teacher expectations should not be the basis for unjust differentiation. All students have the right to engage in tasks they find challenging. Guiding Principle 2: Initial and On-going Assessment (see Chapter 3 for more on the Guiding Principles) based on the Learning Framework in Number provides objective data on which to base instructional decisions around appropriate differentiation (see Chapter 9 for a detailed discussion of differentiation).

In order to support the success of all students, teachers must examine and confront their own particular biases. We all have them (Iqbal, 2019), regardless of our demographics. Our biases may be different from those held by others. We are a product of our own beliefs, education, backgrounds, experiences, and interactions with people from different populations. (For further reading on overcoming racism and bias see DiAngelo, 2018; Kendi, 2019.) One aspect of the classroom environment related to equity is 'Who contributes to the classroom dialogue?' (Reinholz & Shah, 2018). Simply analyzing the contributions during a classroom discussion can be illuminating. Are certain voices dominating the conversation? Is the teacher privileging certain groups of students over others? Videotaping one's own teaching and reviewing the recording for patterns of participation is an excellent first step for a self-reflective teacher. Another strategy is having students place their names on the reverse of their papers. Then, read responses and make comments before determining the owner of the ideas. If you are surprised by the ownership of the work, reflect on why you were surprised.

As educators, it is our responsibility to foster an educational environment in which all students have access to safe learning spaces in which they may thrive. Creating these spaces and confronting biases often require difficult reflection and conversations. While these discussions may be uncomfortable, they are important to ensure all students have the opportunity to excel. If we teach in insular, homogeneous contexts, we may need to seek out individuals who are different from ourselves in order to broaden our perspectives and illuminate our own subtle biases. If we uncover troubling aspects of our own practice and thinking, we should extend ourselves grace, rather than guilt, while purposing to do better going forward.

Students Living in Poverty

In the United States, there are more than 50 million students in 98,311 schools receiving Title 1 funds designated for compensatory education funding for low-achieving students, particularly those living in poverty (National Center for Education Statistics, 2017). In fiscal year 2019, there were 29,537,791 children participating in the National School Lunch Program (US Department of Agriculture Food and Nutrition Service, 2020). In 2018, 74% or roughly 22 million of those participants were provided free or reduced-price meals (US Department of Agriculture, 2019). Those students come from households living at or below 130% of the poverty rate. From these two indicators, it is apparent that millions of school-aged children are living in poverty in the United States. In addition to poverty common in urban communities, suburban and rural poverty (such as found in Appalachian communities) also abound. Few schools are without students living in poverty.

This fact likely has a far-reaching impact on education beyond the nutritional and other basic needs of students. When promoting Inquiry-based Learning, Guiding Principle 1, one must take care when selecting contexts for mathematical problems. For example, when discussing compound interest, students living in poverty might more readily identify with and understand the context of borrowing debt over interest accrued in a savings account or investment. Poverty also likely impacts the number of children who have access to technology at home such as reliable, high-speed Internet service. When making assignments outside of school, accessible alternatives must be considered for students without such access at home.

Homeless Students and Those in Temporary Housing Situations

An estimated 1.6 million youth are homeless in the United States (Aviles, 2019). There are 114,085 'doubling up' or homeless students in New York City alone (Emdin, 2020). The **McKinney–Vento legislation** mandates that every US school district must have a liaison for homeless students, and states must ensure schools provide these students with access to free, appropriate education (US Department of Education, 2017). If students are stressed because of their living situation, mathematics and school in general will likely suffer. The language 'I stay at…' rather than 'I live…' is a clue of an instable housing situation (Aviles, 2019). Some students are staying with relatives in overcrowded dwellings. These situations tend to be unstable. It is not just an urban problem. It may fall on the teacher to use keen observation to identify students in unstable living situations and connect those students with the McKinney–Vento liaison or team in larger districts.

Scenario

Tiffany was a struggling student in a small suburban school. Unbeknownst to her teachers, she was living in a van in sub-freezing temperatures with her mother, Joyce, after they fled Joyce's abusive domestic partner. While Joyce was working with the county Social Services to secure transitional housing, several area churches put Joyce and Tiffany up in hotels on the nights the temperature dipped below zero. Joyce dropped Tiffany off at school each day where she was able to have two meals. Her teachers noticed that she often wore the same few clothes and appeared tired frequently. They were unaware of her living situation because Joyce, fearing that her daughter would be taken away from her, instructed Tiffany not to share their situation. Tiffany was never the recipient of assistance from the liaison for homeless students. Unsurprisingly, Tiffany was struggling in school. Fortunately, with the assistance of a minister in town, Joyce and Tiffany were able to secure a temporary safe place to live while Habitat for Humanity helped them build a home of their own in the community.

English Language Learners/English Learners

Meeting the needs of English learners has become more prominent since the 2001 passage of the No Child Left Behind Act in the United States. The WIDA Consortium has developed standards for teaching English learners (ELs). These standards governing all subject areas can be found at: https://wida.wisc.edu/sites/default/files/resource/2012-ELD-Standards.pdf. The third standard, 'Language of Mathematics,' states: 'English language learners communicate information, ideas and concepts necessary for academic success in the content area of mathematics' (WIDA Consortium, 2012, p. 4). Updated standards are scheduled for release in 2020. These standards will place a greater focus on equity and teaching language with content (WIDA Consortium, 2020).

In an excellent article on constructivism with English Language Learners (ELLs), Mvududu and Thiel-Burgess list several different educational approaches to teaching ELs:

There have been a number of programs designed to assist ELLs to develop English language skill. While the following is not an exhaustive list, it provides an overview of instructional programs implemented over the last decade or so.

1) <u>Transitional bilingual education</u>: Students are taught in their primary language. Over time (1–3 years) there is a gradual decrease in the use of the primary language and a transition to English-only instruction.
2) <u>Maintenance bilingual education:</u> Students are taught in both English and their primary language in the earlier grades (K-6) so that they become academically proficient in both languages.
3) <u>Dual language programs</u>: Students for whom English is the primary language and students for whom it is not are instructed together. The goal is for each group to become bilingual and bi-literate.
4) <u>Sheltered English:</u> Students are initially instructed at low levels of English and gradually move up the levels. The students' primary languages are not used.
5) <u>English as a second language:</u> No instruction is given in the primary language of the students. The goal is to mainstream students as fast as possible.

These programs are not mutually exclusive and many school districts use them in some blended form. Just as there are various ELL programs, there are various pedagogical approaches to teaching ELL students. Regardless of the program chosen, an approach that appears compatible with the goal of reaching all students is the constructivist approach. (2012, p. 109)

In the literature, the term 'emerging bilingual' has become more popular as educators seek to have learners retain their identities as dual-language learners. Moschkovich prefers the term 'bilingual' because it emphasizes what the students know (two languages) rather than the deficit (lack of English proficiency) and because she believes when people use the term 'English learner' they are actually referring to Latinx students who are from poor schools and who are struggling in school (Phakeng & Moschkovich, 2013).

Reflections on Terminology (Pamela D. Tabor)

I have intentionally chosen not to use the term 'bilingual' because of my teaching background. I taught in a public school that serviced the military dependents of a major military installation. This installation included an ordinance school to which individuals from all over the world would come for a relatively short period of time. Their military dependents came from a variety of native languages and were frequently the only person in the class or even school who spoke that language. Within one classroom,

(Continued)

you might have native speakers of English, Arabic, Spanish, and Icelandic. Some of these children were already conversant, if not fluent, in more than one language other than English. Thus, emerging bilingual is not always appropriate for all English Learners (ELs). In using the term English learners, I am referring to any individual, regardless of ethnicity, who is learning English regardless of how many languages they already speak. I also do not use it to highlight what they cannot do. I choose to focus on what they are doing – learning an additional language and using that additional language for instruction.

Out of necessity, the school in which I taught functioned in an English as a second language format as described above. Students who qualified for English learner services received up to two hours a week of pull-out small group instruction and support from the itinerate teacher of ELs. Even this small group lesson was not instructed in the students' primary languages. In fact, the teacher did not speak most of their languages.

Because so many different first languages were spoken, supporting ELs took on a slightly different character than in a classroom in which one common first language was shared by all ELs, as is frequently the case in the research literature. One emerging theme from the literature applies regardless: teacher moves and classroom structures that support ELs also benefit their monolingual peers (Maldonado et al., 2009).

From the literature, there are several pedagogical structures, teacher moves, and classroom cultural aspects that support ELs.

1.   Development of socio-mathematical norms (Cobb, Stephan, McClain, & Gravemeijer, 2001) that are culturally responsive and support ELs.

These norms have been used successfully in inclusive, linguistically diverse classrooms (Merritt et al., 2017):

a.   Every person (students and educators) has an obligation to value and try to understand the contributions of others, giving necessary wait-time without interrupting. (See Chapter 3 for a discussion of wait-time.)

b.   Every student has an obligation to communicate his or her thinking. This communication may take the form of spoken words, visual representations, notations, gestures, and/or demonstrations with manipulatives.

c.   Any person may voice his or her explanation in his or her native language first prior to attempting the explanation in English even if no one else in the room knows that language.

d.   Any person may attempt to **re-voice** an explanation in order to seek clarity, focusing on how and why.

e.   Notation of strategies will remain visible after the discussion has moved on to provide a **residue** of the discussion (Kelemanik & Lucenta, 2019 in Sofrona, 2019).

f.   A word bank will be maintained to facilitate the use of mathematical language. New words will be added as they emerge in the dialogue. Every person has the responsibility for nominating new words for the bank. Students will have access to and may also consult a content-specific bilingual dictionary as needed. (For a discussion of the **Sheltered Instruction Observation Protocol (SIOP)** approach to building content vocabulary in all subject areas, consult Echevarria & Short, 2011.)

g. Educators will strive to provide an individual or small group setting in which students may practice their explanations prior to attempting the explanation in a whole group as students are developing feelings of comfort and confidence.

2. Educators believe that every student can and will make meaningful, substantive contributions to the classroom discourse (Moschkovich, 2013). Every student is held accountable to contribute, even if it is in their first language supported by visual representations, gestures, and demonstrations.

Teacher expectations have long been found to correlate strongly with student performance as first studied in Rosenthal's classic work *Pygmalion in the Classroom* (Rosenthal & Jacobson, 1968) and related subsequent research (Good, Sterzinger, & Lavigne, 2018). Increasing students' own **self-efficacy** is seen as critically related to student performance (Ashcraft, 2019). By supporting and ensuring the voice of all students in the classroom, teachers send subtle messages about their expectations. This discourse is made more accessible to ELs by notating the thinking shared during the discourse. This notion also serves as a residue of the discussion which can provide additional support for ELs over time (Kelemanik et al., 2016, in Sofrona, 2019).

3. Collaborative approaches of instruction often provide additional support for ELs (Merritt et al., 2017; Mvududu & Thiel-Burgess, 2012). These collaborative experiences allow those with developing English skills to formulate and express thoughts in a smaller, less intimidating setting prior to expressing them to the whole class.
4. The more successful a student is academically in their native language, the more likely they will be successful in English. Allowing students to use their primary language first to order thinking may enable the student to be more successful overall as opposed to forcing them to speak only English (Mvududu & Thiel-Burgess, 2012). Even if the student is the only speaker of their language present, having the freedom to initially express ideas in the language of their choice can allow students to focus on the mathematical ideas rather than worrying about the language. This reduces the cognitive load significantly.
5. Teachers make efforts to learn about the student, their culture, religion, etc. not for assimilation, but to celebrate the student's cultural identity. This will help the students feel appreciated and safe to contribute to the classroom in which they are valued (Mvududu & Thiel-Burgess, 2012).

Teachers may need to investigate the culture and norms of the home country. One such source of information is Cultural Crossings Guide (http://guide.culturecrossing.net/index.php). This site provides users with the predominate cultural norms of other countries that may enable the teacher and other students to better understand cultural practices of recent immigrants. The website lists cultural norms common in different countries. The user can click a country and discover information about greetings, communication style, personal space, eye contact, views of time, gestures, gender roles, taboos, dress codes, school/university class norms, and student socializing. This information could be invaluable to promoting good communication and developing culturally responsive, safe educational environments for ELs.

6. ELs need to be afforded autonomy and self-direction (Mvududu & Thiel-Burgess, 2012).

Establishing predictable norms and routines (Kelemanik, Lucenta, & Creighton, 2016) may enable ELs greater autonomy.

There is evidence that teacher participation in Add+VantageMR Course 1 and 2 is associated with closing the achievement gap between students who are native speakers of English and those who are ELs. It takes approximately three years for those ELs to catch up to their native speaking peers within the domain of structuring number (Bradley, 2019) (see Chapter 1 for more detail on the Learning Framework in Number). Many of these students who are recent immigrants also have limited or interrupted formal schooling (see https://www.matsol.org/slife-resources for more information). Recent immigrants, particularly those who are refugees, have likely experienced trauma as well (Persyn & Valbrun-Pope, 2020). For more information on trauma-informed instruction and schools, consult the March 2016 special issue of *School Mental Health* (Overstreet & Chafouleas, 2016). Some ELs may have dual designations as an English learner and a student with disabilities. It may be necessary to coordinate services with other professionals to meet the educational and social–emotional needs of the students.

A free resource that may help teachers explore successful strategies in teaching ELs is the Highest Aspirations podcast found at https://ellevationeducation.com/ell-community/type/podcast. Consult de Araujo, Roberts, Willey, and & Zahner (2018) for a comprehensive review of research related to English learners in K–12 mathematics from 2000 to 2015.

Culturally Responsive Teaching

Culturally responsive teaching, pioneered by Ladson-Billings (1994), intentionally treats diversity as an asset. 'Culturally responsive educators… consider students' diversity as a strength in the classroom rather than a challenge that they must overcome, and they see the incorporation of cultural perspectives as a necessary educational commitment' (Peterek & Adams, 2009, p. 151). Hammond (2017), author of *Culturally Responsive Teaching and the Brain*, contends relationships are the single most important aspect of culturally responsive teaching. Wlodkowski and Ginsberg (1995) highlight four critical aspects of culturally responsive teaching: creating an inclusive atmosphere in which all feel respected and connected; developing an attitude favorable to learning that is personally relevant; including an opportunity to engage with rigorous content that considers student values and perspectives; and expecting students to develop expertise when they value the content. Learning more about a student's culture is necessary for engaging in culturally responsive teaching. More recently in a research commentary, Bartel et al. propose nine equitable practices for the teaching of mathematics:

1. Draw on students' funds of knowledge [For a research review see also Hogg, 2011]
2. Establish classroom norms for participation
3. Position students as capable
4. Monitor how students position each other
5. Attend explicitly to race and culture
6. Recognize multiple forms of discourse and language as a resource
7. Press for academic success
8. Attend to students' mathematical thinking
9. Support development of a sociopolitical disposition. (2017, Table 1, pp. 11–12)

These practices help the teacher promote Students' Intrinsic Satisfaction (Guiding Principle 9).

Culturally responsive teaching is not limited to EL students. Emdin (2016) writes compellingly about the needs of urban students whom he calls **neoindigenous** to draw attention to the similarities in their education to the experiences of indigenous students of the past. Emdin's **reality pedagogy** leverages cultural aspects common among urban students of color to better meet their educational needs. Emdin asserts:

> If we are truly interested in transforming schools and meeting the needs of urban youth of color who are the most disenfranchised within them, educators must create safe and trusting environments that are respectful of students' culture. Teaching the neoindigenous requires recognition of the spaces in which they reside, and an understanding of how to see, enter into, and draw from these spaces... Reality pedagogy is an approach to teaching and learning that has a primary goal of meeting each student on his or her own cultural and emotional turf. It focuses on making the local experiences of the student visible and creating contexts where there is a role reversal of sorts that positions the student as the expert in his or her own teaching and learning... Together, the teacher and students co-construct the classroom space.

> Reality pedagogy allows for youth to reveal how and where teaching and learning practices have wounded them. The approach works toward making students wholly visible to each other and to the teacher and focuses on open discourse about where students are academically, psychologically, and emotionally. In a reality-pedagogy-based classroom, every individual is perceived as having a distinct perspective and is given the opportunity to express that in the classroom. (2016, p. 27)

Emdin describes 'Seven C's': cogenerative dialogues, coteaching, cosmopolitanism, context, content, competition, and curation (Emdin, 2016, p. 60) which are central to his reality pedagogy. His approach is particularly effective when the teacher has a different ethnicity from most of the students as is often the case in urban education. His book, *For White Folks Who Teach in the Hood... and the Rest of Y'all Too: Reality Pedagogy and Urban Education*, elaborates on these strategies in a highly engaging manner.

Gifted Students

Every student has the right to learn and engage in productive struggle to engender new, more sophisticated, learning. This is also true for students who have already mastered the grade-level content at pretest. Many of these students who have demonstrated great promise have underperformed traditionally (National Association for Gifted Children Math/Science Task Force et al., n.d.). In some states, giftedness falls under the umbrella of special education for exactly that reason. Additionally, students of color have been under-identified historically for gifted services (Reis & Renzulli, 2010; Renzulli, 2019). Not only do Add+VantageMR assessments enable teachers to diagnose areas of need, but they also allow teachers to identify areas of strength in need of enrichment. This enrichment should not be simply more of the same or busy work. It should afford students the opportunity to grapple with new mathematical ideas and Engender More Sophisticated Strategies (Guiding

Principle 5; see Chapter 3). Using independent centers and project-based learning with rich, open-ended problems (Singer, Sheffield, Freiman, & Brandl, 2016) is one strategy to address the needs of these students who have already demonstrated mastery of the grade-level content (Reis & Renzulli, 2010). The students also should be afforded the opportunity to communicate those ideas to others. This can pose unique challenges to the teacher attempting to address a wide range of instructional needs (see Chapter 9 on differentiation). Additionally, finding appropriate mentors for these exceptional students from the community is another effective strategy (Bisland, 2001; Gavin & NEAG Center for Gifted Education and Talent Development, n.d.).

Furthermore, it should be noted that these students may also be ELs or have handicapping conditions. Consult the National Center for Research on Gifted Education (National Center for Research on Gifted Education, 2018) for guidelines on identifying EL students for gifted services and Reis and Renzulli (2010) for research summarizing the benefits of gifted services to twice exceptional students.

Mathematics Anxiety

Mathematics anxiety, often defined as 'feelings of tension and anxiety that interfere with the manipulation of numbers and the solving of mathematical problems in a wide variety of ordinary life and academic situations' (Richardson & Suinn, 1972, p. 551), has been extensively studied over the years. It is related to low performance in mathematics (Ashcraft, 2019), specifically with respect to performing calculations and retrieving basic facts (Passolunghi et al., 2016) and more strikingly with how individuals view their own math ability. Those who rate themselves poorly are more likely to be anxious regardless of their actual performance (Dowker, Sarkar, & Looi, 2016). Mathematics anxiety is reported to seriously impact approximately 17% of the population (Ashcraft & Moore, 2009). Students with higher levels of mathematics anxiety tend to demonstrate lower performance in mathematics, are less likely to pursue STEM (Science, Technology, Engineering, and Mathematics) majors, and take less mathematics electives (Ashcraft, 2019; Herts, Beilock, & Levine, 2019). However, the relationship between mathematics anxiety and performance is complex. Dowker argues for the existence of 'a significant bidirectional relationship between mathematics anxiety and low attainment in mathematics' (2019, p. 72). In other words, repeatedly experiencing failure in mathematics likely leads to higher levels of anxiety and fear of more failure. This higher anxiety impedes working memory, which leads to greater difficulty in problem solving and mental calculations, likely further increasing the level of anxiety. Mathematics anxiety is more likely under stressful situations such as when an assessment is timed (Boaler, 2014; Dowker, 2019). Mathematics anxiety can activate the same portion of the brain that governs visceral fear and pain (Lyons & Beilock, 2012) and tax working memory (Ashcraft & Kirk, 2001; Ashcraft & Moore, 2009; Ng & Lee, 2019; Passolunghi, Živković, & Pellizzoni, 2019) and thus reduces resources that would ordinarily be available for problem solving and mental calculations (see Chapter 7 of this work for a discussion from a neuroscience perspective). Having parents or teachers who suffer from mathematics anxiety is associated with the development of mathematics anxiety among students (Herts et al., 2019). This was particularly true for young female students (Ashcraft, 2019) and for those taught in a manner that requires memorization of procedures divorced from conceptual understanding (Petronzi, Staples, Sheffield, & Hunt, 2019). Female preservice elementary teachers are more likely to suffer from mathematics anxiety than other college majors (Hembree, 1990). Most studies show that mathematics anxiety increases with age during childhood (Dowker et al., 2016).

The good news about mathematics anxiety is there are research strategies that seem promising to mitigate and prevent it. The most successful interventions not only include techniques to control negative emotional responses (Petronzi et al., 2019) but also focus on improving numeracy and **mathematical self-efficacy** (that is, self-confidence to learn and perform mathematics) (Ashcraft, 2019). Critical to this intervention is determining the reason for the underlying mathematical difficulty in order to provide the specific strategies tailored to the individual (Caviola, Mammarella, & Kovas, 2019). The role of diagnostic, Initial and On-going Assessment (Guiding Principle 2; see Chapter 5 of this work for a detailed discussion) is crucial here. Researchers have also been successful with interventions designed to break the cycle between parental mathematics anxiety and that of their children. These strategies focus on low-stress, highly enjoyable activities in which parents and children can learn together (Herts et al., 2019). Wright et al. (2012, 2015) provide many games that may be employed in this manner. Additionally, adults seem to benefit from writing about their feelings prior to engaging in mathematical activities (Mammarella, Caviola, & Dowker, 2019a) and reinterpreting their physiological reactions in a more positive light. This reinterpretation sees the physiological response as providing resources to overcome calculational difficulties (Ashcraft, 2019; Herts et al., 2019).

This chapter includes only an overview of some of the most salient aspects of mathematics anxiety. The reader is encouraged to consult the book *Mathematics Anxiety: What is Known and What is Still to be Understood* for a more in-depth, comprehensive treatment of the subject (Mammarella et al., 2019b).

Developing a Mathematical Mindset

Boaler's (2016) work on mathematical mindsets, building on Dweck's (2006) psychological work regarding mindset, focuses on helping students develop a positive growth mindset for learning mathematics. Boaler contrasts a growth mindset with that of a fixed brain mindset. The fixed brain mindset is the belief that each person is born with a static intelligence – some gifted and some who will never be able to learn a given subject. Those with a growth mindset think they can learn, through hard work and persistence, any subject. They see mistakes as an opportunity to learn and they do not fear making them, nor do they allow struggle and mistakes to derail their goals. They are persistent in the face of difficulties.

Teachers can promote a growth mindset by communicating that brains grow when we struggle and learn from our mistakes, not when we immediately get an answer right (see Chapter 7). Battey and Stark (2009) encourage teachers to see misconceptions as an opportunity for mathematical learning, not an indication of a deficit. Teachers should foster a classroom culture of risk-taking. Boaler (2016) contends that numeracy, that is, flexibility with numbers, is critical for developing a mathematical mindset. Students must also be afforded the opportunity to grapple with rich mathematical tasks. Furthermore, teachers can help students make connections between different mathematical ideas, thus improving their numeracy.

Boaler sees the development of a **mathematical mindset** as a path to greater equity. Resilience is a hallmark of those who are successful both in math and in life more generally. Students must learn to channel anger into productive avenues that lead to perseverance, tenacity, and resilience, exhibiting an attitude of 'I've got something to prove! I'll show them.' *The Common Core State Standards for*

Mathematics lists perseverance first among the mathematical practices for a reason (*CCSSM*, 2010a). A critical goal for teachers is to promote this 'overcomer's mindset' despite challenges, be they neurological differences, bias and prejudice, or difficult circumstances. Research has shown a 'stable and dependable relationship with an adult' is the most important factor in students' ability to develop resilience (Persyn & Valbrun-Pope, 2020, slide 23). The first step in engendering this resilience is for teachers to believe their students can learn well. The research on the impact of teacher expectations is compelling, particularly for students living in poverty (Baker et al., 2015; Good et al., 2018; Hinnant, O'Brien, & Ghazarian, 2009; Sorhagen, 2013; Timmermans, Rubie-Davies, & Rjosk, 2018).

Math Recovery as a Vehicle for Improved Equity of Access to Quality Educational Opportunities

As teachers develop a thorough understanding of the Learning Framework in Number and the Guiding Principles of Math Recovery pedagogy, subtle but powerful transformations occur. The following is a composite protocol typical of discussions that occur in awareness sessions about Math Recovery with both teachers and parents:

Teacher (T):   How many of you are fluent in Spanish? [2 of 29 raise their hands. Indicating those two,] T says: For the next few minutes, you are not allowed to respond orally unless I ask you to.

T: I would like for you to do a little experiment with me. How many of you can count to ten in Spanish? [Nearly all raise their hands.] Sesame Street, right? Let's do it together. [Participants all (27 non-Spanish speakers) chorally count to ten in Spanish with near 100% participation and accuracy.]

T: You did that very well with a high degree of fluency. Now, let's start at *diez* and count to *uno*. [Participants (27 non-Spanish speakers) chorally produce *diez* and then pause, one voice leads to produce *nueve, ocho*, down to *uno*, pausing for a second or two between each number.]

T: What happened? You guys were really facile producing the forward number word sequence from *uno* to *diez*. Why can't you do it backward?

P1:   I've never done it before!

P2:   I just have rote knowledge of counting to ten in Spanish. I don't really know what the sounds mean.

T: What would you need to do in order to be able to develop facility with the backward number word sequence?

P3:   Practice a whole lot!

T: Hmmm. Let's try this. I am going to ask you a question. Give me a thumbs up [holds thumb up at mid-chest] when you have a response, but don't respond out loud. You two can participate in this [indicating the two participants fluent in Spanish].

T:	Ready? What number comes right after *cinco*? [Three participants immediately raise a thumb. After about 2 seconds a couple others begin raising a thumb until all participants raise a thumb after about 6 seconds.]
T:	Okay, we all have a response now. I was watching you. I noticed some interesting variation in response time. Did any of you notice anything?
P4:	Yeah, some raised their thumbs right away, and it took me forever!
T:	Indeed. I noticed that these two [indicates fluent Spanish speakers] immediately raised a thumb before the word *cinco* had finished coming out of my mouth. Others of you took up to 6 seconds. What's going on there?
P3:	That wasn't fair – they speak Spanish!
T:	What do you mean?
P3:	I was having to count in my head to work it out.
T:	I see. How many of you needed to do some counting to work out the answer? [The majority of the participants raise their hands.] How many of you started with *uno*? [More than half raise their hands.] How many of you started with a number other than *uno*? [Several raise their hands.]
P5:	I started with *cuatro*.
T:	Why?
P5:	I already know *uno, dos, tres,* but I wasn't sure about the order after that.
T:	How long did it take you to work out an answer?
P5:	I don't know, a second or two?
T:	What would have happened if I had allowed our Spanish speakers to shout out an answer as soon as they knew it or if I had called on one of them as soon as their thumb went up? What would have happened to our non-Spanish speakers?
P6:	I would have stopped working on it.
T:	Indeed. I would have **stolen** your ability to think and work on the problem. Wait-time is critical to give all students an opportunity to think, be they students with disabilities, English learners, or reticent participators. [The discussion then went on to discuss the Learning Framework in Number with respect to Number Word Sequences.]

In this protocol, one can easily see how issues of equity naturally arise in a conversation about Math Recovery methods such as the Guiding Principles of Instruction and Key Elements of Instruction (a detailed discussion of these critical ideas is contained in *LFIN*). We argue that teachers make subtle changes in their practice after participating in Math Recovery professional development such as increasing wait-time in order to promote the eighth Guiding Principle, Encouraging Sustained Thinking and Reflection (see Chapter 3). We further contend that these changes are not limited to the instruction of mathematics but carry over into the instruction of other subjects, becoming normative teacher practices. This simple change in teacher practice of increased wait-time becomes a powerful vehicle to promote equitable access to education by all learners. Similarly, the Learning Framework in Number allows teachers to understand how students develop critical ideas of numeracy. This knowledge, coupled with dynamic assessments and a bank of teaching procedures, allows teachers to capitalize on student assets and provide targeted instruction to address areas of weakness. When teachers pitch instruction just at the students' cutting edge, the students are more likely to be successful, which leads to greater success and enjoyment of the subject. This can have a powerful effect on improving attitudes toward mathematics and lowering or preventing the development of debilitating mathematics anxiety. Although improving attitudes toward mathematics and lowering mathematics anxiety do not address all the issues raised in this chapter, they are tools for supporting students with the special needs that have been discussed.

Conclusion

This chapter does not constitute a comprehensive treatment of any of these very important topics. Nor does it contain an exhaustive list of other students who have special educational needs. Rather, it is intended to raise awareness, engender dialog, and point toward sources of more information. Attending to issues that impact environment and relationships is critical to set the stage for educators to be successful applying the Guiding Principles of Math Recovery (see Chapter 3 for a detailed discussion of the Guiding Principles). Becoming a more constructivist teacher and pedagogical engineer who skillfully wields principles of dynamic assessment and targeted teaching procedures is a pedagogical journey fraught with challenges, but the success of all students depends on our progress. With diligence and care, we can help all students develop a profound understanding of numeracy that will form a solid foundation for their future mathematical endeavors.

Note

1. The authors acknowledge the limitations of this term in that it does not acknowledge indigenous roots and can be traced to colonial structures of oppression. It is not our intention to offend or exclude, but we find ourselves lacking a more inclusive term.

Glossary

Acalculia – acquired dyscalculia.

Accessibility – the extent to which individuals with special needs may fully participate in activities and access places.

Accommodation – in a Piagetian sense, a change in thinking and reasoning as a result of organizing new experiences or information.

Accommodations – affordances offered to students with special needs that grant them access to assessment and instructional tasks that would otherwise be inaccessible due to their disability or special need. Verbatim reading and dictation are examples of accommodations frequently given during written assessment.

Addends – the quantities being added together in the operation of addition. In the equation 2 + 3 = 5, 2 and 3 are the addends.

ADHD – Attention Deficit Hyperactivity Disorder.

Algorithm – a step-by-step procedure to complete a task. In arithmetic, this refers to a written procedure used to complete multi-digit operations. Algorithms may be considered standard or alternative.

Arrow cards – cards used to draw attention to the value of each place in multi-digit numbers (Figure G.1). Having each place in a different color adds additional scaffolding support to the materials. Removing the color scaffolding (that is, all card on white background) provides less support.

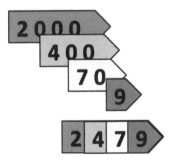

Figure G.1 Arrow cards in color

Source: Wright et al. (2012)

Augmentative and Alternative Communication (AAC) – a system of communication used to replace or supplement speech and/or writing.

Automated structures – cognitive systems for assimilating, or making meaning, of a mathematical situation.

Behaviorism – the belief that changing students' observable behavior (that is, through training) is all that is required to change their understanding. Behaviorists subscribe to behaviorism.

Bias – a belief, either positive or negative, about an individual that likely impacts the perceptions of the holder and the treatment of the other individual. Biases may be either explicitly stated or implicitly held notions of which the individual may be unaware.

Bundling Sticks – a setting in which craft sticks gathered into groups of ten and loose units are used to model numbers (Figure G.2). Ten bundles are often bound together to form a mega bundle of ten 10s or 100.

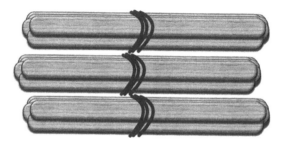

Figure G.2   Three bundles

Source: Wright et al. (2012)

Cardinality Principle – the notion that the last number word said when counting a collection of objects indicates the number of items in the collection.

Central executive – the central component of working memory and executive function.

Choice problems – the same task posed to all students with different number choices.

Cognitive demand – the relative load (sequences of information or actions) placed on working memory while solving a task.

Color coding – the judicious use of color to draw attention to particular aspects of a setting.

Common Core State Standards for Mathematics (CCSSM) – a standards document commissioned by a group of US state governors in an attempt to develop a rigorous, consistent national curriculum in the United States.

Composite unit – a unit made up of other units (for example, 7 as a unit of seven units of 1).

Conceptual understanding – mathematical idea that must be constructed by each individual such as strategies for adding and subtracting.

Constructivism – the belief that students construct their knowledge through their actions and experiences and use those constructions to organize the worlds they experience. Constructivists subscribe to constructivism.

Conventions of mathematics – socially constructed conventions of mathematics can only be known if one is informed of the convention (for example, the names of numerals).

Culturally responsive teaching – pioneered by Ladson-Billings (1994), intentionally treats diversity as an asset. 'Culturally responsive educators… consider students' diversity as a strength in the classroom rather than a challenge that they must overcome, and they see the incorporation of cultural perspectives as a necessary educational commitment' (Peterek & Adams, 2009, p. 151).

Cutting edge – the upper edge of the student's conceptual understanding that constitutes the optimal zone in which to develop new learning (that is, the child's zone of proximal development or ZPD).

Decuple – the numbers that are multiples of ten (that is, 20, 60, 80, 90, 120, 480) as opposed to a decade which is ten numbers in the sequence.

Difference – the remaining portion or amount obtained after the operation of subtraction. In the equation $7 - 5 = 2$, 2 is the difference.

Differentiation – proactively tailoring instruction to students' mathematical thinking while developing a cohesive classroom community.

Dimensions of Progressive Mathematization/Dimensions of Mathematizing – give teachers a roadmap for increasing or decreasing the rigor of problems presented to students by following the various dimensions and are discussed in Chapters 3 and 7.

Disembedding units – separating a segment of a number from a larger number, or a part from a whole, without destroying the structure of or relationship to the larger number or whole. This is a critical concept needed to understand fractions.

Distancing the instructional setting – posing tasks that are contextually removed from the setting in which students first learned to solve them.

Diversity – the state of having individuals who differ on characteristics (for example, from varying backgrounds, races, ethnicities, genders, social status, native languages, disabilities, and the like).

Dyscalculia – a specific learning disability affecting performance in mathematics in approximately 5% of students.

Dysgraphia – a specific learning disability that impacts a person's ability to write.

Dyslexia – a specific learning disability that impacts a person's ability to read.

Empty number line (ENL) – a model developed in the Netherlands (Beishuizen, 1999) consisting of a simple line and arcs to notate jump strategies used to solve addition and subtraction tasks (Figure G.3).

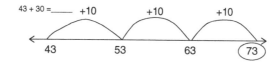

Figure G.3 ENL sample

English learners (ELs) – any individual, regardless of ethnicity, who is learning English regardless of how many languages they already speak. English language learners (ELLs) and emerging bilinguals are similar terms.

Equity – the state of having equal opportunities to learn. To provide equal opportunities for all does not imply that everyone's experience will be the same. To provide equal opportunities means to provide appropriate support and resources, and people need different supports and resources depending on their experiences, backgrounds, etc. Equity also involves creating an environment in which issues of identity and power or agency are addressed (for a detailed discussion see Gutiérrez, 2013). 'Issues of equity' is often used to denote a lack of equitable opportunity to learn.

Executive function – the cognitive resource used to consciously solve problems; it includes working memory.

Extending the range of numbers – expanding the set of numbers that might be used in a task (for example, asking students to work with fractions that have larger denominators).

Figurative materials – physical objects a student can see and manipulate (for example, drawings and manipulatives). The term figurative images refers to mental images of the figurative materials.

Finger patterns – using fingers to display a given quantity. Finger patterns may be in standard five plus patterns, double patterns, or non-standard patterns.

Flashing – the instructional technique of allowing the student to briefly see a setting before obscuring it. Subitizing patterns are often briefly flashed to promote mental figural images.

Folding back – returning to strategies and settings that make sense to the student.

Formalizing – building on students' intuitions by connecting them to the language and notation of the broader mathematics community.

Fragmenting – breaking a whole apart into pieces.

Frontal lobe – the foremost part of the neocortex (the outer region of the brain unique to mammals); it is heavily involved in executive functioning.

Frontal-to-parietal shift – a change in neural activity from the frontal lobe to the parietal lobe as students develop mathematical structures.

Grounded habituation – the development of greater fluency and reasoning in solving problems, over time.

IDEA – Individuals with Disabilities Education Act, the US federal legislation that governs education for students with disabilities.

IEP – Individualized Education Program, a legally binding document as defined in the IDEA US federal legislation which details education goals, accommodations, and modifications for the students which must be afforded to the student. The document is often referred to as an IEP plan at the school level.

Inclusion – the practice of educating individuals with special needs in settings with same-age peers who do not have special needs.

Intraparietal sulcus – the valley between the upper and lower regions of the parietal lobe, associated with hand–eye coordination and numerical reasoning.

Iterating – making identical and connected copies of a unit.

Jump strategy – strategy for solving multi-digit addition and subtraction problems in which one quantity is kept in its entirety and the other is decomposed into quantities that are added or subtracted in a series of jumps.

Learning Framework in Number for the Classroom (LFIN-C) – provides a series of developmental progressions for the domains of early number: Number Words and Numerals, Addition and Subtraction to 20, Addition and Subtraction to 100, Multiplication and Division, and Fractions (Figure G.4).

Manipulatives – settings that are used to illustrate mathematical concepts, typically with a physical material, that students and teachers may manipulate. Bundling sticks is an example of a manipulative.

Marginalized populations – groups who have been prevented historically from having equitable access to education and other opportunities accessible to the majority.

Mathematics anxiety – 'feelings of tension and anxiety that interfere with the manipulation of numbers and the solving of mathematical problems in a wide variety of ordinary life and academic situations' (Richardson & Suinn, 1972, p. 551). In the United States the term math anxiety is more frequently used.

Mathematical mindset – focuses on helping students develop a positive growth mindset for learning mathematics (Boaler, 2016).

Mathematical objects – concepts that a student can act upon, such as numbers, that are themselves products of prior activity – actions coordinated within reversible and composable systems.

Mathematical self-efficacy – self-confidence to learn and perform mathematics.

McKinney–Vento legislation – US federal legislation that mandates each public school district to establish a liaison for homeless students, and states must ensure schools provide these students with access to free, appropriate education **(US Department of Education, 2017)**.

Mental actions – actions that can be performed in imagination, such as partitioning a whole into equal parts.

Mental number line – 'The mental number line describes a spatial representation of number magnitude along an analog number line which is assumed to be activated automatically whenever we encounter a number' **(Link, Moeller, Huber, & Fischer, 2013, p. 75)**.

THE LEARNING FRAMEWORK IN NUMBER

for the classroom

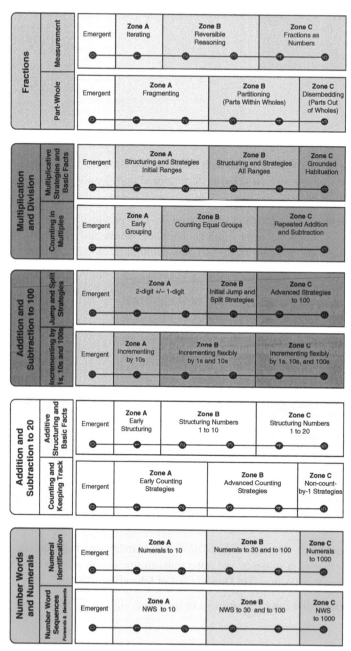

Figure G.4 Learning Framework in Number for the Classroom (as Figure 1.1)

Source: Ellemor-Collins et al. (forthcoming)

Micro-adjusting – 'Making small moment-by-moment adjustments in interactive teaching which are informed by one's observation of student responses.' (*TNC* p. 209)

Minuend – the initial quantity before commencing subtraction. In the equation 7 – 5 = 2, 7 is the minuend.

Modifications – changes made to what a student is expected to learn.

Neocortex – the outer region of the brain, unique to mammals.

Neoindigenous – term coined by Christopher Emdin referring to urban students of color, used metaphorically to draw attention to similarities between their educational experiences and those of indigenous students of the past.

Non-count-by-ones strategies – a collection of strategies that employ units other than one to solve problems. Non-count-by-ones strategies include the use of doubles, near doubles, making-a-ten, compensation, constant differences, and any other strategy that does not involve using counting by ones.

Notating – inscriptions, such as symbols, students use to represent mathematical objects or actions.

Number Word After (NWA) – the number that comes immediately after a number in a forward number word sequence. For example, 'five' is the number word after four when counting by ones.

Number Word Before (NWB) – the number that immediately precedes a number in a forward number word sequence. For example, 'four' is the number word before five when counting by ones.

Numeracy – the ability to flexibly use arithmetic to solve problems and connect mathematical ideas.

Numeral – the written symbol(s) (for example, 498, XII) that represent(s) a number.

Numeral identification – the student generates the name of a numeral when shown the symbol in isolation.

Numeral recognition – the student identifies the requested numeral when presented with a field of numerals in a non-sequential order.

Numeral roll – an instructional setting constructed similarly to a measuring tape, with the sequence of numerals, typically from 1 to 120 on one side and a partially filled 120 × 1 grid on the other (Figure G.5); available from www.mathrecovery.org/store

Figure G.5 Numeral roll

Numeral track – an instructional setting constructed of cardboard with a base and five hinged doors that can be opened to reveal a segment of a number word sequence below; available from www.mathrecovery.org/store

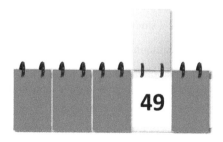

Figure G.6   Numeral track segment

One-to-one correspondence – the assigning of one and only one number word to each item when counting a set of items.

Parallel tasks – a set of two or three different problems designed to target different levels of thinking yet address closely related mathematical ideas (Small & Lin, 2010).

Parietal lobe – the region of the neocortex toward the back of the brain, responsible for numerical and spatial reasoning.

Partitioning – the mental action of breaking a continuous whole into equal parts.

Perturbation – an experience that does not align with one's current understanding that can lead to accommodation.

Prefrontal cortex – the foremost area of the frontal lobe, largely responsible for executive functioning.

Premotor cortex – the area of the frontal lobe that sits just in front of the sensorimotor cortex.

Productive struggle – consciously working through a difficult problem in a manner that leads to new ideas or strategies.

Progress monitoring – a systematic means of measuring progress of students with special needs.

Reality Pedagogy – a culturally responsive pedagogy designed by Christopher Emdin which leverages cultural aspects common among urban students of color to better meet their educational needs.

Recapitulating – the activity of teachers summarizing or highlighting strategies used by students.

Rehearsal mode – time spent with instructional activities intended to afford students the opportunity to build facility with skills through repeated practice (that is, rehearsal) after conceptual understanding is developed. Games provide a setting that allow students to rehearse previously gained skills.

Re-presentation – a mental replay of previous mathematical activity.

Residue (notational) – a notation that remains in sight to allow for further contemplation after the classroom discussion has moved away from the problem.

Reversible reasoning – the ability to perform mental actions in both directions – from a problem to a solution and vice versa.

Reversible structures – the organization of mental actions within a system for reversing them (for example, partitioning and iterating are part of a reversible structure for partitioning wholes into parts and reproducing the whole by iterating one of those parts).

Re-voice – rephrase or repeat previously stated comments, particularly to see clarity.

Scaffolding – the series of supports a teacher provides and fades to enable students to experience success in developing new learning.

Screening – an assessment or instructional technique in which an opaque screen or cover is used to obscure objects in a collection. This is used to assess for or promote the development of figurative images.

Segmenting – using a unit length to measure off another length.

Self-efficacy – see mathematical self-efficacy.

Sensorimotor activity – observable behavior.

Sensorimotor cortex – the region of the neocortex between the frontal and parietal lobes, at the top of the head; responsible for initiating physical actions and receiving signals back from the body.

Sheltered Instruction Observation Protocol (SIOP) – a system of instruction commonly used with English Learners first developed by Jana Echevarria (Echevarria & Short, 2011).

Socio-mathematical norms – the behavioral norms established to govern inter-personal interactions and intra-personal behaviors during mathematics instruction.

Spatial–numerical reasoning – manipulating numbers and objects in space.

Spatial–numerical transformations – manipulating objects in space by mental actions such as partitioning, rotating and reflecting.

Split strategy – strategy for solving two-digit and greater addition and subtraction problems in which each addend is decomposed into tens and ones (Figure G.7). Operations occur on each place individually, regrouping to or from a higher place as needed, prior to the entire quantity being recomposed to determine the final sum or difference.

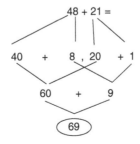

Figure G.7 Split example

Structuring numbers – establishing relationships between numbers, such as 30 as three 10s.

Subitizing – from the Italian *subito* meaning suddenly or instantaneously. It is the identification of a small quantity of items or dots without counting.

Subtrahend – in subtraction, the quantity being removed from the initial quantity. In the equation 7 − 5 = 2, 5 is the subtrahend.

Sum – in addition, the final quantity that is obtained after the operation of addition. In the equation 2 + 3 = 5, 5 is the sum. *Note*: In the UK this is sometimes used to indicate the quantity found in any operation.

Systemically underserved population – term popularized by the New Teacher Center to indicate groups who have been denied equitable access to education due to systemic racism prevalent in education such as underfunding urban schools when compared to suburban schools.

Teaching and Learning Cycle – a framework developed by Math Recovery that includes a series of questions designed to help teachers meet the instructional needs of students (Figure G.8).

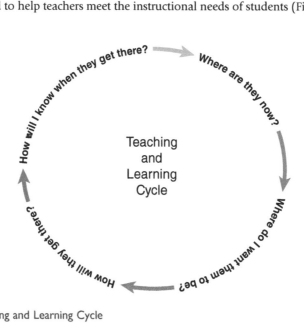

Figure G.8   Teaching and Learning Cycle

Source: Wright et al. (2006b, p. 52)

Tiering instruction – designing different sequences of problems and activities for different groups of students based on conjectures about what will best support students' learning needs (Pierce & Adams, 2005; Tomlinson, 2005).

Underserved groups or populations – groups who have been prevented historically from having equitable access to education and other opportunities accessible to the majority.

Unitizing – attending to an aspect of experience (for example, a collection of objects or a span of time) as a unit of 1.

Units – discrete 1s or measurement units.

Units coordination – distribution and insertion of units across other units, establishing relationships between two different levels of units (for example, a 1-to-7 relationship between 1/7 and the whole).

Universal screener – a brief assessment administered to all students for the purpose of identifying students who may need intervention.

Wait-time – a period of silence used to allow students to process concepts and formulate responses.

Working memory – the cognitive capacity to hold in mind a sequence of information or actions and manipulate them.

References

Alkahtani, M. A., & Kheiralla, S. A. (2016). Background of individual education plans (IEPs) policy in some countries: A review. *Journal of Education and Practice, 7*(24), 15–26. Retrieved from https://files.eric.ed.gov/fulltext/EJ1112737.pdf

Alwell, M., & Cobb, B. (2009). Functional life skills curricular interventions for youth with disabilities. *Career Development for Exceptional Individuals, 32*(2), 82–93.

Ansari, D., & Dhital, B. (2006). Age-related changes in the activation of the intraparietal sulcus during nonsymbolic magnitude processing: An event-related functional magnetic resonance imaging study. *Journal of Cognitive Neuroscience, 18*(11), 1820–1828.

Apps, M., & Carter, M. (2006). When all is said and done, more is said than done: Research examining constructivist instruction for students with special needs. *Australasian Journal of Special Education, 30*(2), 107–125.

Ashcraft, M. H. (2019). Models of math anxiety. In I. C. Mammarella, S. Caviola, & A. D. Dowker (Eds.), *Mathematics anxiety: What is known and what is still to be understood* (pp. 1–19). London: Routledge.

Ashcraft, M. H., & Kirk, E. P. (2001). The relationship among working memory, math anxiety, and performance. *Journal of Experimental Psychology: General, 130*(2), 224–237.

Ashcraft, M. H., & Moore, A. M. (2009). Mathematics anxiety and the affective drop in performance. *Journal of Psychoeducational Assessment, 27*(3), 197–205. doi: 10.1177/0734282908330580

Aviles, A. M. (2019). *Towards justice: Homelessness, education policy and race.* Paper presented at the University of Delaware: Scholar in the library lunchtime lectures on May 8, 2019, Newark, DE.

Aydeniz, F. (2018). *Elementary pre-service teachers distributive reasoning and proportional reasoning.* Unpublished doctoral dissertation, Indiana University, Bloomington.

Babtie, P., & Emerson, J. (2015). Understanding dyscalculia and numeracy difficulties: A guide for parents, teachers, and other professionals. London: Jessica Kingsley.

Baker, C. N., Tichovolsky, M. H., Kupersmidt, J. B., Voegler-Lee, M. E., & Arnold, D. H. (2015). Teacher (mis)perceptions of preschoolers' academic skills: Predictors and associations with longitudinal outcomes. *Journal of Educational Psychology, 107*(3), 805–820.

Bartell, T., Wager, A., Edwards, A., Battey, D. S., Foote, M., & Spencer, J. (2017). Research commentary: Toward a framework for research linking equitable teaching with the standards of mathematical practice. *Journal for Research in Mathematics Education, 48*(1), 7–21.

Battey, D. S., & Stark, M. (2009). Inequitable classroom practices: Diagnosing misconceptions as inability in mathematics: 15. In D. Y. White & J. S. Spitzer (Eds.), *Mathematics for every student: Responding to diversity: Grades Pre-K–5* (pp. 167–177). Reston, VA: National Council of Teachers of Mathematics.

Behrend, J. L. (2003). Learning-disabled students make sense of mathematics. *Teaching Children Mathematics, 9*(5), 269.

Beishuizen, M. (1999). The empty number line as a new model. In I. Thompson (Ed.), *Issues in teaching numeracy in primary schools* (pp. 157–168). Philadelphia: Open University Press.

Bell, M. A., & Fox, N. A. (1997). Individual differences in object permanence performance at 8 months: Locomotor experience and brain electrical activity. *Developmental Psychobiology: The Journal of the International Society for Developmental Psychobiology, 31*(4), 287–297.

Biddlecomb, B., & Olive, J. (2000). JavaBars [Computer software]. Retrieved June 4, 2002 from http://math.coe.uga.edu/olive/welcome.html#Software%20developed%20through%20the%20 Fractions%20Project

Bielaczyc, K., Kapur, M., & Collins, A. (2013). Cultivating a community of learners in K-12 classrooms. In C. E. Hmelo-Silver, A. M. O'Donnell, C. Chan, & C. A. Chinn (Eds.), *International handbook of collaborative learning* (pp. 233–249). New York: Taylor & Francis. doi: 10.4324/9780203837290.ch13

Bisland, A. (2001). Mentoring: An educational alternative for gifted students. *Gifted Child Today, 24*(4), 22–64. doi: 10.4219/gct-2001-550

Boaler, J. (2014). Research suggests timed tests cause math anxiety. *Teaching Children Mathematics, 20*(8), 469–474.

Boaler, J. (2016). *Mathematical mindsets: Unleashing students' potential through creative math, inspiring messages and innovative thinking.* San Francisco: Jossey-Bass.

Boaler, J., Wiliam, D., & Brown, M. (2000). Students' experiences of ability grouping – disaffection, polarisation and the construction of failure. *British Educational Research Journal, 26*(5), 631–648. doi: 10.1080/713651583

Booth, J. L., & Siegler, R. S. (2008). Numerical magnitude representations influence arithmetic learning. *Child Development, 79*(4), 1016–1031.

Bouck, E. C., Park, J., & Nickell, B. (2016a). Using the concrete-representational-abstract approach to support students with intellectual disability to solve change-making problems. *Research in Developmental Disabilities, 60*, 24–36.

Bouck, E. C., Satsangi, R., & Bartlett, W. (2016b). Comparing a number line and audio prompts in supporting price comparison by students with intellectual disability. *Research in Developmental Disabilities, 53–54*, 342–357.

Boyd, B., & Bargerhuff, M. E. (2009). Mathematics education and special education: Searching for common ground and the implications for teacher education. *Mathematics Teacher Education and Development, 11*, 54–67.

Bradley, K. J. (2019). *English learner advancement in AVMR structuring.* Masters of Arts, Minnesota State University Moorhead. Retrieved from https://red.mnstate.edu/thesis

Brighton, C. M., & Hertberg, H. L. (2004). Reconstructing the vision: Teachers' responses to the invitation to change. *Research in Middle Level Education Online, 27*(2), 1–20.

Brown, L. D., Branston, M. B., Hamre-Nietupski, S., Pumpian, I., Certo, N., & Gruenewald, L. (1979). A strategy for developing chronological-age-appropriate and functional curricular content for severely handicapped adolescents and young adults. *Journal of Special Education, 13*(1), 81–90.

Bruner, J. S. (1977). *The process of education.* Cambridge, MA: Harvard University Press.

Brunosson, A., Brante, G., Sepp, H., & Sydner, Y. M. (2014). To use a recipe – not a piece of cake: Students with mild intellectual disabilities' use of recipes in home economics. *International Journal of Consumer Studies, 38*, 412–418. doi: 10.1111/ijcs.12109

Buccino, G., Binkofski, F., Fink, G. R., Fadiga, L., Fogassi, L., Gallese, V., ... & Freund, H. J. (2001). Action observation activates premotor and parietal areas in a somatotopic manner: An fMRI study. *European Journal of Neuroscience, 13*(2), 400–404.

Bugden, S., & Ansari, D. (2016). Probing the nature of deficits in the 'Approximate Number System' in children with persistent developmental dyscalculia. *Developmental Science, 19*(5), 817–833.

Bull, R., & Scerif, G., (2001). Executive functioning as a predictor of children's mathematics ability: Inhibition, switching, and working memory. *Developmental Neuropsychology, 19*, 273–293.

Butler, F. M., Miller, S. P., Lee, K., & Pierce, T. (2001). Teaching mathematics to students with mild-to-moderate mental retardation: A review of the literature. *Mental Retardation, 39*(1), 20–31.

Butterworth, B., Varma, S., & Laurillard, D. (2011). Dyscalculia: From brain to education. *Science, 332*, 1049–1053. doi: 10.1126/science.1201536

Butterworth, B., & Walsh, V. (2011). Neural basis of mathematical cognition. *Current Biology, 21*(16), R618–R621. doi: 10.1016/j.cub.2011.07.005

CAST (2018). Universal Design for Learning Guidelines version 2.2. Retrieved from http://udlguide lines.cast.org/

Caviola, S., Mammarella, I. C., & Kovas, Y. (2019). Math anxiety in children with and without mathematical difficulties: The role of gender and genetic factors. In I. C. Mammarella, S. Caviola, & A. D. Dowker (Eds.), *Mathematics anxiety: What is known and what is still to be understood* (pp. 141–155). London: Routledge.

CCSSM. National Governors Association Center for Best Practices and Council of Chief State School Officers. (2010a). Common Core State Standards for mathematics. Retrieved from http://www. corestandards .org/assets/CCSSI_Math%20Standards.pdf

CCSSM. National Governors Association Center for Best Practices and Council of Chief State School Officers. (2010b). Common core state standards for mathematics. Retrieved from www.corestand ards.org/Math/Content/5/NF/

Clements, D. H., & Battista, M. T. (1990). Constructivist learning and teaching. *Arithmetic Teacher, 38*(1), 34–35.

Cobb, P. (1988). The tensions between theories of learning and instruction in mathematics education. *Educational Psychologist, 23*(2), 87–103. doi: 10.1207/s15326985ep2302_2

Cobb, P. (2005). Where is the mind? A coordination of sociocultural and cognitive constructivist perspectives. In C. T. Fosnot (Ed.), *Constructivism: Theory, perspectives, and practice* (pp. 39–57). New York: Teachers College Press.

Cobb, P., Boufi, A., McClain, K. J., & Whitenack, J. W. (1997). Reflective discourse and collective reflection. *Journal for Research in Mathematics Education, 28*(3), 258–277.

Cobb, P., Stephan, M. L., McClain, K. J., & Gravemeijer, K. P. E. (2001). Participating in classroom mathematical practices. *Journal of the Learning Sciences, 10*(1–2), 113–163.

Cohen, M. S., Kosslyn, S. M., Breiter, H. C., DiGirolamo, G. J., Thompson, W. L., Anderson, A. K., … & Belliveau, J. W. (1996). Changes in cortical activity during mental rotation: A mapping study using functional MRI. *Brain, 119*(1), 89–100.

Collins, B. C., Karl, J., Riggs, L., Galloway, C. C., & Hager, K. D. (2010). Teaching core content with real-life applications to secondary students with moderate and severe disabilities. *Teaching Exceptional Children, 43*(1), 52–59.

Copur-Gencturk, Y., Cimpian, J. R., Lubienski, S. T., & Thacker, I. (2020). Teachers' bias against the mathematical ability of female, black, and Hispanic students. *Educational Researcher, 49*(1), 30–43.

CEC [Council for Exceptional Children] (2015). Ethical Principles and Professional Practice Standards for Special Educators. Retrieved from https://www.cec.sped.org/Standards/Ethical-Principles-and-Practice-Standards

Davis, R. B., Maher, C. A., & Noddings, N. (1990a). Introduction: Constructivist views on the teaching and learning of mathematics. In R. B. Davis, C. A. Maher, & N. Noddings (Eds.), *Constructivist views on the teaching and learning of mathematics: Journal for Research in Mathematics Education: Monograph number 4* (pp. 1–3). Reston, VA: National Council of Teachers of Mathematics.

Davis, R. B., Maher, C. A., & Noddings, N. (Eds.). (1990b). *Constructivist views on the teaching and learning of mathematics: Journal for Research in Mathematics Education: Monograph number 4*. Reston, VA: National Council of Teachers of Mathematics.

de Araujo, Z., Roberts, S. A., Willey, C., & Zahner, W. (2018). English learners in K-12 mathematics education: A review of the literature. *Review of Educational Research, 88*(6), 879–919.

Denny, P. J., & Test, D. W. (1995). Using the one-more-than technique to teach money counting to individuals with moderate mental retardation: A systematic replication. *Education and Treatment of Children, 18*(4), 422–432.

Department of Employment, Education, Training and Youth Affairs. (1997). *Numeracy = everyone's business*. The Report of the Numeracy Education Strategy Development Conference. Adelaide: Australian Association of Mathematics Teachers.

Desoete, A., Ceulemans, A., Roeyers, H., & Huylebroeck, A. (2009). Subitizing or counting as possible screening variables for learning disabilities in mathematics education or learning? *Educational Research Review, 4*(1), 55–66. doi: 10.1016/j.edurev.2008.11.003

Desoete, A., Roeyers, H., & De Clercq, A. (2004). Children with mathematics learning disabilities in Belgium. *Journal of Learning Disabilities, 37*(1), 50.

DiAngelo, R. (2018). *White fragility: Why it's so hard for white people to talk about racism*. Boston, MA: Beacon Press.

Doabler, C. T., Baker, S. K., Kostky, D. B., Smolkowski, K., Clarke, B., Miller, S., & Fien, H. (2015). Examining the association between explicit mathematics instruction and student mathematics achievement. *Elementary School Journal, 115*(3), 303–333.

Dowker, A. D. (2009). *What works for children with mathematical difficulties? The effectiveness of intervention schemes*. Department for Children, Schools and Families. Retrieved from www.mathsrecovery. org.uk/doc/Dowker-what-works%202009.pdf

Dowker, A. D. (Ed.) (2019). *Mathematics anxiety and performance*. London: Routledge.

Dowker, A. D., Sarkar, A., & Looi, C. Y. (2016). Mathematics anxiety: What have we learned in 60 years? *Frontiers in Psychology, 7*, Article 508.

Drijvers, P. H. M. (2003). *Learning algebra in a computer algebra environment*. PhD dissertation, Utrecht University.

Duhaney, L. M. G., & Duhaney, D. C. (2000). Assistive technology: Meeting the needs of learners with disabilities. *International Journal of Instructional Media, 27*(4), 393–401.

Dweck, Carol S. (2006). *Mindset: The new psychology of success: How we can learn to fulfill our potential*. New York: Ballantine Books.

Dyer, E. B., & Sherin, M. G. (2016). Instructional reasoning about interpretations of student thinking that supports responsive teaching in secondary mathematics. *Zentralblatt für Didaktik der Mathematik*. doi: 10.1007/s11858-015-0740-1

Dymond, S. K., & Orelove, F. P. (2001). What constitutes effective curricula for students with severe disabilities? *Exceptionality, 9*(3), 109–122. doi: 10.1207/ S15327035EX0903_2

Echevarria, J., & Short, D. (2011). The SIOP model: A professional development framework for a comprehensive school-wide intervention. *CreateBriefs*. Retrieved from http://www.cal.org/create/publications/briefs/professional-development-framework.html

Ehrlich, S. B., Levine, S. C., & Goldin-Meadow, S. (2006). The importance of gesture in children's spatial reasoning. *Developmental Psychology, 42,* 1259–1268.

Ellemor-Collins, D., Kinsey, K., MacCarty, L. P., & Wright, R. J. (forthcoming). *Journey to numeracy: Mapping and guiding classroom number learning.* London: Corwin.

Ellemor-Collins, D., & Wright, R. J. (2008). Assessing student thinking about arithmetic. *Teaching Children Mathematics, 15*(September), 6.

Ellis, M. W. (2009). Moving from deficiencies to possibilities: Some thoughts on differentiation in the mathematics classroom: 14. In D. Y. White & J. S. Spitzer (Eds.), *Mathematics for every student: Responding to diversity: Grades Pre-K–5* (pp. 161–166). Reston, VA: National Council of Teachers of Mathematics.

Emdin, C. (2016). *For White Folks Who Teach in the Hood… and the Rest of Y'all Too: Reality pedagogy and urban education.* Boston, MA: Beacon Press.

Emdin, C. (2020). *Reality pedagogy to accelerate collective impact for equity in education: Presession C.* Paper presented at the Accelerate: Collective Impact for Equity in Education: New Teacher Center Symposium 2020, Atlanta, GA.

Eriksson, G. (2008). Arithmetical thinking in children attending special schools for the intellectually disabled. *Journal of Mathematical Behavior, 27,* 1–10.

Eysenck, M. W., & Calvo, M. G. (1992). Anxiety and performance: The processing efficiency theory. *Cognition & Emotion, 6*(6), 409–434.

Faragher, R., & Brown, R. I. (2005). Numeracy for adults with Down syndrome: It's a matter of quality of life. *Journal of Intellectual Disability Research, 49*(10), 761–765.

Fayol, M., Barrouillet, P., & Marinthe, C. (1998). Predicting arithmetical achievement from neuropsychological performance: A longitudinal study. *Cognition, 68,* B63–B70. doi: 10.1016/S0010-0277(98)00046-8

Featherstone, H., Crespo, S., Jilk, L. M., Oslund, J. A., Parks, A. N., & Wood, M. B. (2011). *Smarter together! Collaboration and equity in the elementary math classroom.* Reston, VA: National Council of Teachers of Mathematics.

Fischer, B., Gebhardt, C., & Hartnegg, K. (2008). Subitizing and visual counting in children with problems in acquiring basic arithmetic skills. *Optometry & Vision Development, 39*(1), 24–29.

Fischer, D., & Frey, N. (2014). *Better learning through structured teaching: A framework for the gradual release of responsibility* (2nd ed.). Alexandria, VA: ASCD.

Flores, A. (2007). Examining disparities in mathematics education: Achievement gap or opportunity gap? *The High School Journal, 91*(1), 29–42.

Franke, M. L., Carpenter, T. P., Levi, L., & Fennema, E. (2001). Capturing teachers' generative growth: A follow-up study of professional development in mathematics. *American Educational Research Journal, 38*(3), 653–689. doi: 10.3102/00028312038003653

Frankl, C. (2005). Managing individual education plans: Reducing the load of the special education needs coordinator. *Support for Learning, 20*(2), 77–82.

Furlong, M., McLoughlin, F., McGilloway, S., & Butterworth, B. (2015). Interventions to improve mathematical performance for children with dyscalculia (Protocol). *Cochrane Database of Systematic Reviews* (3). doi: 10.1002/14651858.CD012130

Furner, J. M., & Berman, B. T. (2003). Review of research: Math anxiety: *Overcoming a major obstacle to the improvement of student math performance. Childhood Education, 79*(3), 170–174.

Gamoran, A., & Hannigan, E. C. (2000). Algebra for everyone? Benefits of college-preparatory mathematics for students with diverse abilities in early secondary school. *Educational Evaluation and Policy Analysis, 22,* 241–254. doi: 10.3102/01623737022003241

Gavin, M. K., & NEAG Center for Gifted Education and Talent Development. (n.d.). Meeting the needs of talented elementary math students. Retrieved from https://gifted.uconn.edu/projectm3/m3_meeting_the_needs/#

Gearhart, M., & Saxe, G. B. (2014). Differentiated instruction in shared mathematical contexts. *Teaching Children Mathematics, 20*(7), 426–435. doi: 10.5951/teacchilmath.20.7.0426

Gersten, R. M., Chard, D. J., Jayanthi, M., Baker, S. K., Morphy, P., & Flojo, J. R. (2009). Mathematics instruction for students with learning disabilities: A meta-analysis of instructional components. *Review of Educational Research, 79*(3), 1202–1242. doi: 10.3102/0034654309334431

Gifford, S., & Rockliffe, F. (2007). *In search of dyscalculia.* Paper presented at the Proceedings of the British Society for Research into Learning Mathematics, University of Manchester.

Gillum, J. (2012). Dyscalculia: Issues for practice in educational psychology. *Educational Psychology in Practice, 28*(3), 287–297.

Ginsburg, H. P. (1997). Mathematics learning disabilities: A view from developmental psychology. *Journal of Learning Disabilities, 30*(1), 20–33.

Good, T. L., Sterzinger, N., & Lavigne, A. (2018). Expectation effects: Pygmalion and the initial 20 years of research. *Educational Research and Evaluation, 24*(3–5), 99–123. doi: 10.1080/13803611.2018.1548817

Gravemeijer, K. P. E. (1994). *Developing realistic mathematics education.* PhD dissertation, Utrecht University.

Gresalfi, M. S., & Lester, F. K. (2009). What's worth knowing in mathematics? In S. Tobias & T. M. Duffy (Eds.), *Constructivist instruction: Success or failure?* (pp. 264–290). New York: Routledge.

Grobecker, B. (1999). Mathematics reform and learning differences. *Learning Disability Quarterly, 22*(Winter), 43–58.

Gutiérrez, R. (2008). Research commentary: A 'gap-gazing' fetish in mathematics education? Problematizing research on the achievement gap. *Journal for Research in Mathematics Education, 39*(4), 357–364.

Gutiérrez, R. (Ed.) (2013). *Journal for Research in Mathematics Education: Special Equity Issue, 44*(1).

Hackenberg, A. J. (2010). Students' reasoning with reversible multiplicative relationships. *Cognition and Instruction, 28*(4), 383–432.

Hackenberg, A. J. (2013). The fractional knowledge and algebraic reasoning of students with the first multiplicative concept. *Journal of Mathematical Behavior, 32*(3), 538–563.

Hackenberg, A. J., Creager, M., & Eker, A. (2020). Teaching practices for differentiating mathematics instruction for middle school students. *Mathematical Thinking and Learning.* doi: 10.1080/10986065.2020.1731656

Hackenberg, A. J., & Lee, M. Y. (2015). Relationships between students' fractional knowledge and equation writing. *Journal for Research in Mathematics Education, 46*(2), 196–243. doi: 10.5951/jresematheduc.46.2.0196

Hackenberg, A. J., & Lee, M. Y. (2016). Students' distributive reasoning with fractions and unknowns. *Educational Studies in Mathematics, 93*(2), 245–263.

Hackenberg, A. J., Norton, A., & Wright, R. J. (2016). *Developing fractions knowledge.* London: Sage.

Hackenberg, A. J., & Tillema, E. S. (2009). Students' whole number multiplicative concepts: A critical constructive resource for fraction composition schemes. *Journal of Mathematical Behavior, 28*(1), 1–18. doi: 10.1016/j.jmathb.2009.04.004

Hammond, Z. (2017). Start with responsive. Retrieved from https://crtandthebrain.com/start-with-responsive/

Heacox, D. (2002). *Differentiating instruction in the regular classroom: How to read and teach all learners, grades 3–12*. Minneapolis, MN: Free Spirit.

Hembree, R. (1990). The nature, effects, and relief of mathematics anxiety. *Journal for Research in Mathematics Education, 21*(1), 33–46.

Herts, J. B., Beilock, S. L., & Levine, S. C. (2019). The role of parents' and teachers' math anxiety in children's math learning and attitudes. In I. C. Mammarella, S. Caviola, & A. D. Dowker (Eds.), *Mathematics anxiety: What is known and what is still to be understood* (pp. 190–210). London: Routledge.

Hinnant, J. B., O'Brien, M., & Ghazarian, S. R. (2009). The longitudinal relations of teacher expectations to achievement in the early school years. *Journal of Educational Psychology, 101*(3), 662–670.

Hockett, J. A. (2010). *The influence of lesson study on how teachers plan for, implement, and understand differentiated instruction*. Unpublished doctoral dissertation, University of Virginia.

Hoffer, W. W. (2012). *Minds on mathematics: Using math workshop to develop deep understanding in grades 4–8*. Portsmouth, NH: Heinemann.

Hogg, L. (2011). Funds of knowledge: An investigation of coherence within the literature. *Teaching and Teacher Education, 27*(3), 666–677. doi: 10.1016/j.tate.2010.11.005

Howard, A., Alliaga, A., Reese, E., Everett, M., & Robellard, M. (2020). *How can teachers better meet their students' needs? Presession.* Paper presented at the Accelerate: Collective Impact for Equity in Education: New Teacher Center Symposium 2020, Atlanta, GA.

Hubbard, E. M., Piazza, M., Pinel, P., & Dehaene, S. (2005). Interactions between number and space in parietal cortex. *Nature Reviews Neuroscience, 6*(6), 435.

Hume, K., & Carnahan, C. (2008). Steps for implementation: Structured work systems. Retrieved from https://csesa.fpg.unc.edu/sites/csesa.fpg.unc.edu/files/ebpbriefs/StructuredWorkSystems_Steps_0.pdf

Hunt, J., & Tzur, R. (2017). Where is difference? Processes of mathematical remediation through a constructivist lens. *Journal of Mathematical Behavior, 48*, 62–76.

Hunt, J. H., MacDonald, B. L., & Silva, J. (2019). Gina's mathematics: Thinking, tricks, or 'teaching'? *Journal of Mathematical Behavior, 56*, 100707. doi: 10.1016/j.jmathb.2019.05.001

Hunt, J. H., & Silva, J. (2020). Emma's negotiation of number: Implicit intensive intervention. *Journal for Research in Mathematics Education, 51*(3), 334–360.

Hunt, J. H., Tzur, R., & Westenskow, A. (2016). Evolution of unit fraction conceptions in two fifth-graders with a learning disability: An exploratory study. *Mathematical Thinking and Learning, 18*(3), 182–208.

Iqbal, N. (2019, 16 February). Interview: Academic Robin DiAngelo: 'We have to stop thinking about racism as someone who says the N-word'. *Guardian*. Retrieved from https://www.theguardian.com/world/2019/feb/16/white-fragility-racism-interview-robin-diangelo

Jacobs, V. R., & Empson, S. B. (2016). Responding to children's mathematical thinking in the moment: An emerging framework of teaching moves. *ZDM – The International Journal on Mathematics Education, 48*(1–2), 185–197. doi: 10.1007/s11858-015-0717-0

Kane, M. J., & Engle, R. W. (2002). The role of prefrontal cortex in working-memory capacity, executive attention, and general fluid intelligence: An individual-differences perspective. *Psychonomic Bulletin & Review, 9*(4), 637–671.

Kaufmann, L. (2008). Dyscalculia: Neuroscience and education. *Educational Research, 50*(2), 163–175.

Kelemanik, G., Lucenta, A., & Creighton, S. J. (2016). *Routines for reasoning: Fostering mathematical practices for all students*. Portsmouth, NH: Heinemann.

Kendi, I. X. (2019). *How to be an antiracist.* New York: One World.

Kermoian, R., & Campos, J. J. (1988). Locomotor experience: A facilitator of spatial cognitive development. *Child Development, 59,* 908–917.

Kilpatrick, J., Swafford, J. O., & Findell, B. (2001). *Adding it up: Helping children learn mathematics.* Retrieved from www.nap.edu/openbook/0309069955/html/index.html

Kirk, S. A., Gallagher, J., & Coleman, M. R. (2015). *Educating exceptional children* (14th ed.). Stamford, CT: Cengage Learning.

Knight, J. (2002). Crossing boundaries: What constructivists can teach intensive-explicit instructors and vice versa. *Focus on Exceptional Children, 35*(4), 1–14.

Kotok, S. (2017). Unfulfilled potential: High-achieving minority students and the high school achievement gap in math. *High School Journal, Spring,* 183–202.

Kroesbergen, E. H., & VanLuit, J. E. H. (2005). Constructivist mathematics education for students with mild mental retardation. *European Journal of Special Needs Education, 20*(1), 107–116.

Kucian, K., Grond, U., Rotzer, S., Henzi, B., Schönmann, C., Plangger, F., ... & von Aster, M. (2001). Mental number line training in children with developmental dyscalculia. *NeuroImage, 57*(3), 782–795.

Kumar, P., & Raja, B. W. D. (2009). Minimising dyscalculic problems through visual learning. *The Primary Teacher, 24*(3), 4.

Ladson-Billings, G. (1994). *The dreamkeepers: Successful teachers of African American children.* San Francisco: Jossey Bass.

Lampert, M. (2001). *Teaching with problems and the problems of teaching.* New Haven, CT: Yale University Press.

Land, T. J. (2017). Teacher attention to number choice in problem posing. *Journal of Mathematical Behavior, 45,* 35–46. doi: 10.1016/j.jmathb.2016.12.001

Land, T. J., Drake, C., Sweeney, M., Franke, N., & Johnson, J. M. (2014). *Transforming the task with number choice: Kindergarten through grade 3.* Reston, VA: NCTM.

Laud, L. (2011). *Using formative assessment to differentiate mathematics instruction, grades 4–10: Seven practices to maximize learning.* Thousand Oaks, CA, and Reston, VA: Corwin and NCTM.

Lempp, J. (2017). *Math workshop: Five steps to implementing guided math, learning stations, reflection, and more.* Sausalito, CA: Houghton Mifflin Harcourt.

Link, T., Moeller, K., Huber, S., & Fischer, U. (2013). Walk the number line – An embodied training of numerical concepts. *Trends in Neuroscience and Education, 2*(2), 74–84.

Liss, D. R., II. (2015). *Students' construction of intensive quantity.* Unpublished doctoral dissertation, The University of Georgia, Athens, GA.

Lynch, S. D., Hunt, J. H., & Lewis, K. E. (2018). Productive struggle for all: Differentiated instruction. *Mathematics Teaching in the Middle School, 23*(4), 194–201.

Lyons, I. M., & Beilock, S. L. (2012). When math hurts: Math anxiety predicts pain network activation in anticipation of doing math. *PLoS One, 7*(10), e48076.

Mader, J., & Butrymowicz, S. (2020). The vast majority of students with disabilities don't get a college degree: How better soft skills might boost low college persistence and employment rates. Retrieved from https://hechingerreport.org/vast-majority-students-disabilities-dont-get-college-degree/

Maldonado, L. A., Turner, E. E., Dominguez, H., & Empson, S. B. (2009). English-language learners learning from, and contributing to, mathematical discourse: 1. In D. Y. White & J. S. Spitzer (Eds.), *Mathematics for every student: Responding to diversity: Grades Pre-K–5* (pp. 7–22). Reston, VA: National Council of Teachers of Mathematics.

Mammarella, I. C., Caviola, S., & Dowker, A. D. (2019a). Concluding remarks. In I. C. Mammarella, S. Caviola, & A. D. Dowker (Eds.), *Mathematics anxiety: What is known and what is still to be understood* (pp. 211–221). London: Routledge.

Mammarella, I. C., Caviola, S., & Dowker, A. D. (Eds.). (2019b). *Mathematics anxiety: What is known and what is still to be understood*. London: Routledge.

Martin, L., LaCroix., L., & Fownes, L. (2005). Folding back and the growth of mathematical understanding in workplace training. *Adults Learning Mathematics – An International Journal, 1*(1), 17.

Mastropieri, M. A., Scruggs, T. E., Norland, J. J., Berkeley, S., McDuffie, K., Tornquist, E. H., & Connors, N. (2006). Differentiated curriculum enhancement in inclusive middle school science: Effects on classroom and high-stakes tests. *Journal of Special Education, 40*(3), 130–137. doi: 10.1177/00224669060400030101

Mazzocco, M. M. M., Feigenson, L., & Halberda, J. (2011). Impaired acuity of the approximate number system underlies mathematical learning disability (dyscalculia). *Child Development, 82*(4), 1224–1237.

McMillen, S., & Hernandez, B. O. (2008). Taking time to understand telling time. *Teaching Children Mathematics, 15*(4), 248–256.

Meltzer, L., & Reid, D. K. (1994). New directions in the assessment of students with special needs: The shift toward a constructivist perspective. *Journal of Special Education, 28*, 338–355.

Mercer, C. D., Jordan, L., & Miller, S. P. (1996). Constructivistic math instruction for diverse learners. *Learning Disabilities Research & Practice, 11*(3), 147–156.

Merritt, E. G., Palacios, N., Banse, H. W., Rimm-Kaufman, S. E., & Leis, M. (2017). Teaching practices in Grade 5 mathematics classrooms with high-achieving English learner students. *Journal of Educational Research, 110*(1), 17–31. doi: 10.1080/00220671.2015.1034352

Messenger, C., Emerson, J., & Bird, R. (2007). Dyscalculia in Harrow. *Mathematics Teaching Incorporating Micromath, 204*, 37–39.

Mevarech, Z., & Kramarski, B. (1997). Improve: A multidimensional method for teaching mathematics in heterogeneous classrooms. *American Educational Research Journal, 34*(2), 365–394. doi: 10.3102/00028312034002365

Michaelson, M. T. (2007). An overview of dyscalculia: Methods for ascertaining and accommodating dyscalculic children in the classroom. *Australian Mathematics Teacher, 63*(3), 17–22.

Miller, C., Gabrielson, M., Scholla, J., & Jobin, L. (2016). *Addition and subtraction to 100: Bead string activities*. Eagan, MN: US Math Recovery Council.

Moljord, G. (2018). Curriculum research for students with intellectual disabilities: A content-analytic review. *European Journal of Special Needs Education, 33*(5), 646–659. doi: 10.1080/088 56257.2017.1408222

Monei, T., & Pedro, A. (2017). A systematic review of interventions for children presenting with dyscalculia in primary schools. *Educational Psychology in Practice, 33*(3), 277–293.

Montague, M. (2003). Teaching division to students with learning disabilities: A constructivist approach. *Exceptionality, 11*(3), 165–175. doi: 10.1207/ S15327035EX1103_04

Morsanyi, K., Busdraghi, C., & Primi, C. (2014). Mathematical anxiety is linked to reduced cognitive reflection: A potential road from discomfort in the mathematics classroom to susceptibility to biases. *Behavioral and Brain Functions, 10*(1), 31.

Moscardini, L. (2010). 'I like it instead of maths': How pupils with moderate learning difficulties in Scottish primary special school intuitively solved mathematical word problems. *British Journal of Special Education, 37*(3), 130–138. doi: 10.1111/j.1467-8578.2010.00461.x

Moschkovich, J. N. (2013). Principles and guidelines for equitable mathematics teaching practices and materials for English Language learners. *Journal of Urban Mathematics Education, 6,* 45–57.

Munn, P., & Reason, R. (2007). Arithmetical difficulties: Developmental and instructional perspectives. *Educational and Child Psychology, 24*(2), 5–15.

Mvududu, N., & Thiel-Burgess, J. (2012). Constructivism in practice: The case for English language learners. *International Journal of Education for Social Justice, 4*(3), 108–118. doi: 10.5296/ije.v4i3.2223

National Association for Gifted Children Math/Science Task Force, Adams, C., Chamberlin, S., Gavin, M. K., Schultz, C., Sheffield, L. J., & Subotnik, R. (n.d.). The STEM promise: Recognizing and developing talent and expanding opportunities for promising students of science, technology, engineering, and mathematics. Retrieved from https://www.nagc.org/sites/default/files/Position%20Statement/STEM%20White%20Paper.pdf

National Center for Education Statistics. (2017). Table 2. Number of operating public schools and districts, student membership, teachers, and pupil/teacher ratio, by state or jurisdiction: School year 2016–17. Retrieved from https://nces.ed.gov/ccd/tables/201617_summary_2.asp#f2

National Center for Learning Disabilities. (2020). Supporting Academic Success. Retrieved from https://www.ncld.org/research/state-of-learning-disabilities/supporting-academic-success/

National Center for Research on Gifted Education. (2018). *Exploratory study on the identification of English learners for gifted and talented programs.* Retrieved from https://ncrge.uconn.edu/wp-content/uploads/sites/982/2018/06/NCRGE-EL-Report-1.pdf

National Council of Teachers of Mathematics. (2014a). *Principles to actions: Ensuring mathematical success for all.* Reston, VA: National Council of Teachers of Mathematics.

National Council of Teachers of Mathematics. (2014b). Procedural Fluency in Mathematics, 2. Retrieved from https://www.nctm.org/Standards-and-Positions/Position-Statements/Procedural-Fluency-in-Mathematics/

National Numeracy. (n.d.). Retrieved from https://www.nationalnumeracy.org.uk/what-numeracy

Nation's Report Card. (2007). Mathematics 2007: Students with Disabilities – NAEP. Retrieved from https://www.nationsreportcard.gov/math_2007/m0014.aspx

NCTM [National Council of Teachers of Mathematics] (2018). *Catalyzing change in high school mathematics: Initiating critical conversations.* Reston, VA: NCTM.

Newton, N. (2017). *Guided math in action: Building each student's mathematical proficiency with small-group instruction.* New York: Routledge.

Ng, E. L., & Lee, K. (2019). The different involvement of working memory in math and test anxiety. In I. Mammarella, S. Caviola, & A. D. Dowker (Eds.), *Mathematics anxiety: What is known and what is still to be understood* (pp. 126–140). London: Routledge.

Noddings, N. (1990). Constructivism in mathematics education. In R. B. Davis, C. A. Maher, & N. Noddings (Eds.), *Constructivist views on the teaching and learning of mathematics: Journal for Research in Mathematics Education: Monograph number 4* (pp. 7–18). Reston, VA: National Council of Teachers of Mathematics.

Noël, M. E. (2005). Finger gnosia: A predictor of numerical abilities in children? *Child Neuropsychology, 11,* 413–430. doi: 10.1080/09297040590951550

Norton, A., Ulrich, C., Bell, M. A., & Cate, A. (2018). Mathematics at hand. *Mathematics Educator, 27*(1), 33–59.

NSW Department of Education and Training, Professional Support and Curriculum Directorate. (1996). *Count Me In Too Professional Development Package.* Ryde, NSW.

O'Connor, M. C. (2001). 'Can any fraction be turned into a decimal?' A case study of a mathematical group discussion. *Educational Studies in Mathematics, 46*, 143–185. doi: 10.1023/A:1014041308444

Overstreet, S., & Chafouleas, S. M. (2016). Trauma-informed schools: Introduction to the special issue. *School Mental Health: A Multidisciplinary Research and Practice Journal, 8*(1), 1–6.

Passolunghi, M. C., Caviola, S., De Agostini, R., Perin, C., & Mammarella, I. C. (2016). Mathematics anxiety, working memory, and mathematics performance in secondary-school children. *Frontiers in Psychology, 7*(Article 42), 1–8. doi: 10.3389/fpsyg.2016.00042

Passolunghi, M. C., Živković, M., & Pellizzoni, S. (2019). Mathematics anxiety and working memory: What is the relationship? In I. Mammarella, S. Caviola, & A. D. Dowker (Eds.), *Mathematics anxiety: What is known and what is still to be understood* (pp. 103–125). London: Routledge.

Penner-Wilger, M., & Anderson, M. L. (2013). The relation between finger gnosis and mathematical ability: Why redeployment of neural circuits best explains the finding. *Frontiers in Psychology, 4*, 877. doi: 10.3389/fpsyg.2013.00877

Persyn, M. K., & Valbrun-Pope, M. (2020). *The impact of trauma-sensitive care on learning within the optimal learning environment: Supporting students and building resilience.* Paper presented at the New Teacher Center 2020 Symposium: Accelerate: Collective Impact for Equity in Education, Atlanta, GA.

Peterek, E., & Adams, T. L. (2009). Meeting the challenge of engaging students for success in mathematics by using culturally responsive methods: 13. In D. Y. White & J. S. Spitzer (Eds.), *Mathematics for every student: Responding to diversity: Grades Pre-K–5* (pp. 149–159). Reston, VA: National Council of Teachers of Mathematics.

Petronzi, D., Staples, P., Sheffield, D., & Hunt, T. (2019). Acquisition, development and maintenance of maths anxiety in young children. In I. Mammarella, S. Caviola, & A. D. Dowker (Eds.), *Mathematics anxiety: What is known and what is still to be understood* (pp. 77–102). London: Routledge.

Phakeng, M. S., & Moschkovich, J. N. (2013). Mathematics education and language diversity: A dialogue across settings. *Journal for Research in Mathematics Education, 44*(1), 119–128.

Piaget, J. (1970). *Structuralism* (C. Maschler, Trans.). New York: Basic Books (Original work published 1968).

Piazza, M., Facoetti, A., Trussardi, A. N., Berteletti, I., Conte, S., Lucangeli, D., … Zorzi, M. (2010). Developmental trajectory of number acuity reveals a severe impairment in developmental dyscalculia. *Cognition, 116*(1), 33–41.

Pierce, R. L., & Adams, C. M. (2005). Using tiered lessons in mathematics. *Mathematics Teaching in the Middle School, 11*(3), 144–149.

Pirie, S. K., & Kieren, T. (1989). A recursive theory of mathematical understanding. *For the Learning of Mathematics, 9*(3), 7–11.

Poplin, M. S. (1988). Holistic/constructivist principles of the teaching/learning process: Implications for the field of learning disabilities. *Journal of Learning Disabilities, 21*(7), 401–416.

Price, G. R., & Ansari, D. (2013). Dyscalculia: Characteristics, causes, and treatments. *Numeracy, 6*(1). doi: http://dx.doi.org/10.5038/1936-4660.6.1.2

QCA (Qualification and Curriculum Authority) (2007). *Functional skill standards*, London: QCA.

Raja, B. W. D., & Kumar, S. P. (2012). Findings of studies on dyscalculia – A synthesis. *Journal on Educational Psychology, 5*(3), 41–51.

Reinholz, D. L., & Shah, N. (2018). Equity analytics: A methodological approach for quantifying participation patterns in mathematics classroom discourse. *Journal for Research in Mathematics Education, 49*(2), 140–177.

Reis, S. M., McCoach, D. B., Little, C. A., Muller, L. M., & Kaniskan, R. B. (2011). The effects of differentiated instruction and enrichment pedagogy on reading achievement in five elementary schools. *American Educational Research Journal, 48*(2), 462–501. doi: 10.3102/0002831210382891

Reis, S. M., & Renzulli, J. S. (2010). Is there still a need for gifted education? An examination of current research. *Learning and Individual Differences, 20*, 308–317.

Renzulli, J. S. (2019, November 11). What we're getting wrong about gifted education: Opinion. *Education Week.*

Richardson, F. C., & Suinn, R. M. (1972). The mathematics anxiety rating scale: Psychometric data. *Journal of Counseling Psychology, 19*, 551–554.

Rivera, S. M., Reiss, A. L., Eckert, M. A., & Menon, V. (2005). Developmental changes in mental arithmetic: Evidence for increased functional specialization in the left inferior parietal cortex. *Cerebral Cortex, 15*(11), 1779–1790. doi: 10.1093/cercor/bhi055

Rosenberg-Lee, M., Lovett, M. C., & Anderson, J. R. (2009). Neural correlates of arithmetic calculation strategies. *Cognitive, Affective, & Behavioral Neuroscience, 9*(3), 270–285. doi: 10.3758/CABN.9.3.270

Rosenthal, R., & Jacobson, L. (1968). *Pygmalion in the classroom: Teacher expectations and pupils' intellectual development.* New York: Holt, Rinehart, and Winston.

Rubin, B. C. (2006). Tracking and detracking: Debates, evidence, and best practices for a heterogeneous world. *Theory into Practice, 45*(1), 4–14. doi: 10.1207/s15430421tip4501_2

Rubin, B. (2008). Detracking in context: How local constructions of ability complicate equity-geared reform. *Teachers College Record, 110*(3), 646–699.

Rusconi, E., Walsh, V., & Butterworth, B. (2005). Dexterity with numbers: rTMS over left angular gyrus disrupts finger gnosis and number processing. *Neuropsychologia, 43*(11), 1609–1624. doi: 10.1016/j.neuropsychologia.2005.01.009

Rykhlevskaia, E., Uddin, L. Q., Kondos, L., & Menon, V. (2009). Neuroanatomical correlates of developmental dyscalculia: Combined evidence from morphometry and tractography. *Frontiers in Human Neuroscience, 3*, 51.

Sammons, L. (2010). *Guided math: A framework for mathematics instruction.* Huntington Beach, CA: Shell Education.

Santamaria, L. J. (2009). Culturally responsive differentiated instruction: Narrowing gaps between best pedagogical practices benefiting all learners. *Teachers College Record, 111*(1), 214–247.

Sato, M., Cattaneo, L., Rizzolatti, G., & Gallese, V. (2007). Numbers within our hands: Modulation of corticospinal excitability of hand muscles during numerical judgment. *Journal of Cognitive Neuroscience, 19*(4), 684–693. doi: 10.1162/jocn.2007.19.4.684

Saxe, G. B., Diakow, R., & Gearhart, M. (2013). Towards curricular coherence in integers and fractions: A study of the efficacy of a lesson sequence that uses the number line as the principal representational context. *ZDM – The International Journal on Mathematics Education, 45*, 343–364. doi: 10.1007/s11858-012-0466-2

Schleifer, P., & Landerl, K. (2011). Subtizing and counting in typical and atypical development. *Developmental Science, 14*(2), 280–291. doi:10.1111/j.1467-7687.2010.00976.x

Sella, F., Berteletti, I., Martina, B., Lucangeli, D., & Zorzi, M. (2013). Number line estimation in children with developmental dyscalculia. *Learning Disabilities: A Contemporary Journal, 11*(2), 41–49.

Siegler, R. S., & Ramani, G. B. (2008). Playing linear numerical board games promotes low-income children's numerical development. *Developmental Science, 11*(5), 655–661. doi: 10.1111/j.1467-7687.2008.00714.x

Simon, M. A. (1995). Reconstructing mathematics pedagogy from a constructivist perspective. *Journal for Research in Mathematics Education, 26*(2), 114–145.

Simpson, M. (1997). Developing differentiation practices: Meeting the needs of pupils and teachers. *Curriculum Journal, 8*(1), 85–104. doi: 10.1080/09585176.1997.11070763

Singer, F. M., Sheffield, L. J., Freiman, V., & Brandl, M. (2016). Research on and activities for mathematically gifted students. In F. M. Singer et al. (Eds.), *Research into Practice: Programs and pedagogy.* New York: Springer.

Small, M., & Lin, A. (2010). *More good questions: Great ways to differentiate secondary mathematics instruction.* New York and Reston, VA: Teachers College Press and NCTM.

Sofrona, S. (Host). (2019). Routines for reasoning: English learners and math with Grace Kelemanik and Amy Lucenta: Part 1: Highest Aspirations, Season 4/Episode2. Retrieved from https://ellevationeducation.com/podcast/routines-reasoning-english-learners-and-math-grace-kelemanik-and-amy-lucenta-part-1

Sorhagen, N. S. (2013). Early teacher expectations disproportionately affect poor children's high school performance. *Journal of Educational Psychology, 105*(2), 467–477. doi: 10.1037/a0031754

Sowell, E. J. (1989). Effects of manipulative materials in mathematics instruction. *Journal for Research in Mathematics Education, 20*(5), 498–505.

Special Educational Needs Code of Practice. (2001). Retrieved from https://assets.publishing.service.gov.uk/government/uploads/system/uploads/attachment_data/file/273877/special_educational_needs_code_of_practice.pdf

Steele, M. M. (2005). Teaching students with learning disabilities: Constructivism or behaviorism? *Current Issues in Education [Online], 8*(10).

Steele, S. D., Minshew, N. J., Luna, B., & Sweeney, J. A. (2007). Spatial working memory deficits in autism. *Journal of Autism and Developmental Disorders, 37*(4), 605–612.

Steffe, L. P. (1991). The constructivist teaching experiment: Illustrations and implications. In E. von Glasersfeld (Ed.), *Radical constructivism in mathematics education* (pp. 177–194). Dordrecht: Kluwer.

Steffe, L. P. (1992). Schemes of action and operation involving composite units. *Learning and Individual Differences, 4*(3), 259–309. doi: 10.1016/1041-6080(92)90005-Y

Steffe, L. P. (1994). Children's multiplying schemes. In G. Harel & J. Confrey (Eds.), *The development of multiplicative reasoning in the learning of mathematics* (pp. 3–39). Albany, NY: State University of New York Press.

Steffe, L. P. (2013). On children's construction of quantification. In R. L. Mayes & L. L. Hatfield (Eds.), *Quantitative reasoning in mathematics and science education: Papers from an international STEM research symposium* (pp. 13–41). Laramie, WY: University of Wyoming.

Steffe, L. P. (2017). Psychology in mathematics education: Past, present, and future. In E. Galindo & J. Newton (Eds.). *Proceedings of the Thirty-ninth Annual Meeting of the North American Chapter of the International Group for the Psychology of Mathematics Education* (pp. 27–56). Indianapolis, IN: Hoosier Association of Mathematics Teacher Educators.

Steffe, L. P., Cobb, P., & von Glasersfeld, E. (1988). *Construction of arithmetical meanings and strategies.* New York: Springer.

Steffe, L. P., & Olive, J. (2010). *Children's fractional knowledge.* New York: Springer. doi: 10.1007/978-1-4419-0591-8

Steffe, L. P., von Glasersfeld, E., Richards, J., & Cobb, P. (1983). *Children's counting types: Philosophy, theory, and application.* New York: Praeger.

Stein, M. K., Engle, R. A., Smith, M. S., & Hughes, E. K. (2008). Orchestrating productive mathematical discussions: Five practices for helping teachers move beyond show and tell. *Mathematical Thinking and Learning, 10*(4), 313–340. doi: 10.1080/10986060802229675

Steinberg, R. M., Empson, S. B., & Carpenter, T. P. (2004). Inquiry into children's mathematical thinking as a means to teacher change. *Journal of Mathematics Teacher Education, 7*, 237–267. doi: 10.1023/B:JMTE.0000033083.04005.d3

Stiff, L. V., Johnson, J. L., & Akos, P. (2011). Examining what we know for sure: Tracking in middle grades mathematics. In W. F. Tate, K. D. King, & C. R. Anderson (Eds.), *Disrupting tradition: Research and practice pathways in mathematics* (pp. 63–75). Reston, VA: NCTM.

Szűcs, D., & Goswami, U. (2013). Developmental dyscalculia: Fresh perspectives. *Trends in Neuroscience and Education, 2*, 33–37. doi: 10.1016/j.tine.2013.06.004

Ta'ir, J., Brezner, A., & Ariel, R. (1997). Profound developmental dyscalculia: Evidence for a cardinal/ordinal skills acquisition device. *Brain and Cognition, 35*, 184–206.

Tabor, P. D. (2008). *An investigation of instruction in two-digit addition and subtraction using a classroom teaching experiment methodology, design research, and multilevel modeling.* PhD dissertation, Southern Cross University, Lismore, NSW. Retrieved from https://epubs.scu.edu.au/theses/68/

Test, D. W., Howell, A., Burkhart, K., & Beroth, T. (1993). The one-more-than technique as a strategy for counting money for individuals with moderate mental retardation. *Education and Training in Mental Retardation, 28*(3), 232–241.

Thomas, J. N., & Tabor, P. D. (2012). Developing quantiative mental imagery: Use these descriptions of diagnostic and instructional tools to help young learners move beyond reliance on physical materials to negotiate arithmetic tasks. *Teaching Children Mathematics, 19*(3), 174–183.

Timmermans, A. C., Rubie-Davies, C. M., & Rjosk, C. (2018). Pygmalion's 50th anniversary: The state of the art in teacher expectation research: Editorial. *Educational Research and Evaluation,* (3–5), 91–98. doi: 10.1080/13803611.2018.1548785

Tobin, R., & Tippitt, C. (2014). Possibilities and potential barriers: Learning to plan for differentiated instruction in elementary science. *International Journal of Science and Mathematics Education, 12*, 423–443.

Tomlinson, C. A. (1995). Deciding to differentiate instruction in middle school: One school's journey. *Gifted Child Quarterly, 39*, 77–87. doi: 10.1177/001698629503900204

Tomlinson, C. A. (2005). *How to differentiate instruction in mixed-ability classrooms* (2nd ed.). Upper Saddle River, NJ: Pearson.

Tran, T. L. (2016). *Targeted, one-to-one instruction in whole-number arithmetic: A framework of key elements.* Doctor of Philosophy dissertation, Southern Cross University, Lismore, NSW. Retrieved from http://epubs.scu.edu.au/theses/472/ (Thesis: 1481)

Trent, S. C., Artiles, A. J., & Englert, C. S. (1998). From deficit thinking to social constructivism: A review of theory, research, and practice in special education. *Review of Research in Education, 23*, 277–307.

Tsui, G. H. H., & Rutherford, M. D. (2014). Video self-modeling is an effective intervention for an adult with autism. *Case Reports in Neurological Medicine, 2014*, 6.

Ulrich, C. (2015). Stages in constructing and coordinating units additively and multiplicatively (part 1). For the Learning of Mathematics, 35(3), 2–7.

Ulrich, C. (2016). Stages in constructing and coordinating units additively and multiplicatively (part 2). For the Learning of Mathematics, 36(1), 34–39.

US Department of Agriculture. (2019). Decline in school lunch participation driven by drops in full- and reduced-price participation. Retrieved from https://www.ers.usda.gov/data-products/charts-of-note/charts-of-note/?topicId=14873

US Department of Agriculture, Food and Nutrition Service. (2020). Child Nutrition Tables. Retrieved from https://www.fns.usda.gov/pd/child-nutrition-tables

US Department of Education. (n.d.). Definitions: Race to the Top District Competition Draft. Retrieved from https://www.ed.gov/race-top/district-competition/definitions

US Department of Education. (2017). Education for homeless children and youths program: Non-regulatory guidance: Title VII-B of the McKinney-Vento Homeless Assistance Act, as amended by the Every Student Succeeds Act. Retrieved from https://www2.ed.gov/policy/elsec/leg/essa/160240ehcyguidance072716updated0317.pdf

US Department of Education. (2019). A Guide to the Individualized Education Program. Retrieved from https://www2.ed.gov/parents/needs/speced/iepguide/index.html

US Math Recovery Council. (2016). *Add+VantageMR fractions course teacher handbook* (C. Miller, J. Scholla, K. Kinsey, & M. Grabrielson, Eds.). Apple Valley, MN: USMRC.

Van de Walle, J. A., Karp, K. S., & Bay-Wiilliams, J. M. (2013). *Elementary and middle school mathematics: Teaching developmentally.* The professional development edition (8th ed.). Upper Saddle River, NJ: Pearson.

von Aster, M. G., & Shalev, R. S. (2007). Number development and developmental dyscalculia. *Developmental Medicine & Child Neurology, 49,* 868–873.

von Glasersfeld, E. (1984). An introduction to radical constructivism. In P. Watzlawick (Ed.), *The invented reality* (pp. 17–40). New York: Norton.

von Glasersfeld, E. (1991). *A constructivist's view of learning and teaching.* Paper presented at the Research in physics 135 learning: Theoretical issues and empirical studies, Kiel, Germany.

Weng, P.-L., & Bouck, E. C. (2014). Using video prompting via iPads to teach price comparison to adolescents with autism. *Research in Autism Spectrum Disorders, 8*(10), 1405–1415.

WIDA Consortium. (2012). The English Language Development Standards: 2012 Amplification of: Kindergarten–Grade 12. Retrieved from https://wida.wisc.edu/sites/default/files/resource/2012-ELD-Standards.pdf

WIDA Consortium. (2020). https://wida.wisc.edu/teach/standards/eld/2020

Wilcox, B., & Bellamy, G. T. (1987). *A comprehesive guide to the activities catalog: An alternative curriculum for youth and adults with severe disabilities.* Baltimore, MD: Paul H. Brookes.

Wilkins, J. L., Woodward, D., & Norton, A. (2020). Children's number sequences as predictors of later mathematical development. *Mathematics Education Research Journal.* doi:10.1007/s13394-020-00317-y

Wilson, A., Revkin, S., Cohen, D., Cohen, L. D., & Dehaene, S. (2006). An open trial assessment of 'The Number Race,' an adaptive computer game for remediation of dyscalculia. *Behavioral and Brain Functions, 2*(1). doi:10.1186/1744-9081-2-20

Witzel, B., & Mize, M. (2018). Meeting the needs of students with dyslexia and dyscalculia. *SRATE Journal, 27*(1), 31–39.

Wlodkowski, R., & Ginsberg, M. B. (1995). A framework for culturally responsive teaching. *Educational Leadership, 53*(1), 17–21.

Wood, D., Bruner, J. S., & Ross, G. (1976). The role of tutoring in problem solving. *Journal of Child Psychology and Psychiatry, and Allied Disciplines, 17*(2), 89–100.

Woodward, J., & Montague, M. (2002). Meeting the challenge of mathematics reform for students with LD. *Journal of Special Education, 36*(2), 89–101.

Woodward, J., & Tzur, R. (2017). Final Commentary to the Cross-Disciplinary Thematic Special Series: Special Education and Mathematics Education. *Learning Disability Quarterly, 43*(3), 146–151. doi: https://doi.org/10.1177/0731948717690117

Wright, R. J. (1989). *Numerical development in the kindergarten year: A teaching experiment*, PhD thesis, University of Georgia, Athens, GA (*DAI, 50A*(1588), DA8919319).

Wright, R. J. (2000). Professional development in recovery education. In L. P. Steffe & P. W. Thompson (Eds.), *Radical constructivism in action: Building on the pioneering work of Ernst von Glasersfeld* (pp. 134–151). London: RoutledgeFalmer.

Wright, R. J., & Ellemor-Collins, D. (2018). *The Learning Framework in Number: Pedagogical tools for assessment and instruction*. London: Sage.

Wright, R. J., Ellemor-Collins, D., & Tabor, P. D. (2012). *Developing number knowledge: Assessment, teaching and intervention with 7–11-year-olds*. London: Sage.

Wright, R. J., Martland, J., & Stafford, A. K. (2000). *Early numeracy: Assessment for teaching and intervention*. London: Sage.

Wright, R. J., Martland, J., & Stafford, A. K. (2006a). *Early numeracy: Assessment for teaching and intervention* (2nd ed.). London: Sage.

Wright, R. J., Martland, J., Stafford, A. K., & Stanger, G. (2006b). *Teaching number: Advancing children's skills and strategies* (2nd ed.). London: Sage.

Wright, R. J., Stanger, G., Stafford, A. K., & Martland, J. (2015). *Teaching number in the classroom with 4–8 year olds* (2nd ed.). London: Sage.

Xin, Y. P., Grasso, E., Dipipi-Hoy, C. M., & Jitendra, A. K. (2005). The effects of purchasing skill instruction for individuals with developmental disabilities: A meta-analysis. *Exceptional Children, 71*(4), 379–400.

Xin, Y. P., Liu, J., Jones, S. R., Tzur, R., & Si, L. (2016). A preliminary discourse analysis of constructivist-oriented mathematics instruction for a student with learning disabilities. *Journal of Educational Research, 109*(4), 436–437. doi: http://dx.doi.org/10.1080/00220671.2014.979910

Yackel, E., & Cobb, P. (1996). Sociomathematical norms, argumentation, and autonomy in mathematics. *Journal for Research in Mathematics Education, 27*(4), 458–477. doi: 10.2307/749877

Index